▶ FOCUS ON ◀

Proficiency

 LONGMAN

FULL COLOUR EDITION

SUE O'CONNELL

► Acknowlegements

I would like to thank the Proficiency students at Filton College and the Abon Language School in Bristol for their enthusiastic co-operation in the development of the materials which form this book.

The author and publishers are grateful to the following for permission to reproduce the material on the pages indicated:

Extracts: Bower and Bower and Addison Wesley 64–66 (from *Asserting Yourself*, Addison Wesley, 1976), James Burke and Macmillan, 172, Nigel Buxton, 49 (Extract C) (from *American*, Cassell, 1979); John Carter, 54, Richard Cootes and Longman, 72, Daily Telegraph, 106 (B-E, 1–4), Gillian Dyer and Methuen and Co, 175, 194 (from Advertising as Communication, 1982); Express Newspapers, 2B 148 (from the Daily Star); Fitzgerald, Margolis and Young and Pan, 55 (questions 1 and 2), 95–96 (from Know your Society, 1981), Guardian, 20, 42, 60, 67, (Listening text), 81,119, 122, 132, 147 (2A, 5A); Middle East Centre, Cambridge and World of Islam Festival Publishing Co, 15 (Listening text), Mirror Group 148 (IB from Sunday Mirror, 3B from Daily Mirror); New Society, 56, 57, 73, 77, 96, 113, the Observer, London, 5, 23, 58, 94, 128, (Extract 3), 136, 177; Open University Guide to the Associate Student Programme, The Open University Press, 1984, 128 (Extract l); Pan Books, 82 (from the Good Health Guide, 1980); A D Peters Ltd, 134, The Press Agency (Yorkshire) Ltd, 147 (5A); Penguin Books Ltd, 21 (from *Work*, ed. Ronald Fraser, Pelican 1968 ©) New Left Review 1965, 1966, 1967); Salman Rushdie and Jonathan Cape, 12 (Extract D, from Midnight's Children); St Martins USA, 49 (Extract D from Let's Go 1982), the Sun, 148 (4B), Paul Theroux and Cape Cod Scriveners Company 1979, (Hamish Hamilton UK and Houghton Mifflin and Co USA, 1979) 39, Times Newspapers, 7 (19 Feb 1978), 37 (25 April 1982), 89 (Extract 4) from 'Join the Chain Gang' by Tony Osman in the Sunday Times Magazine, 16 May 1982); 105 (Listening text from 'How to steal a march on the burglar' by Lindsay Bareham in The Times, 5–11 Feb 1983); TSB Family Magazine, 68; TV Times, 120-2;1 Which? and the Consumers Association, 12 (Extracts A and C), 28, 186, 189–190.

As far as the publishers can ascertain, in the cases of Miss Jackson and Miss White mentioned on pages 146 and 147 there was no appeal.

Exam Practice - Interview reading passages: Focus magazine (from *Quote marks - Football* by Danny Blanchflower and *Animal magic – the healing power of pets*), 213, 215, The Observer Magazine ©) (from *Are you ready to take the plunge?* by Irma Kurtz; Drama in the ghetto by Martin Plimmer and *The glory, glory kids* by Peter Nicholls), 213, 219, 223; Wilson, Etchels and Tulloh and Virgin Publishing (extract from *The Marathon Book,* 1984), 213; John James (Letter to the Editor in *The Times*), 213; Woman magazine (from *Close encounters of the furred kind* by Bruce Fogle), 215; Pan Books in association with Channel 4 (from *Battle For the Planet* by Andre Singer), 215; New Internationalist (from *Zooooooh* by Tess Lemmon), 215; ©) Phaidon Press Limited (from *The Story of Art* by Professor Ernst Gombrich), 217; (© The Telegraph Plc, London, 1986 (from *Every portrait tells a story* by Philip Oakes), 217; © Times Newspapers Ltd. 1988/92 (from *Fraudsters and thieves join forces in art trade* by Sarah Jane Checkland; *Mad driuers in the fast lanes* by Neville Hodgkinson; Why motorists are driven to

distraction by Nick Rufford and A car to put the thieves out of business by Peter Evans), 217, 221 The Museum of Modern Art, New York (from Henri Matisse, 1931 published in The Museum of Modern Art Catalogue), 217; Sally Jones and Times Newspapers Ltd. (from If only England's men could be more like sporting women), 219; Reprinted by permission of the Peters Fraser & Dunlop Group Ltd (The Leader by Roger McGough), 219; Living magazine (from Should parents be taught a lesson by Michele Jaffe), 223; Reproduced by kind permission of London Regional Transport (extract from London Underground advertisement), 223; Penguin Books, 1987 (from Pearls of Wisdom - A Book of Aphorisms by Vivian Foster), 223.

Exam Practice - Listening material: Adrian Burchall, 202; Steve Berry, 203; Martin Matthews, 205; GWR and Margo Horsley, 210.

Photographs and illustrations: Advertising Archives, 173, 174, 220; Gareth Boden Photography, 29, 67, 145, 161; Railways – Milepost 921/2, 220; J Allan Cash, 15, 216; (© Environmental Transport Association for Green Transport Week logo 221; Getty Images, 23, 47, 158, 203, 212, 214, 218; Sally and Richard Greenhill, 81; Health Education Authority, 74; The Hulton Picture Company, 134; Hutchison, 38; The Image Bank, 88; Lifelife, 88; Leila Miller Photography, 41, 114, 222; Network Photographers/Goldwater, 42; Network Photographers/ Gupta, 23; Network Photographers/lgnatiev, 222; Network Photographers/Lowe, 27; Network Photographers/ Matthews, 222; Network Photographers/Sturrock, 7; Network Photographers/Sykes 114, 122; Pictor International, 38, 49, 218, Rex Features, 23, 38, 42, l14, l4l, 214, 216; Frank Spooner Pictures, 100; The Times Newspaper/ Martin Beddall, 212; Margaret Welbank, 221.

The publishers have made every effort to contact owners of copyright, but this was not possible in all cases. They apologise for any omissions, and if details are sent, will be glad to rectify these when the title is reprinted.

Other artwork by Chartwell Illustrators, Geraldine Finn, Douglas Hall, Chris Pavely, John Plumb, Caroline Porter, Gina Smart, Alastair Taylor, Hugh Tisdale.

The author would like to give special thanks to Lindsay White for her substantial contribution to the Exam Practice Listening section, and to Peter Watkins for the Communication activity in Unit 3 .

Special thanks also go to Margaret Hanson, and to Peter Rutherford at the British Institute, Madrid; Stephen Parkin and Graham Sullivan at the English Centre, Madrid; Tony Buckby at the British Institute, Florence; Luke Prodromou at the British Council, Thessaloniki; Rod Joyce at Westminster College.

For my parents

Addison Wesley Longman Limited
Edinburgh Gate, Harlow,
Essex CM20 2JE, England
and Associated Companies throughout the world.

© Sue O'Connell 1984, 1989, 1995
First published by Harper Collins 1984
This edition published Addison Wesley Longman Limited 1996
Fifth impression 1998

Contents

Unit 1 Homes *4*

Unit 2 Work *19*

Unit 3 Tourist or traveller? *38*

Unit 4 Relationships *55*

Unit 5 Health *73*

Unit 6 Crime and punishment *95*

Unit 7 Learning and teaching *114*

Unit 8 The media *133*

Unit 9 Science and technology *154*

Unit 10 The consumer society *173*

Answer key *195*

Exam practice Listening *201*

Interview *212*

Index *224*

UNIT 1 Homes

▶ Lead-in

1

a Describe the building and people in the cartoon above.
b What do you think the cartoonist is suggesting?
c How far do you agree with the cartoonist? Why?

2

a Describe the two houses on page 4.
b What are the main differences between them and what do they have in common?
c Which would you prefer to live in and why?
d Think about a typical house in your country (perhaps your own). What differences would there be? Can you account for them?

▶Text 1 · Finding friends

Reading for gist   Read through the passage fairly quickly and answer the following questions.

1 What does the holiday organisation aim to do for its customers?
2 How does it acquire the information that it needs?
3 Was the holiday a success or not? In what way?

It was an enquiring mind that took me to Texas and my spare room that put me in touch with the Sattersfield family. Between the two – acting as a kind of marriage broker –
5 was an organisation called *Home and Awaystay Holidays*.

The machinery is set in motion following completion of a comprehensive questionnaire detailing the requirements of the guest family,
10 their interests and preferences. This information allows *HAH* to set about arranging an introduction with a compatible host family from their records.

When a likely match is found the applicant
15 is sent a full description of the potential hosts and, if approved both ways, the address is released. Only then is the agency fee payable.

Then you are on your own. In direct contact the guest and host family can make
20 whatever arrangements they choose including that of the 'return match' that would normally follow. Me, I had gone alone to Texas on a voyage of discovery to see how the system worked subsequent to *HAH*'s initial
25 commitment.

An oil township out West they had said, so I expected the worst; a timber saloon bar and Joe's Place community centre with, maybe, an oil derrick or two on the horizon. And, as my
30 comfortable Trailways bus headed out of Downtown Dallas on Interstate 20 and into the limitless horizons of central Texas, I believed it.

Imagine my surprise, therefore, when nine
35 hours and 300 miles later, Midland, my destination, loomed before me. There, rising phoenix-like from a semi-desert of scrub and tumbleweed, was a concrete city of soaring skyscrapers.
40   Though a three-bedroomed home like my own, the Sattersfield residence was more spacious and lavish. It was an open-plan single-storey construction but not at all the sort of house you would call a bungalow. An
45 enclosed patio, fully equipped for a barbecue party, led to a sizeable lawn and orchard. A utility room contained an automatic washer, washing-up machine and 'trash-compressor', and a large garage housed two cars with a
50 third standing on the 'drive-in'. With a

husband away at frequent intervals as a pilot of an oil-tycoon's private jet, Jean Sattersfield, like my own wife married to a travel writer, was something of a grass widow.[1] They had a
55 married daughter, aged 26; a working son of 22. In my family we have a married daughter – 21 next birthday – and a son of 17 mad keen on flying. I could raise but one car. Yes, the match was as good as one could expect from
60 the sparse completion of a questionnaire I had been sent.

Midland was an enclave of great wealth, high-powered business activity and aggressive Texan bonhomie. It might be situated in a
65 kind of desert and collect the odd summer dust storm but its residents were certainly no nomads. Many lived in stupefying luxury and I began to wish *my* hometown stood on a large proportion of my country's entire supply of
70 crude oil and natural gas.

In one of the three cars I explored the region and learnt of the vast distances that are taken for granted in the United States. The sea is 500 miles away – yet is still in Texas. The
75 famous Carlsbad caverns in New Mexico are 150 while Midland's neighbour, the slightly larger Odessa, is 30 miles or 20 breezy minutes down Interstate 20 or Highway 80. With cars that cost a third less than ours to put
80 on the road and petrol prices half our own, such travel is cheap while the sheer size, power and comfort of the vehicles themselves make short work of the miles. Midland alone sports two airports seething with private
85 aircraft that are relatively cheap to run.

The lower cost of living compared to our own, further enhanced by higher incomes, was a fact that became increasingly clear as I delved into the lives of my new Texan friends
90 and, in turn, their friends who soon became my own. The variety of goods in shops and supermarkets, the choice in restaurants, is astounding.

Learning how the other half of the English-
95 speaking world goes round can be an exasperating exercise but getting to the grass roots[2] of a country is no bad thing. America has learnt much from us; maybe she can return the compliment as I shall my new
100 Texan friends' astounding hospitality.

from an article in the Observer, London

Notes
1 *grass widow* – a wife whose husband is temporarily not living with her as a result of his job or hobby.
2 *grass roots* –   the ordinary people, often in the sense of those remote from political decisions but affected by them.

Extending your vocabulary Look at paragraphs 7–10 and find the word or words which mean the same as:

a luxuriously equipped (7) ....

b fairly large (7) ....

c not thorough (7) ....

d self-contained territory (8) ....

e pleasantness of manner (8) ....

f occasional (8) ....

g possesses proudly (9) ....

h crowded with (9) ....

i improved (10) ....

j researched (10) ....

Reading for detail Complete these statements by choosing the answer which you think fits best. Why are the other answers unsuitable?

1 The writer applied to the holiday organisation because he
  a wanted to get to know the Sattersfields.
  b intended to try out the new scheme.
  c needed a change from his busy job.
  d wanted to take his family to America.

2 Payment to the agency is required
  a when a suitable family has been found.
  b at the time when the initial application is made.
  c before the address of the host family is supplied.
  d as soon as both parties agree to proceed.

3 The writer was surprised by Midland because it
  a seemed to be so far from anywhere.
  b was more industrial than he had expected.
  c seemed to be so empty of people.
  d was more impressive than he had expected.

4 One important way in which the two families were well-matched was that
  a they both lived in three-bedroomed houses.
  b they both enjoyed a similar level of income.
  c both wives were in a similar situation.
  d both husbands had the same occupation.

5 The aspect of the holiday which the writer seems to feel he can learn from was
  a the friendliness of his Texan hosts.
  b the luxury of the Texan lifestyle.
  c the enormous range of goods in the shops.
  d the speed and ease of travel.

▶Focus on writing 1 · Description

A house A written description can either take the place of a picture or diagram or supplement it by drawing attention to important points and supplying details which are not shown.

When describing a house a number of features can be mentioned: age, style, size, location and condition. Individual houses will also have special features such as a garden or a fine view. There is no fixed order in which to mention these but the writer should give a reader a clear picture with all the information they need for their purposes. Obviously the needs of a prospective purchaser will be different from those of a holiday guest!

Writing assignment Imagine that you have applied to *Home and Awaystay Holidays* and been given the address of the Sattersfield family. Write a letter to them describing your family and home (real or imaginary) and inviting them to do the same.

▶ Text 2 · Tower slums wait for the hammer

FEW people now believe that system-built tower blocks are the answer to the country's housing problem. For any lingering doubters, the story of Towerhill, on Merseyside, could be instructive.

5 Less than five years after their completion, 16 huge blocks were standing forlorn, wrecked and uninhabitable – an ugly and costly memorial to the bulk-building policies that spawned them.

10 SIXTEEN blocks of flats at Towerhill, on Merseyside, were built between 1971 and 1973 to house 3,000 people. They stand now – damp, derelict and wrecked – as the ghastliest, most expensive folly in the history of British local authority housing.

15 The only problem still facing the owners, Knowsley District Council, is how best to demolish them. Only 80 families remain to endure the wetness and decay; and their recriminations echo loudly in the emptiness.

20 In the block called Stanforth House, opened on November 4, 1972, the Joyce family are one of the last four households to remain. All six of them – two adults and four children – sleep in one bedroom.

Spreading patches of damp mould have made the 25 others unusable.

"I'm terrified at night," says Mrs Patricia Joyce, who is expecting her fifth child. "The doors of all the empty flats slam in the wind. It's eerie. I'm frightened to be left alone. Outside, the place is like 30 a battlefield."

Along the abandoned landing, several of the empty flats have suffered fires. Walls are blackened; doors and cupboards badly charred. The flat next door to the Joyces' has been smashed by a gas 35 explosion. Others overflow with household rubbish, broken cots, twisted prams, fragments of wastepipe and heaps of insulating material. The copper piping, water tanks and other fittings have been looted, and the walls are being devoured by 40 mould.

On the fifth floor of Lime Court, opened on November 24, 1971, lives the Rev Dave Thomas. The water seeping through his bedroom ceiling trickles down the electric light flex and drips from 45 the bulb into an orange plastic bucket.

"The flats become flooded when the pipes are ripped out of empty flats above them," he says. "The places are not boarded up and you don't see a policeman around here from one day to the next. 50 The council itself has removed the window frames and the rain just rushes in, collects in huge puddles and finds its way down here."

Thomas is the driving force behind the Towerhill Flat Dwellers' Association, which has campaigned 55 for years to have the flats evacuated. "The problem is that the council regards us as the scum of the earth, the butt end of the borough. These were dud buildings to start off with. They sent all the social problem families here – all the people they thought 60 wouldn't protest."

Radshaw Court, opened on March 29, 1973, also now houses only four families. It was in this block that the Towerhill Flat Dwellers' Association commissioned Liverpool architect Jim Hunter to report 65 on the flats' construction and design.

Hunter found water penetration in every room of the flat he examined. Throughout his report he stressed the building's poor weather-resistance. Last year he asked Knowsley Council for access to 70 construction drawings so that he could more precisely pinpoint the structural shortcomings, but permission was refused.

Towerhill was the last great example of system-built council homes – vast slabs of concrete crane-75 hoisted together. The flats were never popular with tenants, who disliked the curiously interlocking designs. Some families had to walk upstairs from their front doors to their living rooms; others had to step down. And it was hardly a favourite feature 80 that one family's bedroom would adjoin another's living room.

Knowsley Director of Housing, Kenneth Hodgson, told *The Sunday Times*: "We'd rather be living quietly without all this attention. The only thing we 85 can do is empty those flats and seal them off. I would admit that there are the problems of modern concrete construction, but it's the people living up there who have wrecked the place. It's been a bloody shambles."

90 Chairman of the council's Housing Committee is Jim Lloyd. He blames the Towerhill disaster on a combination of failed housing policies and the wilful behaviour of tenants. "The truth is when we do something up there it doesn't last four hours. But 95 what has failed here is system-building, which the Government pressured councils into adopting so that it could get quick results in terms of homes built."

This month Knowsley commissioned its own 100 report from structural engineers, designed to discover just how difficult the flats will be to demolish.

"It's not a simple matter of a dumper truck with two bloody navvies and a 5lb hammer," says Lloyd. "These places are built of pre-stressed concrete with 105 special steel reinforcing."

The flats won't fall without a struggle. It will take Knowsley 60 years to pay off the debts incurred in *building* them – and winning further Government loan sanction for their demolition is not likely to be 110 easy.

by Rob Rohne in the Sunday Times

Find words in the article which mean:

a most awful (2) ....
b foolish mistake (2) ....
c accusations (3) ....
d blackened by
   burning (6) ....
e pieces (6) ....
f stolen (6) ....
g eaten (6) ....

h torn (8) ....
i emptied (9) ....
j sub-standard/
   useless (9) ....
k defects (11) ....
l mess (13) ....
m approval (17) ....

Now answer the following questions.

1   Explain why the Towerhill flats are seen as a foolish mistake ....
   ....
   ....
   ....

2   In what way were the flats 'like a battlefield' (lines 29-30)? ....
   ....
   ....
   ....

3   How might the council have improved the situation for the remaining tenants? ....
   ....
   ....
   ....
   ....

4   What two phrases are used to illustrate the council's low opinion of the tenants? ....
   ....
   ....
   ....

5   Explain what is meant by 'driving force' (line 53) ....
   ....
   ....
   ....

6   Why did the Flat Dwellers' Association commission an architect to report on the flats'
   construction and design? ....
   ....
   ....

7   Explain in your own words why Jim Hunter wanted to see the construction
   drawings ....
   ....
   ....
   ....

8   Why was the layout of the flats unpopular with tenants? ....
   ....
   ....
   ....

9   What justification does the council representative give for failing to maintain the
   buildings properly? ....
   ....
   ....
   ....

10 'The flats won't fall without a struggle.' (line 106) What *two* kinds of struggle will be
   involved? ....
   ....
   ....

▶ Focus on writing 2 · A letter of complaint

Structure   Look at this letter:

13 April 19___

Dear Sir,

I am writing to express my concern about the dangerous state of the pavements in the suburb of Clifton, where I live.

Severe weather last winter caused many of the old paving stones to crack and distort so that they now provide a very uneven surface to walk on. The worst affected areas are in Gloucester Lane, Queen's Street, and on the corner of Victoria Avenue and Windsor Road.

As you well know, many retired people live in the district and these pavements present a particularly serious hazard for them. Walking unsteadily, and perhaps suffering from poor eyesight, an elderly person could all too easily fall and badly hurt himself.

I must urge you to take immediate action to repair the damaged paving stones in order to prevent such accidents from occurring.

Yours faithfully,

OPENING PARAGRAPH
states the reason for the letter

MIDDLE PARAGRAPH
gives the precise nature
of the complaint

MIDDLE PARAGRAPH
explains the implications
of the matter

CLOSING PARAGRAPH
describes what action is
needed to put the matter
right

Notes   1   In the *opening paragraph* you should state clearly and concisely the reason for writing the letter so that the reader is prepared for the detail which follows. Names of people dealt with, places, dates and any other necessary information should be mentioned.

2   In the *middle paragraphs* you should outline the exact nature of your complaint simply and logically. Include enough detail to emphasise your point but not so much that your letter becomes rambling and ineffective. Avoid irrelevancies. Separate points are best made in separate paragraphs.

3   In the *closing paragraph* it is important to suggest clearly and firmly what action you think should be taken in order to resolve the matter.

Criticise the following letter:

Dear Sir,
    I'm writing to complain about a pair of shoes I bought recently in one of your stores. They were a most unusual colour and I couldn't resist buying them even though they were a bit pricey. I'd only been wearing them for a short while when one of the heels fell off and you can imagine how awkward that was in the middle of the High Street! When I took them back, the manager had the nerve to tell me that they were supposed to be fashion shoes and not meant for a lot of wear and tear.
    I think it's disgusting and I want some action from your company or you'll be hearing from my solicitor.
    Yours,

Writing assignment

Imagine that you are a member of the Towerhill Flat Dwellers' Association. Write a letter to Jim Lloyd, the Chairman of the council's Housing Committee, outlining the difficulties and dangers faced by the remaining tenants and suggesting what action he should take, both in the short and in the long term.

Useful language

1 I'm writing to express my | deep / grave | concern about | the state of the roads. / the fact that a new car park is being planned.

2 I must draw your attention to the fact | that . . .

I would like to emphasise | that I am in no way responsible. / the importance of the matter.

3 I must insist | that you put matters right. / on your immediate action in this matter.

I feel that / It seems to me that / It would appear to me that | you should . . . / the least you can do is . . . / you have a responsibility to . . . | as soon as possible. / without further delay. / immediately.

I should therefore be grateful if you could . . .

STUDY BOX
Do's and Don'ts of Letter Writing

Do	Don't
— write **your address** in the top right-hand corner.	— write your name before your address.
— write **the date** immediately below your address (eg 28th March 19__)	— write the date 28/3/19__
— write the **recipient's name and address** on the left-hand side of the page, just below the date, in formal letters only.	— write the recipient's name and address on the left in informal letters.
— use *Dear Sir/Madam* only when you don't know the person's name.	— begin *Dear Friend* – use the person's name.
— begin the letter on the left-hand side, next to the margin.	— begin the letter in the middle of the page.
— in a handwritten letter **indent each paragraph.** (You start a little way inside the margin.)	— forget to use paragraphs.
— write a short **final sentence** on a separate line, before the ending eg *I'm looking forward to hearing from you.*	
— end with *Yours faithfully* if you begin with *Dear Sir*; if you begin with *Dear Mr X*, end with *Yours sincerely,* (formal letters).	— Use *Dear Sir* with *Yours sincerely,* or *Dear Mr X* with *Yours faithfully.*
— use *Yours, Best wishes* or *Love* in informal letters, depending on how well you know the person!	

▶Communication activity

This activity will give you an opportunity to *work with a partner* using language in a freer, more creative way. One of you should look at the notes for the Housebuyer on this page and the other should turn to the notes for the Estate Agent on page 195.

Before you begin, read the notes for your role very carefully and mark any points that you need to keep in mind. If you are not sure about something, discuss it with your teacher or another student with the same role.

When you start, base your conversation on the notes but don't be afraid to use your imagination!

Role A Housebuyer

You are anxious to buy a house as soon as possible because your own has been sold and you and your family are having to stay with friends at the moment. You have £70,000 to spend although you *could* raise a further £10,000 if absolutely necessary. These are your requirements:

Central location, near shops (there is only one car in the family)

Three bedrooms (you have two children)

Good condition (you are no do-it-yourself fan)

Large garden if possible; *some* garden essential

Central heating if possible

Garage if possible but not essential

Storage space

Find out about the five homes which the estate agent has to offer. Remember that estate agents don't always mention the snags and be prepared to ask detailed questions. You can try offering a lower price if you like.

Make your notes about the choices like this.

	1	2	3	4	5
Address *(Location)* *(Price)* *(Beds)* *(Heating)* *(Garden)* *(Garage)* *(Storage)* *(Condition/notes)*					
Decision:					

▶Focus on register

The following four extracts share a common theme but they come from very different sources and have different characteristics of style, depending on the writer's purpose.

Read the four extracts carefully and consider (a) where such a piece of writing might be found, and (b) what the writer's purpose was. Then read the statements which follow and say which of the extracts they each refer to.

A

Cover your loft with at least 100 mm of insulation. Do the same around and over the top of your cold water tank (but not under it, or the water may freeze). You may be able to get a grant to help with the cost. Draught-proof your doors, windows and floorboards (also unused fireplaces) – but leave some ventilation to avoid condensation in the chimney.

B

Probably the most common way of connecting radiators to the boiler is the smallbore system (Fig. 1). Hot water is pumped from the boiler along flow pipes to the radiators. These give off heat and the cooler water is returned to the boiler along return pipes.

C

Each house is individually designed for each owner and built up to a standard, not down to a price, by country craftsmen using the best quality materials. As soon as you turn the key you become the owner of a home that is ready for you to live in. Fitted kitchens with ample worktops and cupboard space, lots of power points, bathroom suites in your own colour choice and much more.

D

My grandfather's large old stone house stood in the darkness, set back a dignified distance from the road. There was a walled-in garden at the rear and by the garden door was a low outhouse rented cheaply to the family of old Hannard and his son, Rashid, the rickshaw boy.

1 This passage describes a process in a neutral style.
2 A persuasive style is the characteristic of this passage.
3 This passage gives instructions to householders.
4 This passage is least likely to be accompanied by a diagram.
5 This passage is probably aimed at readers with a technical interest.
6 The passive voice is a characteristic of this type of writing.
7 This passage probably sets the scene in a novel.

LANGUAGE CHECK
Dependent Prepositions 1: Verb + Preposition

Here is a list of 16 verbs, some of which have been used in the texts in this unit. Write in the preposition which follows them.

Check your answers with your teacher or in the dictionary so that you have an accurate reference list for the future.

apply . . . (eg a job)
approve . . .
believe . . .
blame *something* . . . *somebody*
blame *somebody* . . . *something*
complain . . . *somebody* . . .
   something
cover *something* . . . *something else*

depend . . .
differ . . .
insist . . .
mistake *somebody* . . . *someone else*
overflow . . . *something*
regard *someone/something* . . . .
succeed . . .
suffer . . . eg *a disease*
take advantage . . .

▶ Focus on grammar · The passive voice

Look at these examples of the passive voice from the two texts which you have read and say what tense they are in. The first is done for you.

1 The machinery *is set* in motion (present simple)

2 The walls *are being devoured* by mould. ....

3 The flats *were built* between 1971 and 1973. ....

4 The flat . . . *has been smashed* by a gas explosion. ....

5 The match was as good as one could expect from the sparse completion of a questionnaire I *had been sent.* ....

6 No-one *will be admitted* to the auditorium after the curtain goes up. ....

Main uses of the passive voice

a When the agent is unknown or when it is unnecessary to mention the agent.

    eg Petrol is sold by the litre.
        The factory was designed five years ago.
        My handbag has been stolen

b To avoid using 'one' or 'you'.

    eg Bicycles can be rented cheaply.
        Drinks must not be brought into the football ground.
        Brushes should be washed out immediately.

c To emphasise the action or event rather than the agent.

    eg Coal is cut at the coal face and carried on a conveyor belt to the bottom of the pit shaft. It is then raised to the surface in cages.

d To make a statement more formal and impersonal.

    eg The position which you applied for has now been filled
        New safety procedures are to be introduced next year.
        It has been decided to close the students' bar.

Exercise

Put the verbs in brackets into the appropriate passive tense in the following sentences.

1 You'll hardly recognise our flat. It (*redecorate*) since your last visit.

2 Two players (*send*) off the field during last Saturday's match.

3 The hotel, which (*complete*) only last year, (*equip*) with a solarium and sauna.

4 The theatre company (*give*) a grant of £6,000 and a further £2,000 (*now/seek*) from elsewhere.

5 Applications (*invite*) for the post of Senior Lecturer in the Department of Architecture. Preference (*give*) to applicants with teaching experience.

6 As my car (*repair*) last Friday, I (*give*) a lift to work by a colleague.

7 As soon as your order (*receive*), it (*process*) and an acknowledgement (*send*).

8 Eleven strikers who (*imprison*) for disturbing the peace (*release*) yesterday.

9 The ancient language of Aramaic (*speak*) in only three villages in Syria and (*overtake*) gradually by Arabic nowadays.

10 Your gas cooker (*inspect*) and no fault (*find*). It (*deliver*) to your home in the next week.

▶ Focus on writing 3 · Description of process

Coffee preparation

Tent-dwelling Bedouins in Arabia invariably welcome guests with coffee. This is prepared by the men of the family over an open fire. Using the present simple passive, write a description of the process of coffee preparation which is illustrated below.

Begin: Coffee beans are taken from a skin bag and . . .

▶ Focus on listening

You are going to hear a talk about a typical house in the ancient city of Sana'a in Yemen. Look at the photograph and describe the appearance of such a house.

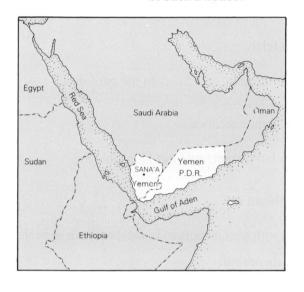

During the talk you should look at the two plans below which are labelled with letters A–O and at the list of rooms and uses. Write one letter by the room or use which it represents. Two are already done for you.

Room/Use	Letter
Kitchen	. . . . .
Living room	. . . . .
Animal stalls	. . . . .
Laundry	. . . . .
Mafraj	. . . . .
Lobby	. . B . .
Entrance hall	. . . . .
Grain store	. . . . .
Wardrobe	. . . . .
Bathroom	. . . . .
Well	. . . . .
Diwan	. . . . .
Loading	. . L . .
Grinding	. . . . .

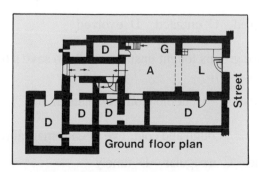

Ground floor plan

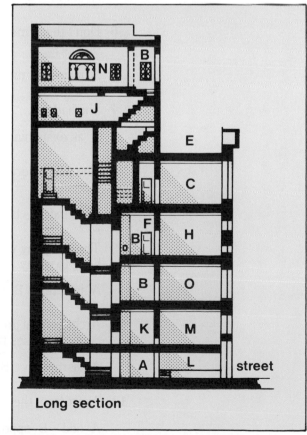

Long section

▶ Vocabulary practice

Review In this section you must choose the word or phrase which best completes each sentence.

The correct answers here, and in all the other vocabulary review sections in the book, will be words or phrases which you have already met in the unit concerned, or in earlier units.

1 The hotel room was .... furnished with only a bed, a wardrobe and an ancient armchair.

   A thinly   B sparsely   C lightly   D sketchily

2 The main disadvantage to our house is that the only .... to the garden is through a bedroom.

   A passage   B doorway   C access   D communication

3 I've had my car examined three times now but no mechanic has been able to .... the problem.

   A pinpoint   B focus   C specify   D highlight

4 Our hosts had prepared a .... meal with seven courses to celebrate our arrival.

   A generous   B profuse   C lavish   D spendthrift

5 Having decided to rent a flat, we .... contacting all the accommodation agencies in the city.

   A set to   B set off   C set out   D set about

6 Don't thank me for helping in the garden. It was .... pleasure to be working out of doors.

   A plain   B mere   C simple   D sheer

7 She had .... mind which kept her alert and well-informed even in old age.

   A an examining   B a demanding   C an enquiring   D a querying

8 The police decided to .... the department store after they had received a bomb warning.

   A abandon   B evacuate   C evict   D expel

9 The company was declared bankrupt when it had .... more debts than it could hope to repay.

   A inflicted   B incurred   C entailed   D evolved

10 Architectural pressure groups fought unsuccessfully to save a terrace of eighteenth century houses from ....

   A disruption   B abolition   C demolition   D dismantling

11 Apart from the .... cough and cold, I've been remarkably healthy all my life.

   A odd   B opportune   C irregular   D timely

12 I had to take out a bank loan when I started up in business and it took me two years to pay it ....

A out   B up   C over   D off

13 The railway line has been closed for ten years and the station buildings are now sadly ....

A decrepit   B derelict   C decomposed   D discarded

14 The school authorities .... the child's unruly behaviour on his parents' lack of discipline.

A attribute   B accuse   C blame   D ascribe

15 After months of bitter arguing the couple had to accept that they were ....

A incongruous   B incompatible   C dissident   D disaffected

16 We can't eat this bread. It's ....

A mouldy   B rotten   C bad   D rancid

17 A special committee was set up to .... on the problem of football hooliganism.

A investigate   B inform   C research   D report

18 After the flash flood, all the drains were overflowing .... storm water.

A from   B with   C by   D for

19 Soldiers were warned that anyone caught .... the shops in the deserted town would be severely punished.

A stealing   B raiding   C embezzling   D looting

20 The BBC has .... a young composer to write a piece of music for the Corporation's centenary.

A ordered   B consulted   C commissioned   D decided

Words describing the movement of liquids

Choose words from the following list and put them in the correct form in the sentences below.

flow   pour   gush   trickle   drip   seep   splash   lap   gurgle   pelt

1 The sound of a tap .... kept me awake all night.
2 The rain is really .... down! We can't possibly go out in it.
3 There was a loud .... sound as the bathwater ran down the plughole.
4 Be careful how you .... my beer!
5 There was a .... as my camera fell into the river.
6 As I lay in my cabin I heard the gentle sound of waves .... against the hull.
7 The River Swift rises in the hills and then .... south west to the sea.
8 A water main had burst and water was .... out of the ground with great force.
9 Moisture from the fish had .... through the paper bag and made the rest of the shopping damp.
10 Rain was falling on my collar and .... unpleasantly down my neck.

▶Grammar practice

1   Fill each of the numbered blanks in the following passage with *one* suitable word.

It is forecast that we can look .... (1) to working fewer hours in the future, but it is necessary for health and tranquillity to work a certain .... (2) of hours per week, ideally doing a variety of jobs – something schools .... (3) always known. It .... (4) be that house building will .... (5) this need. It is a very basic human instinct. Gardening is a related .... (6). It is already cheaper to .... (7) many fruits and vegetables than to buy them in the shops and the house of the next decade should take this into .... (8).

Another important question is .... (9) of energy conservation. The proportion of income .... (10) on keeping warm is steadily going up, and, with the cost of energy .... (11) to double in real terms during the next ten years or .... (12), many large badly-insulated old houses will become extremely expensive to use. The demand will be .... (13) small, well-insulated homes .... (14) in warm protected areas and making the .... (15) use of the sun's warmth. Efficient heating units will be .... (16) prime importance. At .... (17) we waste a lot of space .... (18) planning rooms which are awkward to use.

2   Finish each of the following sentences in such a way that it means exactly the same as the sentence printed before it.

EXAMPLE: I know that he is honest.   ANSWER: I know him *to be honest*

a The house was so badly damaged in the fire that it couldn't be repaired.
  The house was too . . .

b He told me my request was unreasonable.
  He said, 'You can hardly . . .'

c I was exasperated when the appointment was cancelled once again.
  Imagine . . .

d You won't reach the station in less than twenty minutes.
  It will take . . .

e I took my car to the garage last Saturday and they resprayed it.
  I had . . .

f 'Whatever you do, don't give up hope,' they said.
  They urged me . . .

g How often is it necessary to feed your goldfish?
  How often does . . .

h It is possible that she has been delayed.
  She may well . . .

i They didn't prosecute any of the protesters.
  None . . .

j I didn't hear the news until the next day.
  It was not . . .

UNIT 2 Work

▶ Lead-in

1 *a* Of the jobs shown above, which *two* are likely to offer the greatest job satisfaction in your opinion? Explain why.
   b Which *two* are likely to offer the least job satisfaction? Say why.

2 *a* Think of the worst job you have ever had, full-time or part-time, paid or voluntary. Tell the class why it was so bad.
   b What are the most common complaints from people who are dissatisfied with their jobs, apart from low wages?

3 *a* The *Guardian* newspaper sent out a questionnaire to its readers on the subject of work and careers and received more than 11,000 replies. In one section, aspects of work which might contribute to job satisfaction were listed and readers were asked to say how important they were.

Working with a partner, consider the 15 points below and put them in order of importance.

What adds up to job satisfaction?

How important are each of the following to you in providing you with job satisfaction?

- Challenge
- Meeting people through work
- Security
- The respect of colleagues
- Working conditions
- Status in your organisation
- Learning something new
- Personal freedom
- Being part of a team
- Exercising power
- Helping other people
- Being praised by your superiors
- Social status
- Being promoted
- Making money

When you have finished, compare your results with those of another pair. Then turn to page 195 to see how *Guardian* readers responded.

▶Text 1 · The clerk

Read through the passage and answer these questions.

1 Where did the writer begin his working life?
2 What was his brother's opinion of a clerk's work?
3 Which of his jobs did the writer enjoy least? Why?
4 Which did he enjoy to some extent?

"*He's in quite a good mood today.*"

Start at the beginning: Civil Service clerk, temporary, at the local Ministry of Works depot in my home town. Can't get any lower than that. At the base of the bureaucratic pyramid, buried alive in fact, the temporary clerk is the navvy of the Civil Service, without status or security. When I took the job I'd only worked in
5 factories, and so I was a bit in awe of the office world I was about to enter. As an apprentice, queueing in the spotless corridor on Thursdays outside the wages window, peering in at the comparative purity of desks and paper and slick, dandified staff, you got a queer, dizzy sensation. My brother was a clerk himself, at the Council House, but I never connected him with this Thursday vision.
10 On my first day as a clerk, going down the street with my brother, I confessed how nervous I was. 'Listen,' he said, 'you can write your name can't you? You can add up? Then you can be a clerk.'

It was true. The depot was a big old house near the city centre, with the offices upstairs. My boss had a room at the front to himself, and behind him was a door
15 leading to my den, which contained three others. This boss, a big, bumbling, embarrassed man addressed us all with the 'Mr' fixed firmly between, as if to maintain his distance. Everyone accepted his remoteness as inevitable, something which struck me as weird from the beginning, especially as you had to go to and fro behind his chair to the outer door every time you went anywhere. The boss sat
20 through it all encased in silence and dignity, like an Under Secretary.

Holed up in the back room it was snug and at first I liked it, till the novelty wore off and the chronic, stagnant boredom began to take over. An old man, the only other temporary, made tea in the corner where he sat, and he did all the menial labouring jobs, stamping and numbering time-sheets, sorting vouchers: so at first I
25 helped him. The other two did the more skilled entering and balancing, working on wage sheets, PAYE tabulations and other mysteries I never penetrated. It seemed to culminate, their activity, in the grand climax of pay-day, which was Friday. Then the boss, for an hour or so, came out of his fastness and was nearly human. He would march in smiling with the box stuffed full of money, and together they
30 would count and parcel it. Out went the box again, stuffed with pay envelopes.

The old man was treated with amiable contempt by the established clerks, who asserted their superiority now and again, and, as the old man was deaf, kept up a running commentary, half fun and half malice, which they evidently found necessary to break the monotony. Before long I needed it as much as they did. The
35 worst aspect of a clerk's existence was being rubbed into me: it's how prison must be. At first you don't even notice; then it starts to bite in. Because of the terrible limitation of your physical freedom – *chained to a desk* is right – you are soon forced to make your own amusements in order to make life bearable. You have to liven it up. And with the constriction comes inevitably an undertow of bitterness
40 and all kinds of petty behaviour arise out of the rubbing frustration, the enforced closeness. Plenty of it is malicious.

Another clerical job, at a builder's merchants, was redeemed to some extent by the fact that you were actually in the warehouse, among storemen, sales reps, and all the tangible, fascinating paraphernalia of the trade, racks and bins and lofts
45 stacked with it; one occupational hazard facing a clerk is always the sense of futility he struggles against, or is more often just overwhelmed by. Unlike even the humblest worker on a production line, he doesn't produce *anything*. He battles with phantoms, abstracts; runs in a paper chase that goes on year after year, and seems utterly pointless. How can there be anything else other than boredom in it
50 for him?

'The Clerk' by Philip Callow from 'Work: Twenty Personal Accounts', Pelican

Now look again at paragraphs 4 and 5 and find the word or phrase which means the same as:

a hidden (4) ....   *h* safe place which is hard to reach (4) ......

b cosy (4) ....   *i* good-natured (5) ....

c passed away (4) ....   *j* lack of respect (5) ....

d unchanging (4) ....   *k* displayed (5) ....

e suitable for a servant (4) ....   *l* intention to hurt (5) ....

f understood (4) ....   *m* current (noun) (5) ....

g reach the highest point of development (4)   *n* unimportant (5) ....

....

Now complete these statements. Remember to say why the other possibilities are unsuitable.

1 When the writer first got a job in the Civil Service he
  a felt intimidated by the prospect.
  b looked forward to working in cleaner surroundings.
  c felt sick with anxiety.
  d realised how dull the work was going to be.

2 His boss seemed to him
  a moody and unpredictable.
  b formal and aloof.
  c cold and hostile.
  d shy and forgetful.

3 The writer seems to have become disillusioned because he
  a disliked dealing with complex calculations.
  b didn't find the work challenging enough.
  c did not get on well with his colleagues.
  d was not allowed to handle money.

4 He regarded his colleagues' behaviour towards the old man as
  a cruel because the man was deaf.
  b an essential element of office life.
  c an enjoyable way to pass the time.
  d a natural result of their environment.

5 His job at the builder's merchants was preferable because he
  a was not required to handle paperwork.
  b had a chance to talk to people.
  c felt more involved in the business.
  d was interested in the firm's records.

▶ Focus on writing · The narrative/descriptive essay

There is a strong temptation, especially in a test or examination situation, to start writing feverishly as soon as you have chosen an essay topic. You may not want to plan your essay in advance or make notes beforehand for fear that it will waste time or interfere with your creative 'flow'. In fact, lack of planning can lead to various problems. Running out of ideas when you are only half way through is a common one. Can you think of any others?

The best approach is to make a list of points, in note form, which you want to include. Each paragraph should develop the theme of your essay one step further. This will enable you to check that all points are relevant and represent a logical and natural progression while maintaining overall balance. You should be able to avoid rambling repetition and irrelevant detail.

Below are points to be included in an essay entitled *My first work experience*. Match them to the appropriate paragraphs.

Para 1 ⎱
     2 ⎰ Scene-setting
     3
     4
     5
     6   Conclusion

a Gaining experience – the daily routine
b Expectations of the job
c Some memorable incidents
d The first day – learning the ropes
e Reflections on the experience in general
f Need for money as a student

Now prepare a plan for the following topic:

> Write an account, true or imaginary, of the least enjoyable job you have ever had.

When you are satisfied with your plan, write your essay in about 300 words.

▶ Text 2 · Equal at work?

Read through the passage and answer these questions:

1 What are the advantages of equality at work?
2 What factors make equality at work hard to achieve?

In the early seventies, when the Department of Employment and EEC alike said the answer to women's low pay – and perhaps to poverty in general – was for
5 women 'to break through the ring-fence of special women's employment', it seemed improbable this social transformation would ever be achieved.

Hedged about by our own self-images,
10 as much as by the opposition of employers, unions and husbands, it looked as if it would be impossible for us to grasp that the roles of Pamela the Great Man's Handmaiden and Dora the tea-lady *were*
15 roles, imposed from outside, and not the limits of our capacities.

Events since have demonstrated the untruth of these impressions. Women of all types have blazed trails in new areas, so
20 that in a matter of a few years the impossible has happened. There are women piloting British airliners, women as navigating and radio officers on ships, women detective superintendents leading
25 murder enquiries, women military officers performing strenuous training exercises – all on equal terms.

The change has not been one of revolutionary speed but it has spread
30 through a wide range of jobs. It is no longer only university graduates and the like who are breaking the boundaries of tradition. The late seventies was the time when June Wilson, a cleaning lady, Alison
35 Crompton, a nightclub hostess, and Rosalba Turi, a clothing factory presser, left their 'traditional' jobs and became crane drivers. It was the time when Colette Clark and Margaret Chairman resisted all
40 their schools' pressure for them to become shopgirls, clerks and seamstresses, to take up electrical trades apprenticeships. When Maureen Marshall gave up assembly work for skilled joinery. When Cristina Stuart,
45 who abandoned her secretarial work to travel the roads of Europe as a rep, became Sales Manager of her Publishing House.

Even without high-flying ambitions, work of a more masculine cast has strong
50 advantages. At Maureen Marshall's factory in Doncaster, work had been traditionally segregated – even though, ironically, all the work involved was of a 'masculine' character in a joinery factory making

55 doors, window-frames and even
housefronts. The bulk of the labour,
however, was female and it was the women
who supplied the joinery work which was
frequently very heavy. Meanwhile the men
60 minded cutting machines and drove fork-
lift trucks at higher rates of pay.

The men were allowed day-release to
become skilled apprentices; the women
remained, in paper terms, uneducated
65 even after 28 years in the same factory, and
even when they were privately skilled in
advanced cabinet-making. The men, as
qualified machinists, had the option of
moving elsewhere if better jobs presented
70 themselves. And they progressed up the
firm to become foremen and managers.
The women, technically unqualified, were
considered good only for the exact job they
were in, however skilled they might
75 individually be. When equal pay
legislation came into force, the work done
by the women, which in the pre-war past
had been done by recognised qualified
joiners, was downgraded by the employer
80 to unskilled, and continued at an unequal
rate to the men's. Maureen, whose
foreman had encouraged her to move into
the male area, was one of the few who got
equal pay, and has a foot on the ladder
85 towards supervisory work, or work options
elsewhere.

Another problem for women, according
to an industrial psychologist, is that 'they
consistently undervalue themselves',
90 taking a humble viewpoint. Cristina
Stuart, in fact, has learned the male
technique of making her own chances.
'There really are things you have to grow
out of once you're moving, that sort of
95 feeling you have at first of just being

grateful for having a place on the bench
alongside the big boys, that initial
wondering when you're talking to directors
and managers in other companies of
100 whether it will come over as what you
intend, or whether they'll take what you
say as female chatter. You have to train
yourself out of that female lack of
assertiveness. At least, I don't think it is
105 specifically female – you see it in men too –
they have to make an effort when they
move into management from another job,
to get the style – though I think it's harder
for women because it goes against a
110 lifetime's training. And you've also got to
counter that female tendency to be
overhelpful, insufficiently competitive and
wary.

'And it is possible. Bit by bit, when you
115 find things work, that you are effective,
that you are indubitably really *there* as far
as work results are concerned, any feeling
that you are wearing a disguise gradually
melts away. Suddenly you wake up one
120 morning and you are a manager in the
whole way you react and act and think, and
it is second nature. There are an awful lot
of girls in jobs below their capacities
simply because of the way they think about
125 themselves. In the end it all boils down to a
matter of attitude.'

It is evident that women can, and are,
adapting themselves to male professions.
But for true equality, why can there not be
130 a further stage – unmentioned as yet –
valuing women's jobs properly. Why
should not a nurse or a home help be
considered as valuable and paid as well as a
carpenter or plumber? When this equation
135 is solved, equality will be here.

from 'Driver, banker, carpenter, sailor' by Lyn Owen in the Observer, London

Now answer the following questions.

1 What do you understand by the phrase 'the ring-fence of special women's
employment' (lines 5–6)?

2 In what way is it suggested that women themselves have contributed to their
inequality at work?

3 What does the expression 'blazed trails' (line 19) suggest about the achievements of
the women mentioned?

4 What was unusual about the choice of crane driving as a job for the three women?

5 Why do you think there was pressure from schools for girls to take certain jobs?

6 Explain the phrase 'in paper terms' (line 64).

7 Why was equal pay legislation ineffective?

8 Explain in your own words what Maureen Marshall has gained, apart from equal pay.

9 What fear do women often have when addressing senior staff, according to Cristina
Stuart?

10 What masculine characteristics does she suggest that women should cultivate in order
to fight inequality at work?

11 What does 'it' (line 114) refer to?

12 Explain 'it is second nature' (line 122).

13 Summarise in a paragraph of 50–100 words the disadvantages which women have
suffered from at work, as described by the author. (For details on how to write a
summary, see STUDY BOX – Summary Writing on page 127.)

▶ Focus on grammar 1 ·
Review of the present perfect

Look at these examples from Text 2:

a Events since *have demonstrated* the untruth of these impressions.
b Women of all types *have blazed* trails in new areas so that in a matter of years the impossible *has happened*
c The change *has not been* one of revolutionary speed but it *has spread* through a wide range of jobs.
d Cristina . . . *has learned* the male technique of making her own chances.

The present perfect tense has a strong connection with present time. When we refer to an event in the present perfect, we are usually concerned with the result or effect of that event as it applies to us now:

eg I'm afraid he's *left* the office.   (= he's not available to see you)
    You've *ruined* the carpet.   (= we'll have to replace it)
    I've *been* to Mexico City.   (= I have some experience of it)

Suggest what the following examples mean as far as the present is concerned:

You've just missed the bus!
The meeting has been cancelled.
We've run out of petrol.
She's been sacked.
Have you tasted Portuguese 'caldeirada'?

There are two main uses of the present perfect:

1 a to express an action which started in the past and has continued until the present:

eg *I've been* off work with 'flu since Monday.

   b to express a number of individual actions which have happened until the present:

eg *He's won* several medals for diving in the last few years.

Time expressions often used: *for, since, lately, so far, up to now,* etc.

2 to express an action which was completed in the past but where the time is not given:

eg *You've seen* the film. Would you recommend me to go and see it?

In this case, it is the present result of the action or event which is important. Indefinite time expressions commonly used with this type of present perfect are: *already, yet, ever, never, before*

The present perfect continuous

The present perfect continuous can often be used as an alternative to the present perfect simple to express an action which began in the past and has continued to the present. There may be a slight difference of emphasis:

1 The present perfect continuous emphasises the process of the action rather than the action as a whole. Compare:

I've been waiting for an hour.
I've waited long enough!

It therefore tends to be used with verbs of continuous action (*stay, lie, work, read, study* etc) and in situations where an action has been repeated:

eg I've been trying to get hold of you all day.

2 The present perfect continuous suggests that a situation is temporary rather than permanent. Compare:

He's been working for the Post Office for the last six months.
He's worked for the Post Office since he was 16.

3 The present perfect continuous is also used when the action in the recent past, which was continuous, is now complete but the results are still apparent:

> eg 'Your hands are dirty.'
> 'Yes, I've been cleaning the car.'

Further points:

a The present perfect continuous is not usually used with those verbs which rarely occur in the present continuous. When it does, there is a special emphasis or a change of meaning. (See STUDY BOX and Exercise 1 below.)

b The present perfect continuous cannot be used to express a completed action, or where a quantity is expressed. Compare:

I've been collecting stamps all my life.
I've collected literally thousands of stamps!
I've been smoking all morning. I've smoked 30 cigarettes!

STUDY BOX
Stative Verbs

These are verbs which describe a state rather than an event, and which are not usually used in the continuous tenses. An example is *know*.

Some of these verbs can be stative in one meaning but non-stative in another meaning. An example is *think*:

> I *think* you're right. = have an opinion (stative);
> Be quiet while I'*m thinking*. = considering, a deliberate activity (non-stative).

These verbs are shown in blue in the list of stative verbs below.

Senses: *see, hear, notice, recognise*

Emotions: *like, dislike, love, hate, want, prefer, mind, care*

Thought processes: *think, feel, know, believe, suppose, understand, realise, recognise, remember*

Possession: *own, possess, belong to*

Inherent Properties/Qualities: *be, have, look, appear, seem, sound, smell, taste, weigh, measure, hold, contain, consist of, fit, cost*

Others: *owe, matter, depend (on), trust, deserve, apply*

Exercise 1   The following verbs are among those listed above as being stative. They may be used in continuous tenses, however, when there is a change of meaning. Remember that verbs are used statively to refer to *involuntary states* while they are used non-statively to refer to *deliberate actions*

1 Look at each verb below and see if you can think of two separate meanings.

> eg *see* means a) observe with the eyes (involuntary), and
> b) meet someone by arrangement (deliberate).

2 Complete the sentences on page 27 by using each of the verbs *twice*, with two different meanings. Use the correct simple or continuous form in each case.

see	depend	fit
hold	apply	look

a Up to now, the discount .... only to children under 10. From next month, we're planning to extend it to children under 16.
b What do you mean, you're past it? In my opinion you (never) .... fitter in your life!
c She .... a lot of Mark lately. Do you think there's anything between them?
d Since I broke my leg, I .... on my daughter to see to the shopping and housework.
e He .... for jobs without success for months now.
f The hall .... 300 people on some occasions, though you'd hardly believe it.
g As you .... the film already, can you tell me if it would be likely to appeal to my young nephew?
h Sorry about the mess! The workmen .... a new boiler in the bathroom all morning.
i The success of the agricultural show .... very much on the weather in recent years.
j Oh there's *The Times*! I .... for it everywhere.
k They .... him as a political prisoner since 1984.
l All the shirts you've sent your father .... him perfectly so far.

Exercise 2 Complete the following passage with the correct form of the verb in brackets. Use the present, present perfect or past, simple or continuous, active or passive:

Case notes of a nurse

Ward Sister Sarah Browne is responsible for the welfare of 28 patients on two wards at the London hospital where she (work 1) for the last 6 years. She (direct 2) a staff of 12 working in three shifts. There are also as many as 15 student nurses who (assign 3) to the ward at any one time. It (calculate 4), she says, that 200 people – doctors, nurses, visitors, students – (move 5) through her general and acute medical ward in a day.

Sister Browne, who is 39, (qualify 6) as a nurse 20 years ago. She (work 7) as a clinical teacher and (do 8) research into psychotherapy for former smokers. Her working week easily (exceed 9) the 37½ hours she is supposed to work.

08.45 The morning report (just/end 10) and Sister Browne (listen 11) as a qualified nurse (explain 12) the insulin injection she is about to give to a diabetic patient.

09.38 Sister Browne (chat 13) by the bedside of an 85-year old woman who (wait 14) for a place in a home for two and a half years.

11.33 Sister Browne (just/interrupt 15) by a telephone call. Whatever she (do 16), she finds herself being summoned to deal with queries and occasional emergencies. Whenever she (enter 17) a room, she (switch 18) on a light by the door to show staff and patients that she (arrive 19).

All the nurses (wear 20) flat white shoes which are essential to lessen the strain of being on their feet virtually all day. The floors are hard but Sister Browne says she (get used to 21) them and hardly (notice 22) her aching feet any more.

12.18 Sister Browne (have 23) a kind word with an elderly patient who (recently/admit 24) and is very concerned about her dog and four cats. Pets are a particular problem for elderly patients who (live 25) alone for some time.

15.01 Sister Browne (joke 26) with a patient who is about to (take 27) to another part of the hospital for an X-ray. The ward (specialise 28) in chest diseases and Sister Browne (ban 29) smoking.

15.55 Now that her shift (finish 30), Sister Browne (snatch 31) a moment's rest before driving home. She will be up again at six tomorrow to do the same shift.

▶ Communication activity · Clothes to wear at work

The consumer magazine *Which?* carried out a survey of its members to find out their general opinion of office clothes and also the kind of clothes which they felt were suitable for different kinds of jobs.

More than 1,000 *Which?* members were involved in the survey which was in two parts. *Work with a partner* to answer the same questions. Then see how your opinion compares with the results of the original survey!

Part 1 Look at the following statements about clothes to wear at work and tick the correct box. You should have reasons for your answers.

		AGREE	DISAGREE
1	The way people dress at work usually indicates how competent they are at their jobs.	☐	☐
2	People should be allowed to wear exactly what they want at work.	☐	☐
3	Firms who want employees to wear particular clothes should pay for those clothes.	☐	☐
4	In most firms, the way you dress will affect your chances of promotion.	☐	☐
5	People work best in the clothes they feel most comfortable in.	☐	☐
6	People wearing unusual clothes to work give a bad impression to clients.	☐	☐
7	As long as a person is good at his job, it shouldn't matter what he/she wears.	☐	☐
8	I object to senior female staff wearing trousers.	☐	☐
9	Sloppy clothes mean sloppy work.	☐	☐
10	I wouldn't have faith in an executive who wore jeans to work.	☐	☐
11	Men shouldn't be allowed to take off their jackets at work even in the summer.	☐	☐
12	Bosses should always be smartly dressed.	☐	☐

Turn to page 196 for the results of the *Which?* survey.

Part 2 With a partner, look at the pictures opposite. Decide which one or two of the following jobs each outfit would be suitable for.

Architect	Middle management executive
Bank manager	Television reporter
Clerk	Personnel manager
Designer	Researcher
Doctor	Schoolteacher
Insurance salesman	

Note You can mention the same job as many times as you like and you needn't use all the jobs mentioned.

Now turn to page 196 and compare your results with those of the *Which?* survey.

1

Shirt, no tie, smart trousers
pale shirt, dark trousers

2

Scruffy suit
dark navy, somewhat battered suit, sober tie

3

Casual shirt and faded jeans
faded, scruffy and old blue denims, red checked shirt, trainers

4

Trendy
denim shirt, jazzy tie, leather jacket, cream trousers, black shoes

5

Sports jacket and trousers
brown check sports jacket, pale blue shirt, cream trousers, sober tie

6

Smart jeans, collar, tie
pale blue shirt, smart tie, new-looking jeans

7

Polo neck sweater,
jacket and trousers all dark coloured

8

Three-piece pin-stripe suit
dark navy suit, white shirt, sober tie

▶ Focus on grammar 2 · Phrasal verbs

Phrasal verbs are an extremely important feature of English. They are used widely in conversation and in informal written English, including many newspaper and magazine articles, to express ideas in a vivid and homely way.

Phrasal verbs are often used in preference to verbs of Latin origin which sound more formal: eg *go down* for *descend*; *rub out* for *erase*. English speakers probably learn phrasal verbs earlier than other sorts of verbs in their childhood.

A foreign learner who is not aware of the most common phrasal verbs is likely to have considerable difficulty in following everyday spoken English. And someone who is unable to use phrasal verbs appropriately in speech will tend to sound stiff and formal to an English listener.

Form and meaning   A phrasal verb is a combination of a verb (*do, make, put* etc) with one or two particles (adverbs or prepositions such as *on, up, out* etc).

The meaning of the phrasal verb can sometimes be guessed easily from the sum of its parts:

eg He *took off* his coat.

More often, the meaning is quite different from the combination of its parts:

eg He *took* me *in* with his story. (deceived)

Some phrasal verbs also have more than one meaning:

eg *go off* – depart
explode
go bad (of food)

Here are some examples of phrasal verbs from the texts in this unit. Which meanings are easy to guess?

Text 1   . . . at first I liked it, till the novelty *wore off* and the chronic, stagnant boredom began to *take over*

(the clerks) *kept up* a running commentary

He . . . runs in a paper chase that *goes on* year after year.

Text 2   . . . to *take up* electrical trades apprenticeships

Maureen Marshall *gave up* assembly work for skilled joinery.

There really are things you have to *grow out of*

Word order   Phrasal verbs can be divided into three main groups:

1 Transitive/separable (adverbial phrasal verbs)

a If the object of the phrasal verb is a *noun*, the particle may either come before or after the noun:
eg She *gave up* her job.   or   She *gave* her job *up*
b If the object is a *pronoun*, the particle must follow it.
eg She got bored with her job and decided to *give* it *up*

2 Transitive/inseparable (prepositional phrasal verbs)

The preposition always comes before the object whether it is a noun or a pronoun:
eg I *ran into* my brother/him in the library today. (met by chance)
Note: All 3-word phrasal verbs (eg *grow out of*) are inseparable.

3 Intransitive (adverbial phrasal verbs)

eg My headache *wore off* after a while.
Rehearsals *went on* all afternoon.

Exercise 1 Give an alternative word for the common phrasal verbs in the following sentences:

a I *gave up* smoking years ago!

b Well, that's my offer. Why don't you *think* it *over* for a few days?

c I've *talked* the matter *over* with my husband and we've decided to accept your offer.

d The police are *looking into* the company's records.

e They've decided to *call off* the strike.

f He *turned up* half an hour late for his appointment.

g Please *put out* your cigarettes before entering the library.

h I found it reasonably easy to *pick up* enough Spanish to *get by* with.

i It was obvious that he was *making up* facts as he went along.

j Numbers in the class have *fallen off* recently.

Exercise 2 Look at the sentences in Exercise 1 again. Which of the phrasal verbs (apart from *b* and *c*) are separable?

Exercise 3 Put crosses on the following grid to show which particle the verbs can be combined with:

	in	down	off	on	out	up
carry			×	×	×	
cut						
fill						
give						
hand						
make						
pay						
turn						

LANGUAGE CHECK
Make vs Do

eg *they have to* **make an effort** *when they move into management* (Text 2)

the **work done** *by women* (Text 2)

Here is a list of 36 words or phrases. Decide whether they are used with **do** or **make** and write the answers in the correct column below.

Check your answers with your teacher or in the dictionary so that you have an accurate reference list for the future.

a suggestion, an offer, an examination, a profit, (someone) a favour, homework, an excuse, an attempt, damage, money, fun of, one's best, sure, a choice, harm, an exercise, a decision, room for (somebody/something), one's duty, a course, the best of, use of, a complaint, business, good, a mistake, certain, a journey, an effort, an arrangement, housework, an enquiry, the most of, a discovery, work, war.

Make	Do

▶ Focus on listening

This advertisement has recently appeared in the newspaper. You are now going to hear one of the applicants being interviewed.

As you listen, complete the interview report form below by putting a tick (✓) in the appropriate boxes and filling in any other necessary details.

Note In some sections it may be appropriate to tick more than one box.

GROUND HOST(ESS)S and RECEPTION STAFF

HAPPY HOLS, the successful coach tour operator, requires staff to handle visitors from Europe and the United States on their arrival at the airport.

Applicants should have a pleasant personality, plenty of initiative and be able to work under pressure at times. A foreign language would be an advantage. Preferably full-time but could be part-time.

Good salary for the right applicants.

INTERVIEW REPORT FORM

1 **Job title:** Ground Hostess / Reception Staff

2 **Name of applicant:** Rosemary Jones

3 **Address:** 12 Regent St. Stanmore Middlesex   permanent accommodation ☐   temporary accommodation ☐

4 **Age:** under 20 ☐   20–24 ☐   25–30 ☐   over 30 ☐

5 **Educational qualifications:**

CSE ☐   O Level ☐   A Level ☐   degree ☐

details of subjects ....

6 **Foreign languages spoken:**

	Fluent	Very good	Good	Fair
a	☐	☐	☐	☐
b	☐	☐	☐	☐
c	☐	☐	☐	☐

Standard

7 **Work experience:**

industrial ☐   commercial ☐   retail ☐
casual labour ☐   voluntary ☐   other ☐
eg building site

details: ....

8 **General health and fitness:**

Excellent ☐   Good ☐   Fair ☐   Poor ☐

9 **Hobbies:**

Sport ☐   Music ☐   Theatre/Cinema ☐
Handicrafts ☐   Other ☐
eg sewing

10 **Personality:**

shy/nervous ☐   cold/distant ☐   relaxed/friendly ☐
too casual/informal ☐   overconfident ☐

11 **Details of availability:** ....

12 **Starting salary offered:** £..........

▶ Focus on register

Read the following advertisements:

A

This dynamic and pioneering company, a member of a well-established group, continues to expand significantly its market share, both through emphasis on technical excellence and a professional business approach. This new appointment is the corner-stone in the company's future diversification programme.

B

If you've got an eye for detail, coupled with secretarial skills, then Bejam the freezer people have just the job for you at their busy, lively offices in Stanmore. You'll be responsible for checking that the prices and spelling are correct on our display material, liaising with the display company and store managers. This involves a lot of telephone work and keeping to deadlines, so you must be capable of working efficiently under pressure.

C

The company is a successful independent operator with turnover now exceeding £30m. It provides a range of services from a number of locations in the UK and on the Continent.

Reporting to the General Manager, responsibility is to manage the finance and accounting functions. Developing controls and advising on financial policy and planning will be major tasks. Success in the role should lead to a Board appointment.

D

Mayfair-based public company is looking for the best sales people in Britain. You must be money motivated, aggressive, hardworking and above all, a good sales person. We sell ad space. If you can as well, you can move to any of our offices all expenses paid.

Now say which advertisement the following statements refer to.

1 This advertisement emphasises the importance of the position in the company's planned development.

    A   B   C   D

2 This advertisement seems to issue a challenge.

    A   B   C   D

3 This advertisement mentions the possibility of promotion.

    A   B   C   D

4 This advertisement promises a special benefit to the successful applicant.

    A   B   C   D

5 This advertisement adopts an informal, almost chatty style.

    A   B   C   D

▶ Vocabulary practice

Review   Choose the word or phrase which best completes each sentence.

1 I explained that I wanted to .... my legal right to consult a solicitor.

   A entertain   B exercise   C grant   D insist

2 We were all rather in awe .... the new computers when they arrived.

   A about   B before   C by   D of

3 The demonstrations .... in one hundred students being arrested.

   A culminated   B erupted   C escalated   D concluded

4 Although he was a hardened criminal, his one .... feature was his love of children.

   A saving   B redeeming   C recovering   D acquitting

5 I meant to sound confident at the interview but I'm afraid I .... as dogmatic.

   A came out   B came through   C came off   D came over

6 The switchboard at Television Centre was so .... by complaints about the programme that they had to take on extra staff.

   A overrun   B overcome   C overwhelmed   D overhauled

7 The restaurant is popular with film stars and the ....

   A like   B same   C similar   D such

8 She was able to .... my argument effectively by quoting actual statistics.

   A retaliate   B counter   C reciprocate   D confront

9 If you wish to .... this offer of a place, you should confirm your acceptance in writing.

   A undertake   B partake   C take up   D take on

10 Although I explained the situation he didn't seem to .... the degree of danger he was in.

   A seize   B grab   C catch   D grasp

11 He's applied for a(n) .... lot of jobs but he's only been short-listed once.

   A dreadful   B awful   C enormous   D wide

12 Before I went to drama school, I had to .... quite a lot of family pressure for me to study medicine.

   A resist   B restrain   C refuse   D reconcile

13 Strong protests were made, ... with demands for an international enquiry.

   A joined   B added   C coupled   D included

14 I've been working .... quite a lot of pressure lately.

A in   B with   C on   D under

15 She's decided to .... her German by attending an evening course.

A brush up   B patch up   C polish off   D dust off

16 Will you .... the baby for a minute, while I make a phone call?

A control   B settle   C attend   D mind

17 Police have warned people to be .... when strangers call at the door and to ask to see proof of identity.

A choosy   B cagey   C wary   D scarey

18 New consumer protection legislation comes into .... next April.

A law   B force   C statute   D act

19 The factory is working below .... because of the shortage of essential materials.

A range   B scope   C capacity   D density

20 If the work-force respected you, you wouldn't need to .... your authority so often.

A assert   B affirm   C maintain   D inflict

21 It's twenty years since I worked in Germany and my German is pretty .... now.

A scratchy   B scruffy   C rusty   D sloppy

22 Every Christmas of my childhood was the same. My father .... late for lunch, weighed down with presents for the family.

A would arrive   B had arrived   C was arriving   D was used to arriving

23 It .... me as strange that my front door was open when I got home.

A seemed   B occurred   C appeared   D struck

24 His English was roughly .... with my Greek, so communication was rather difficult!

A level   B on a par   C equal   D in tune

25 What her problems all seemed to .... to was lack of money.

A analyse   B condense   C boil down   D sum up

Phrasal verbs — TAKE

Look at the following selection of phrasal verbs formed with *take* and their meanings:

take after	resemble an older relative	take out	obtain something officially issued
take in	understand/grasp		
take in	make narrower	take over	take control of
take in	deceive	take to	like instinctively
take off	imitate	take up	adopt as a hobby
take on	accept (responsibility etc)	take up	shorten
		take up	challenge

Now choose the appropriate phrasal verb to complete the following sentences:

1 He only .... golf because his doctor told him he would have to get more exercise.

2 When I first heard the announcement, I was too busy cooking to .... it .... properly.

3 Our local pub hasn't had the same atmosphere since it was .... by one of the big breweries.

4 He's a marvellous mimic. You should see the way he .... the Prime Minister – it's hilarious!

5 The jacket fits you very well round the waist, sir, but if you feel it's too long, we can easily arrange for it to be ....

6 My daughter's not a bit like me. She seems to .... her father in the way she acts.

7 Don't let him .... you .... with his hard luck stories. The truth is that he's never done an honest day's work in his life!

8 However keen you are to make a success of the business, it's important not to .... more work than you can reasonably manage.

9 When our in-laws first met they .... each other immediately and they've been friends ever since.

10 Thank you for that explanation of union views but there is one point I'd like to .... you .... on, if I may. Is it really true to say . . .?

11 Do you have trouble obtaining your copy of *Teacher's Weekly*? Why not .... a regular subscription and be sure of receiving each edition as soon as it's published?

12 The problem with losing weight, I find, is that all your clothes need to be ....

▶ Grammar practice

1 Fill each of the numbered blanks in the following passage with *one* suitable word.

One day it will seem strange, ... (1) retrospect, that we spent much more thought and effort on developing human ability .... (2) on making good use of it, once we had it. There are innumerable examples. We hear them in casual conversation and occasionally they .... (3) a journalist's attention. Doctors provide a good .... (4) of complaints: they have to .... (5) a particularly protracted and detailed training and – at the end of it – many of them .... (6) a substantial part of their working day in relatively routine or clerical operations. Has anyone ever .... (7) how much money could be saved by splitting .... (8) these two .... (9) of a GP's job? Nurses .... (10) recently reiterated their age-old complaint that their scarce and skilled womanpower is frittered .... (11) in quite unskilled work. The educational world is .... (12) of examples of highly paid specialists .... (13) their own letters with two fingers. We promote top research academics .... (14) headships of departments and give them inadequate support services. Even in business, the provision of secretarial help tends to go by seniority and not by the .... (15) of routine work that has to be done.

from an article by Joan Smith in The Sunday Times

2 For each of the sentences below, write a new sentence as similar as possible in meaning to the original sentence, but using the words given: these words must *not be altered* in any way.

EXAMPLE: She stopped asking for advice.
     gave
ANSWER: She gave up asking for advice.

a He seemed to me a highly efficient manager.
  struck

b I assumed that you would ask for a reference.
  granted

c At first the new computer made me feel a bit afraid.
  awe

d Shouldn't you smoke fewer cigarettes?
  cut

e You may choose to take early retirement.
  option

f I only called the police when I had tried everything else.
  resort

g Women in this factory work under the same conditions as men.
  terms

h You can try as hard as you like but you won't succeed.
  however

UNIT 3 Tourist or Traveller?

▶ Lead-in

1

1 What's happening in picture 1?

2 How are the people dressed and why?

3 What else might they be going to do in this area?

2

1 What's happening in picture 2?

2 Describe the women's appearance.

3 Which country do you think this could be? Why?

4 How much do you think the visitors will learn about the country?

3

1 Describe the picture and the people in it.

2 Which country do you think they are in?

3 What are they doing?

4 How do you think they are feeling?

4

1 Where are the men in picture 4? How can you tell?

2 What might they be doing, and why?

3 What problems could they have in that environment?

In buzz groups of about three, discuss what the difference is between a tourist and a traveller. Think particularly about the purpose of the journey in each case and the response of each to the country visited. (3–5 minutes)

Report back to the class.

General discussion points

1 How much do tourists really learn about the countries they visit? Give reasons.
2 Can travel broaden the mind? How?
3 What are the advantages/disadvantages of travelling:
   a alone
   b with a companion
   c in a group with a guide?

▶ Text 1 · Travel

Read the following text to find out how the writer prefers to travel – and why.

Travel is at its best a solitary enterprise: to see, to examine, to assess, you have to be alone and unencumbered. Other people can mislead you; they crowd your meandering impressions with their own; if they are companionable they obstruct your view, and if they are boring they corrupt the silence with non-sequiturs,
5 shattering your concentration with 'Oh, look, it's raining', and 'You see a lot of trees here'. Travelling on your own can be terribly lonely (and it is not understood by Japanese who, coming across you smiling wistfully at an acre of Mexican buttercups tend to say things like 'Where is the rest of your team?'). I think of evening in the hotel room in the strange city. My diary has been brought up to
10 date; I hanker for company; What do I do? I don't know anyone here, so I go out and walk and discover the three streets of the town and rather envy the strolling couples and the people with children. The museums and churches are closed, and toward midnight the streets are empty. If I am mugged I will have to apologize as politely as possible: 'I am sorry, sir, but I have nothing valuable on my person.' Is
15 there a surer way of enraging a thief and driving him to violence?
   It is hard to see clearly or to think straight in the company of other people. Not only do I feel self-conscious, but the perceptions that are necessary to writing are difficult to manage when someone close by is thinking out loud. I am diverted, but it is discovery, not diversion, that I seek. What is required is the lucidity of
20 loneliness to capture that vision, which, however banal, seems in my private mood to be special and worthy of interest. There is something in feeling abject that quickens my mind and makes it intensely receptive to fugitive impressions. Later these impressions might be refuted or deleted, but they might also be verified and refined; and in any case I had the satisfaction of finishing the business
25 alone. Travel is not a vacation, and it is often the opposite of a rest. 'Have a nice time,' people said to me at my send-off at South Station, Medford. It was not precisely what I had hoped for. I craved a little risk, some danger, an untoward event, a vivid discomfort, an experience of my own company, and in a modest way the romance of solitude. This I thought might be mine on that train to Limón.

from 'The Old Patagonian Express' by Paul Theroux

Now complete these statements by choosing the answer you think fits best.

1 Travelling companions are a disadvantage, according to the writer, because they
   a give you the wrong impression about the journey.
   b distract you from your reading.
   c intrude on your private observations.
   d prevent you from saying what you think.

2 It has been assumed by Japanese that he
a belongs to a group of botanists.
b is excessively odd to travel alone.
c needs to be directed to his hotel.
d has wandered away from his party.

3 His main concern in the evenings was to
a take some physical exercise.
b avoid being robbed in the street.
c overcome his loneliness.
d explore the sights of the city.

4 The writer regards his friends' farewell to him as
a inappropriate.
b unsympathetic.
c tactless.
d cynical.

5 We gather from the passage that his main purpose in travelling was to
a test his endurance.
b prove his self-sufficiency.
c experience adventure.
d respond to new experiences.

▶ Focus on grammar 1 · Not only . . . but . . .

INVERSION OF SUBJECT AND VERB AFTER NEGATIVE INTRODUCTIONS

Notice this example from Text 1:
Not only do I feel self-conscious, *but* . . .

The writer could have written 'I feel self-conscious and also . . .' but the effect of starting his sentence with the negative adverb phrase is to make his point more emphatic.

After negative introductions, the subject and verb are inverted as in questions.

Here are some more examples:

Never **have** I seen such a mess!

On no account **must** you touch the machinery.

Not a soul **did** I see, the whole day.

Exercise 1   Rephrase the following sentences so that the negative expression in blue comes first, followed by the question form:

a You *rarely* see such an outstanding bargain.
b We have *seldom* met a ruder person.
c You shouldn't wander away from the path *under any circumstances*
    (Begin: *Under no circumstances* . . .)
d I didn't leave the office *at any time*
    (Begin: *At no time* . . .)
e They would *not* confess to the murder *until the police came*
f She could rely on *nobody* but him.
g The keys couldn't be found *anywhere*
    (Begin: *Nowhere* . . .)
h We *not only* ran into fog but it began to rain.

Further examples

1 *Hardly ... when*
  eg Hardly had the car been mended when something else went wrong with it.

2 *No sooner ... than*
  eg No sooner had I arrived in Greece than it began to rain.

3 *Only* with adverbs of time (*then later* etc) or qualifying an introductory phrase.
  eg Only much later did he realise his fatal mistake.
    Only now can I bear to talk about the experience.
    Only on holiday does he ever relax.

4 *Little, few, so, such* when not followed by a noun.
  eg Little do you know about my plans.
    So severe was the pain that I called an ambulance.
    Such was my dilemma.

Exercise 2 Complete the following:
a Not until the alarm bell rang . . .
b Only in New York . . .
c So frightening . . .
d Only after years of trying . . .
e Never again . . .
f Not a single word . . .
g No sooner . . .
h Hardly . . .

"You'll be fine with me. I know these waters like the back of my hand."

LANGUAGE CHECK
Dependent Prepositions 2: Preposition + Noun

Here is a list of 16 words or phrases, some of which have been used in the texts in this unit. Write in the preposition which precedes them.

Check your answers with your teacher or in the dictionary so that you have an accurate reference list for the future.

..... **sale** (2 possibilities)   ..... **doubt**
..... **cover of**   ..... **the left**
to be ..... **interest**   ..... **the left-hand corner**
..... **contrast to**   ..... **the left-hand end**
to go ..... **a journey/voyage/trip**   ..... **danger of** (+*ing*)
..... **no extra charge**   ..... **the intention of** (+*ing*)
..... **aid of**   *to be* ..... **the opinion that**
..... **the aid of**   ..... **the habit of** (+*ing*)

▶ Text 2 · Amateur photography . . .

In a few short weeks the camera season begins. Loaded down with film and filters and huge black boxes, the first of hordes of tourists will start to
5 flood across the world, an infestation of locusts that give out a myriad of dry clickings as they land. Smile, click. Say cheese, click. A bit to the left, click. Keep still, click.
10 All travel is now merely a means of moving a camera from place to place, all travellers are ruled by the all-powerful lens. Visitors old-fashioned enough to wish only to stand and look
15 with their anachronistic eyes are shoved aside by the photographers, who take it for granted that while they do their ritual focusing, nothing else may move or cross their vision. Those
20 peculiar souls without a camera must step aside for those more properly occupied, must wait while the rituals take place, and must bide their time while whole coaches stop and unleash
25 upon the landscape the Instamatic God. And the populations of whole countries seeing themselves cannibalised, swallowed up, vacuumed into the black-ringed staring eye, wrench what
30 they can from the cannibals. You want take picture me? You pay. You want picture my house, my camel? You pay.

None of this would matter, perhaps, if anything worthwhile was being ac-
35 complished. If all the constant busy-ness and clicking produced, at its end, what had not existed before, images of beauty captured or truth told, then who could complain? But, sadly, this isn't so.
40 The camera is simply graffiti made respectable. Nice people do not cut their initials on walls any more. Nice

people aim their lenses, develop their film, and prove in that way the same age-old human message – Kilroy Was Here.

The camera is the means by which we stamp ourselves on everything we see, under cover of recording the Wonders of the World already wonderfully recorded by professionals and on sale at every corner bookshop and newsagent. But what use to us an illustrated book of perfect photographs? What use to show Aunt Maud, back home, postcards of the Taj Mahal, the Coliseum, the Leaning Tower of Pisa, a Tuscan landscape, since we are not in the picture to prove that we were there?

No stretch of rocks has verity unless I am within it. No monument exists but for my wife, leaning against it. No building is real if it does not contain my husband at its door. No temple is of interest without my face beside it, grinning. With my camera I appropriate everything beautiful, possess it, shrink it, domesticate it, and reproduce it on my blank sitting-room wall to prove to a selected audience of friends and family the one absolutely vital fact about these beauties: I saw them, I was there, I photographed them, and, ergo, they are.

Even this immense ego-mania might be forgivable if some truth, some meaning emerged, albeit in the background, behind the smirking faces. But most amateur photographers show no interest in the world as it is, only in the world as it ideally should be. For tourists, it is a world of images as clichéd as brochures, calculated to arouse envy in the bosoms of the stay-at-homes.

Thus, all photographs of famous tourist sights must, for a start, eliminate their one overwhelming ingredient – other tourists. Patiently, the photographer waits while the crowds surge round about and pounces, clicks, in the one infinitesimal second when his target is clear of all others but Gladys. So Aunt Maud, at home, sees a peaceful idyll, an uncharted ruin far from the haunts of any human but Gladys. And lies are often more deliberate than that. You wish to show that you have been to places ancient, untouched, quite outside the stream of ordinary tourism, quite outside the stream of modern life. You want a picture of the Real Morocco – a scene as old as time. Unfortunately for you, a glassy modern building edges up to the mosque; behind the minaret television aerials spike the sky; beside the camel two Moroccans in unsuitable Western suits stand discussing business; and all around the cars hoot and squeal.

So you must stand and twist your camera, hold it up sideways, shift your position so that the little yellow lines just clear the building, just cut out the aerials and the telegraph wires, just exclude the business men and their cars while retaining the rest. And when all these alien elements have, for a precious moment, been obliterated, click. There, Aunt Maud. The Real Morocco. The Morocco nobody who has actually been there will ever actually see. That is the summit of the amateur photographer's art – total unreality. The World As It Isn't, and our Fred.

Travel with camera wonderfully narrows the mind.

from 'Amateur Photography: the World as it isn't and our Fred' by Jill Tweedie in the Guardian

1 Which words in the first paragraph emphasise the volume of tourist traffic?
2 What does the writer suggest by comparing tourists to locusts?
3 Why is the camera lens described as 'all-powerful' (lines 12–13)?
4 What is implied about the amateur photographer's attitude to those without cameras?
5 What is suggested by the phrase 'their ritual focusing' (line 18)?
6 Explain in your own words how native people 'wrench what they can from the cannibals' (lines 29–30).
7 What is the main purpose of holiday photographs, according to the writer?
8 What is meant by the phrase 'under cover of recording . . .' (line 49)?
9 By using the words 'shrink' and 'domesticate' (line 69), what does the writer suggest about the photographs taken?
10 Explain how holiday photographs can be 'as clichéd as brochures' (lines 83–84).
11 What fundamental rule applies to photographing famous tourist sites, according to the writer?
12 Why are the Moroccans' Western suits described as 'unsuitable' (lines 109–110)?
13 How can tourists be guilty of the most deliberate lies?
14 Summarise in a paragraph of 50–100 words how travel with a camera narrows the mind, according to the writer's argument. (See STUDY BOX – Summary Writing on page 127.)

▶ Focus on grammar 2 ·
Review of conditionals 1 and 2

Conditional sentences show how a *result* depends on a *condition.* That condition, and therefore the result, may be (1) possible and probable, (2) possible but improbable or unreal, or (3) impossible. This section reviews the first two types.

Type 1a Look at these examples from the texts in this unit:

If they are companionable, they obstruct your view . . .

No building is real if it does not contain my husband at its door.

They represent general truths, at least in the view of the writer. The condition is possible and the result virtually inevitable. In sentences like this, *if* could often be replaced by *when*

Form

| IF | present form | present form or imperative |

Any present form may be used – present simple or continuous, present perfect simple or continuous.

eg *If you add sugar to coffee, it dissolves*
It invariably rains if you have forgotten your umbrella.

Type 1b Look at this example from Text 1:

If I am mugged, I will have to apologize . . .

The condition and result here are both *possible* and *probable* in the writer's view.

Form

| IF | present form | future form or imperative |

Again, any present form can be used in the *if*-clause and any future form (simple continuous, perfect) in the main clause. *If* cannot normally be replaced by *when.*

A Complete the following examples:

If that flight is fully booked, we'll reserve . . .

If you have just flown in from Los Angeles, you'll probably be suffering from . . .

If you can't make the meeting on Friday, give me . . .

Will you have finished the report if I call in . . .

Type 2 Look at these examples from Text 2:

None of this would matter if anything worthwhile was being accomplished

Even this ego-mania might be forgivable if some truth . . . emerged

If all the busyness . . . produced . . . what had not existed before, who could complain?

The condition and result here are possible but improbable or unreal.

Form

| IF | past simple or continuous | present conditional simple or continuous |

The past tense in the *if*-clause may be replaced by the form *were to* + infinitive.

B Complete the following examples:

If you took the trouble to phone your parents more often, they wouldn't . . .

I'd have more time to see friends if I weren't . . .

If you were to fail your finals, what would be the . . .

Points to remember

1 Should: *Should* + infinitive (without *to*) may be used in the *if*-clause in these types of conditionals. The effect is to make the condition less probable.

> eg *If I should ever come to Lisbon on business, I'll look you up*
> *Should you change your mind, we'd be only too happy to see you.*

2 Order of clauses: the *if*-clause may come first or second in a statement, depending on which part is uppermost in the speaker's mind.

3 Punctuation: from the examples above, it can be seen that while a comma is necessary when the *if*-clause comes first, no comma is needed when the order is reversed.

4 Other expressions introducing conditional clauses: conditional sentences are usually associated with the conjunction *if* but there are several other expressions which may introduce conditional clauses.

C   Look at these sentences from Text 2 and underline three expressions that introduce conditional clauses.

No stretch of rocks has verity unless I am within it.

No temple is of interest without my face beside it, grinning.

No monument exists but for my wife, leaning against it.

Exercise 1   Choose one of the expressions below to complete the following sentences and put the verbs in brackets into the correct form:

unless	provided (that)	without	given
in case	supposing	on condition that	so/as long as

a I don't anticipate any difficulty in reaching Brussels by Friday .... the ferries (run) to schedule.

b .... the support of my Head of Department, it (be) impossible for me to undertake this research.

c He would only agree to drop legal proceedings against the magazine .... the editor (publish) a formal apology.

d .... your motorbike breaks down in the desert, (can) you mend it yourself?

e .... he can find a financial backer, his scheme (come) to nothing.

f .... I have my health, I (not worry) about getting old.

g You'd better carry a first aid kit .... any untoward events (occur).

h .... a favourable reception from the critics, the show (probably/run) for at least a year.

Exercise 2   Complete the following sentences:

a If you were to address all those envelopes by hand, how long . . .

b You know I'll never forgive you if you . . .

c Unless I hear from you by the first of the month, I . . .

d What on earth would you do if you . . .

e Should there be any trouble, just . . .

f I'd sleep better at night if the neighbours . . .

g I'll lend you the money you want on condition that . . .

h He'll be setting off from base camp next week provided that . . .

i Given a bit of luck, we . . .

j He'll come home from work in a furious temper if he . . .

k I'd have no hesitation in accepting if I . . .

▶Focus on writing · Directed writing

You saw the following advertisement in a magazine called *Holiday Choice*. You sent for the brochure and eventually spent a week at the hotel but were far from satisfied with your holiday. You feel the advertisement and brochure were seriously misleading.

Write a letter to the editor of the magazine explaining why you feel that the advertisement should not be accepted in future. Your answer should not exceed 200 words.

> **Not booked your summer holiday yet? We still have vacancies at our luxury hotel!**
>
> Occupying a prime residential position, only minutes from the sea, the hotel offers spacious, comfortable bedrooms and the highest standards of food and service. Many extras including conducted tours to local places of interest and hotel minibus from station or airport. Superb value!
>
> Write now for our illustrated brochure.

Notes It is important when tackling a composition of this type to make full use of the information given.

Begin by listing each feature mentioned and making notes of how the hotel failed to live up to expectations. Add any further details that you can to complete the picture. Of course, it is unlikely that the holiday was a total disaster and shades of criticism with, perhaps, a little grudging praise will add to the credibility of your account.

Next plan the *structure* of your letter, bearing in mind its purpose. You will need to consider the appropriate ordering of the items as well as suitable opening and closing paragraphs.

Pay special attention to the *tone* of the letter. You are writing to a third party who, while not responsible for the hotel's shortcomings, should have a professional interest in them. The editor should be persuaded that your complaints are to be taken seriously in the interests of his readers. Balance outrage with courtesy!

▶Focus on listening 1

As you listen, complete the following table of information about the five holidays. Use the symbols below for the columns headed *Method(s) of travel* and *Price range*. If a piece of information is not given, put an × in the space.

Destination	Method(s) of travel	Number of days	Price range	Type of accommodation	Extra features
Malta				hotel	
Venice	T				X
India		X			
Scotland		3			
Ireland			1		

KEY

Methods of travel

C – coach P – plane
T – train O – other
S – ship

Price range

4 – More than £350 per person   2 – £150–£250 per person
3 – £251–£350 per person   1 – less than £150 per person

▶ Communication activity ·
Life or death in the Alps

Introduction In this activity you will work in groups of 6–10 to solve a life or death problem. Your survival will depend on your ability to use your judgement as a group to work out the most appropriate course of action to follow in the circumstances.

The situation You and your friends are flying in a light aircraft over the Alps on your way to an adventure holiday centre in Switzerland. Visibility is bad due to low cloud. The engine develops a problem and you begin to lose altitude. The pilot is unable to make radio contact and thinks that you may be as much as 90 kilometres off course. The plane continues to lose altitude and you crash into the mountains.

All of you on board survive the crash uninjured, except for minor cuts and bruises, but the plane is destroyed. It is 11.00 a.m. The temperature is minus 10 degrees Celsius, and there is a light wind. The mountain is covered in a blanket of thick snow. You are all wearing warm jackets and thick boots, and have woollen hats.

You have very little food and you decide that in order to survive you must try to get down the mountain rather than waiting to be rescued. You estimate that descending may mean spending two nights on the mountain, and the climb could be dangerous.

The problem   From the wreckage of the plane you are able to salvage the 15 items illustrated below.

1 Look at the items below. Work individually to decide which items are the most important to your survival as you climb down the mountain. Think about the main dangers and difficulties you will face. Put '1' by the most important down to '15' for the least important. Write the numbers in the first box. Be prepared to give your reasons.

2 Now work with the other people in your group. Agree as a group on a rank order for the items and discuss the reasons for your choices. Write the numbers in the second box. Remember, your survival depends on what you decide.

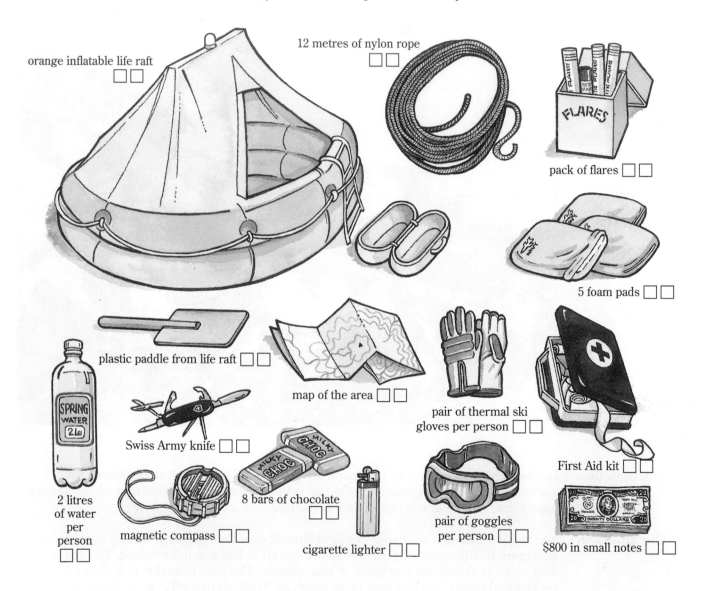

orange inflatable life raft ☐☐

12 metres of nylon rope ☐☐

pack of flares ☐☐

5 foam pads ☐☐

plastic paddle from life raft ☐☐

map of the area ☐☐

pair of thermal ski gloves per person ☐☐

First Aid kit ☐☐

2 litres of water per person ☐☐

Swiss Army knife ☐☐

magnetic compass ☐☐

8 bars of chocolate ☐☐

cigarette lighter ☐☐

pair of goggles per person ☐☐

$800 in small notes ☐☐

Discussion   1 Compare your group's ranking and the reasons for it with that of other groups. Did all the groups put the items in a similar order? Were the group decisions different from those of individual group members?
2 Now read the suggested solution on pages 196/197. Do you agree with it? Do you think you would have survived?
3 People usually find that they would have had a better chance of survival from the group decisions than their individual ones. Why is this, do you think?

▶ Focus on register

Read the following extracts:

A

The most populous metropolis of the Western Hemisphere, New York is, depending on one's point of view any one of four cities: to social scientists it is a laboratory in which to study the challenges of urban life, from ghastliest slum to tycoon luxury; to tourists it is a city of jostling crowds, horn-honking traffic jams, dirty streets, smelly subways – all in dramatic contrast to such international symbols as the skyscraper skyline, the United Nations building, Wall Street, the Statue of Liberty, the Metropolitan Museum of Art, Times Square and Broadway theatres; to commuters it is an enervating beehive of world trade and finance, mass media, business administration, fashion and associated entrepreneurial activities and manufacturing – a place to leave as soon as possible in the evening for the more serene atmosphere of greener suburbia.

B

Okay, so New York is crowded, dirty, noisy and impolite! But it's one of the world's most exciting and beautiful cities and, surprisingly, a very human place.

Other Americans often fear and dislike New York. With a typical shrug, New Yorkers dismiss this as provincial jealousy. Fire sirens may wail all night while steam billows hellishly from the manholes, the subway cars may be defaced by graffiti and people move faster than taxis. So what? New York is the place where it's all happening.

C

New York. If I leave my writing table in the hotel and go to the window I can look down on a corner of Central Park where I was jogging a short while ago.

Spring is still some weeks distant and it was cold out there. Squirrels, not birds, were most evident among the bare trees. The few early morning walkers – mostly with their dogs – were well-wrapped. The exercise followed by the hot, then cold shower that I returned to so stimulated my appetite for breakfast that I ate buckwheat pancakes with maple syrup to preface bacon and eggs.

Such enthusiastic self-indulgence is a vice I am more prone to in New York than in any other city in the world. Although this may owe something to the air, and something to the exercise, and something to that shedding of inhibitions which is one of the most evident consequences and rewards of travel, it owes yet more, I think, to a quality which is peculiar to New York itself.

D

The popular image of New York conjures up a jungle of muggers, dope addicts, and hustlers creating an obstacle course for the city's normal citizens. But the tourist will find that the Big Apple threatens only his budget. New York's menacing streets, while not entirely mythical, fortunately do not approach their notoriety. Common sense and an alert eye should insure the safety of all but the most reckless: steer clear of run-down neighbourhoods (especially after dark) and keep to the more touristed parts of the city and trouble will not find you.

1 A feature of New York mentioned in both extracts A and B is
   a the uncomfortably humid heat of the streets.
   b the spectacular height of the buildings.
   c the characteristic sounds of the traffic.
   d the writing on walls and public transport.

2 In extract C, we understand that in New York the writer
   a enjoys taking exercise more than usual.
   b prefers American breakfasts to English ones.
   c is struck by the strangeness of the environment.
   d is less restrained in his behaviour than usual.

3 Extracts B and C share
   a a relish for the city's particular character.
   b an awareness of the city's imperfections.
   c a sense of the city's startling contrasts.
   d an appreciation of the beauty of the city.

4 In extract D, the writer points out that in New York
   a it is extremely difficult to get about.
   b it is easy to be cheated over prices.
   c the violence has been exaggerated.
   d the traffic can represent a hazard.

5 In extract D, the reader is advised
   a to avoid going out at night.
   b to keep an eye open for crime.
   c not to run unnecessary risks.
   d only to drive in the city centre.

STUDY BOX 1
Prevent vs Avoid

Prevent means to stop another person's (or thing's) action. It can take the
preposition **from**. You can prevent *somebody* from *doing* something, or prevent
something (from *happening*).

> eg *They* **prevented** *me* **from** *leaving.*
> *The firecrew managed to* **prevent** *the fire from* *spreading.*
> *Sunglasses* **prevent** *the harmful effects of intense sun on the eyes.*

Avoid has two main meanings:
1 to stay away from a person, a thing, or a situation yourself.

> eg *I try to* **avoid** *him if possible.*
> *If we leave now, we'll* **avoid** *the rush hour traffic.*
> *She wanted to* **avoid** *an argument, so she said nothing.*

2 to make an effort *not* to do something (in this sense it means prevent yourself from
doing something). It cannot take the preposition *from*.

> eg *They* **avoid** *speaking to each other, as far as possible.*
> *The subway system is safe as long as you* **avoid** *travelling alone in an empty*
> *carriage.*

▶ Focus on listening 2

You are going to hear a conversation between an agent for holiday caravans and a client. Before your listen, look carefully at the diagram showing the layout of a caravan and at the list of fittings and fixtures below. While you are listening, you should label the diagram by writing the number of each item in the correct place. Note that you may use some numbers more than once.

KEY
1	Gasfire	**9**	Dining seats
2	Cupboard	**10**	Single bed/lounge seat
3	Electric cooker	**11**	Double bed
4	Wardrobe	**12**	Bunk beds
5	Wash hand basin	**13**	Shower
6	Sink and drainer	**14**	Toilet
7	Vanity unit	**15**	Lounge seat
8	Dining table		

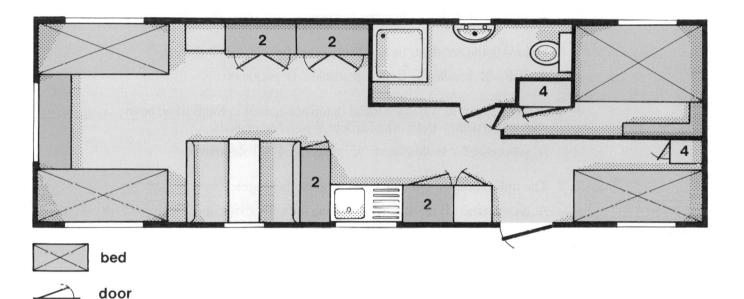

☒ **bed**

◿ **door**

STUDY BOX 2
Phrasal Verbs 1

Look at these examples from this unit:

1 *locusts that* **give out** *a myriad of dry clickings* (Text 2)
   give out means 'send out' (especially a noise).

   NB **give off** also means 'produce or send out' but usually refers to a smell, heat, or smoke.

2 *just* **cut out** *the aerials and the telegraph wires . . .* (Text 2)
   cut out means 'remove'.

   NB **cut out** can also mean 'give up or stop a habit' eg *He had to* **cut out** *his heavy gambling.*

3 *You should* **allow for** *medical insurance as an extra* (Listening 1)
   allow for means 'take into consideration'.

4 *But let's* **get down to** *the costs* (Listening 1)
   get down to means 'turn your attention to a particular subject.'

▶Vocabulary practice

Review   Choose the word or phrase which best completes each sentence.

1   My sunburnt nose made me feel rather .... for the first few days of the holiday.

   A self-effacing   B self-centred   C self-conscious   D self-evident

2   The peace of the public library was .... by the sound of a transistor radio.

   A smashed   B fractured   C demolished   D shattered

3   There were so many people .... me in the crowd that I couldn't hold the camera steady.

   A jostling   B jerking   C obstructing   D agitating

4   'Frankly, I couldn't care less!' he said with a .... of his shoulders.

   A twitch   B flick   C hunch   D shrug

5   Following the accident, he was prosecuted for .... driving.

   A rash   B heedless   C irresponsible   D reckless

6   In many places in Wales we found that place-names in English had been ....
   with green paint – the work of ardent Welsh Nationalists.

   A suppressed   B disguised   C obliterated   D destroyed

7   The radio receiver was .... regular messages.

   A giving over   B giving off   C giving out   D giving up

8   The case was .... by the judge for lack of evidence.

   A disallowed   B dismissed   C abandoned   D discarded

9   Once she's .... a few tears she'll resign herself to the situation.

   A shed   B split   C sobbed   D released

10   If the door has jammed, there's no point in trying to force it open. You'll probably
   .... the handle off!

   A gouge   B wrench   C pluck   D drag

11   The smoke .... from the burning tyres could be seen for miles.

   A bulging   B radiating   C billowing   D sweeping

12   Several of the advertising hoardings had been .... by anti-sexist slogans.

   A deleted   B mutilated   C erased   D defaced

13   Unfortunately, I'm rather .... to forgetfulness in my old age.

   A apt   B prone   C open   D prey

14   You would be well advised to .... clear of the casinos in the city.

   A stray   B stick   C steer   D veer

15 As a result of careless washing, the jeans had .... to a child's size.

A shrunk   B faded   C reduced   D dwindled

16 Only after buying the cottage did we discover that it was .... with mice.

A inflicted   B infested   C invaded   D infected

17 She .... affection from her children but they neglected her shamefully.

A yearned   B craved   C hungered   D desired

18 He told the court that it was his desperate poverty that had .... him to crime.

A driven   B brought   C induced   D compelled

19 I utterly .... your argument. In my opinion, you have distorted the facts.

A confound   B dispute   C decline   D refute

20 I offer you my most .... apologies for offending you as I did.

A repentant   B servile   C candid   D abject

21 The villa has excellent .... for cooking and for washing clothes.

A facilities   B amenities   C utilites   D conveniences

22 There is a feature of dialect .... to Bristol by which an 'l' is added to the ends of some words.

A original   B peculiar   C particular   D proper

23 It is essential to be on the .... for any signs of movement in the undergrowth since there are poisonous snakes in the area.

A guard   B care   C alarm   D alert

24 The hotel, though obviously grand in its day, appeared rather neglected and .... when we checked in.

A tumble-down   B downcast   C run-down   D down-and-out

25 In order to explore the city ...., I left my luggage at the station.

A unladen   B unencumbered   C undeterred   D unrestrained

Words describing facial expression

Choose words from the following list to put in the sentences below.

grin   grimace   frown   smirk   beam   scowl   pout   glare   gape   leer

1 I could tell by the .... on his face that the car wasn't going to be so easy to start as he'd thought.

2 You .... at me so furiously that I knew I'd really put my foot in it!

3 She .... with pleasure at the unexpected compliment.

4 When I saw the figure on the cheque, I just .... in astonishment.

5 He .... as he swallowed the evil-tasting medicine.

6 If the children .... and stamp their feet when you tell them to go to bed, pay no attention.

7 The way the boy just .... when I told him off made me really lose my temper.

8 .... at your boss's wife was just about the worst thing you could have done.

9 Since you can't do anything to change the situation, you'll just have to .... and bear it.

10 By the way he's ...., I'd say he is in a pretty bad mood.

▶ Grammar practice

1   Fill each of the numbered blanks in the following passage with *one* suitable word.

Let's assume that choosing your holiday was trouble-free. A rash assumption, I admit, for I know about the hearthside arguments that brochures .... (1) spark off. However, I must confine .... (2) to the things that could go wrong once you .... (3) out on your travels or after you arrive at your .... (4).

.... (5) I claim no qualification .... (6) an adviser, I do have under my belt practical experience which has been .... (7) over twenty years of globetrotting. First, some basic ground rules that .... (8) in all situations. If something does go wrong, then bear in .... (9) that you are not the first person to have .... (10) something lost or stolen, or to have been .... (11) in accidents or illness. The people to .... (12) you go for help are .... (13) with the proper way of doing things and you can best help by keeping as .... (14) as possible and .... (15) them with the information they need.

.... (16) to say, you should be adequately insured and carry .... (17) of that insurance. .... (18) who travels abroad without proper cover .... (19) little sympathy in the .... (20) of trouble.

from 'Tackling Travel Traumas' by John Carter in Good Housekeeping

2   Fill each of the blanks with a suitable word or phrase.
    eg If I had your address, *I would write* to you.

a .... a decision yet about where you're going on holiday?

b Yes, ... of going to Greece.

c Lucky you! This time next week you .... the beach.

d Actually, sunbathing .... to me at all.

e .... rather see the sights instead then?

f No. What .... is sailing.

g I wish you .... before. Why?

h Because sailing's my hobby, too, but up to now there .... to go with me.

[UNIT **4**] **Relationships**

▶ Lead-in · Quiz

Choose the most likely answer to the following questions and then compare your answers with your neighbour.

1 What age is a woman most likely to be on her wedding day in the United Kingdom?

A Under 18   B 18–20   C 21–24   D 25–29

2 What is the most common size of household in the UK?

A 1 person   B 2 people   C 3 people   D 4 people

3 In a recent national survey, what percentage of people said they were completely or almost completely satisfied with their marriage?

A 15%   B 30%   C 50%   D 80%

4 How likely are single men and women to suffer from mental illness, compared with married people?

A less likely   B equally likely   C more likely

5 How likely are single men and women to die from heart attacks, compared with married people?

A less likely   B equally likely   C more likely

6 True or False?

In a recent survey, significantly more men than women were found to have a close friend.

7 True or False?

In the same survey, the sexes differed significantly on their definition of a 'close friend'.

The answers to the quiz appear on page 197. When you have checked them, see if you can find answers to the following questions.

a Why do married people enjoy better mental and physical health than single people?
b Why do women seem to benefit less from marriage than men?

Now read the following extract:

Successful marriage is the most effective form of social support. It relieves the effects of stress, and leads to better mental and physical health.

While many studies have shown the great importance of 'social support', it is still not clear exactly what this means. Most likely it consists of being a sympathetic listener or offering helpful advice; providing emotional support and social acceptance; giving actual help or financial help; and simply doing ordinary things together, like eating and drinking.

Husbands seem to benefit much more from marriage than wives do. Married women are in better physical and mental health, and are happier than single women, but these effects are nearly twice as great for men. Various explanations have been considered, but the most plausible is that wives provide more social support than husbands. Perhaps men need it more? They are more exposed to stresses at work, and have worse health, and die earlier than women.

In addition, when women get married, their way of life is subject to much greater change and this often leads to boring and isolated work in the home for which they are ill-prepared. Despite the benefits of marriage, women find it stressful, and are in better shape if they also have jobs; their earnings and status increase their power in the home, and they may also get social support at work.

from 'What Makes Marriage Tick?' by Michael Argyle in New Society

"It looks as if the Robinsons have been fighting again."

What is a close friend?   Look at the following definitions of a close friend. Choose the one which is closest to your own understanding of the term. If none seems quite adequate, write your own definition.

someone I can trust
someone I can call on for help
someone I go out with
someone I see often
someone who comes into my home
someone I've known for a long time
someone whose company I enjoy
someone ....

Compare your definition with others in the class. Are there any differences between definitions given by male members of the class and those given by female members of the class?

The table on p. 57 shows the results of a survey of middle-aged couples in Britain who were asked what they meant by the term 'close friend'.

1 What seem to you to be the most significant differences between the two sexes?

2 Can you think of any reasons for the differences?

Definitions of what a close friend is			
	men	women	%
someone I can trust	30	52	28
someone I can call on for help	35	37	26
someone I go out with	26	5	10
someone I see often	17	12	9
someone who comes into my home	21	8	9
someone I've known for a long time	12	11	8
someone whose company I enjoy	19	4	8
other	12	14	8

Note: some people gave more than one definition.

Now read the following extract from a report on the survey:

On four of the definitions, the sexes differed significantly. More women than men emphasised confidentiality and trust; more men than women emphasised pleasure in a friend's company, going out with a friend and having a friend in one's home. This is not surprising. Given the traditional differences in sex roles, women are supposed to be more expressive than men, and working class men, in particular, have often been described as spending their leisure time outside the home, in the company of other men. And since an Englishman's home is supposed to be his castle, it is natural that, apart from relatives, only close friends are allowed or welcomed into it.

More surprising is that as many men as women defined a close friend as someone they can call on for help. It may be that with a nuclear family structure and quite a high level of physical and social mobility, friends are now substitutes for relatives of both sexes. Among the middle-aged men and women in this study, the lack of contact with relatives, even those who lived nearby, was notable, suggesting that friends and relatives are indeed interchangeable.

from 'What is a Friend?' by Marion Crawford in New Society

Discussion points

1 How did your group's results compare with those of the survey?

2 Are women more expressive than men in your opinion? If so, in what way?

3 When might you need to rely on the confidentiality of a friend?

4 In your country, do men tend to spend much of their leisure time outside the home? If so, what kind of activities do they engage in?

5 What does the saying 'An Englishman's home is his castle' suggest? If you are living, or have lived in Britain, do you agree with it?

6 In your country, how freely are people invited into your home?

7 What kind of help might you call on a close friend for?

8 Are close friends as important as relatives, in your opinion?

▶ Text 1 · Quarrelling

Read the following text to find out what the essential characteristics of a quarrel are, according to the author.

Great emotional and intellectual resources are demanded in quarrels; stamina helps, as does a capacity for obsession. But no one is born a good quarreller; the craft must be
5 learned.

There are two generally recognised apprenticeships. First, and universally preferred, is a long childhood spent in the company of fractious siblings. After
10 several years of rainy afternoons, brothers and sisters develop a sure feel for the tactics of attrition and the niceties of strategy so necessary in first-rate quarrelling.
15 The only child, or the child of peaceful or repressed households, is likely to grow up failing to understand that quarrels, unlike arguments, are not *about* anything, least of all the pursuit of truth. The
20 apparent subject of a quarrel is a mere

pretext; the real business is the quarrel itself.

Essentially, adversaries in a quarrel are out to establish or rescue their dignity.
25 Hence the elementary principle: *anything may be said.* The unschooled, probably no less quarrelsome by inclination than anyone else, may spend an hour with knocking heart, sifting the consequences of
30 calling this old acquaintance a lying fraud. Too late! With a cheerful wave the old acquaintance has left the room.

Those who miss their first apprenticeship may care to enrol in the
35 second, the bad marriage. This can be perilous for the neophyte; the mutual intimacy of spouses makes them at once more vulnerable and more dangerous in attack. Once sex is involved, the stakes are
40 higher all round. And there is an unspoken rule that those who love, or have loved,

one another are granted a licence for unlimited beastliness such as is denied to mere sworn enemies. For all that, some of
45 our most tenacious black belt quarrellers have come to it late in life and mastered every throw, from the Crushing Silence to the Gloating Apology, in less than ten years of marriage.
50   A quarrel may last years. Among brooding types with time on their hands, like writers, half a lifetime is not uncommon. In its most refined form, a quarrel may consist of the participants not
55 talking to each other. They will need to scheme laboriously to appear in public together to register their silence.
   Brief, violent quarrels are also known as rows. In all cases the essential ingredient
60 remains the same; the original cause must be forgotten as soon as possible. From here on, dignity, pride, self-esteem, honour are the crucial issues, which is why quarrelling, like jealousy, is an all-
65 consuming business, virtually a *profession*. For the quarreller's very self-hood is on the line. To lose an argument is a brief disappointment, much like losing a game of tennis; but to be crushed in a quarrel . . .
70 rather bite off your tongue and spread it at your opponent's feet.

from 'Flying in the face of authority' by Ian McEwan in the Observer

Look at paragraphs 2–5 and find the words which mean the same as:

a bad-tempered (2)   ....
b brothers and sisters (2)   ....
c process of tiring or weakening (2)   ....
d excuse (3)   ....
e temperament (4)   ....
f examining closely (4)   ....
g novice/beginner (5)   ....
h husbands and wives (5)   ....
i risks (5)   ....
j persistent (5)   ....

Complete these statements by choosing the answer which you think fits best.

1 Unschooled quarrellers are said to be at a disadvantage because
   a their insults fail to offend their opponent.
   b they reveal their nervousness to their opponent.
   c they suffer from remorse for what they've said.
   d they are apprehensive about speaking their minds.

2 According to the writer, quarrels between married couples may be
   a physically violent.
   b extremely bitter.
   c essentially trivial.
   d sincerely regretted.

3 When quarrelling, both children and married couples may, according to the writer,
   a be particularly brutal.
   b use politeness as a weapon.
   c employ skilful manoeuvres.
   d exaggerate their feelings.

4 The difference between a quarrel and an argument is said to be that
   a the former involves individual egos.
   b the former concerns strong points of view.
   c the latter has well-established rules.
   d the latter concerns trivial issues.

5 In the passage as a whole, the writer treats quarrelling as if it were
   a a military campaign.
   b a social skill.
   c a moral evil.
   d a natural gift.

▶Text 2 · Neighbours

The best neighbour I ever had was an Italian restaurant. Emergency lasagne available night and day, change for the launderette on Sundays, a permanent
5 door-keeper against gatecrashers and policemen with parking tickets. Even if our fourth floor bath water did run dry every time they filled up the Expresso machine, I miss them still.
10 Bad neighbours can blight a house worse than dry rot but there is no insurance against them, no effective barricades in the compulsory intimacy except a decent caution and conversation
15 ruthlessly restricted to matters of meteorology. And it only takes a tiny breach in the wall of platitudes to unleash appalling dramas of persecution and passion.
20 And what can be done if the people next door breed maggots or wake up to the Body Snatchers (or some other punk group) in quadrophonic or poison the cat with their slug doom? What happens
25 when one man's trumpet practice is another's thumping headache, when two neighbouring life styles are just incompatible? There are three basic responses to what the law calls Nuisance:
30 surrender, retaliate or sue.
Joan and Andrew live next to a couple who have been having screaming, shouting and banging fights two or three times a week for the best part of five
35 years. 'It sometimes gets so bad that our whole house shakes, pictures rattle on the wall,' said Joan. She has tried sympathetic chats, face to face confrontation and even recourse to the local social services
40 department and the police when she feared that the child of the family might be at risk. 'Every time I say something, she is apologetic but says she can't help it. I don't think the child is subject to
45 physical abuse, but the verbal onslaughts are frightful. It's worrying as well as infuriating but it seems there's nothing to be done. There would be no point in bringing an action against them, it's just
50 how they are.'
Retaliation – or crash for crash – is a dangerous game which calls for nerves of steel and considerable perseverance. It is a winner take all strategy from which
55 there is no turning back, because it becomes a war of escalation and the side which is prepared to go nuclear wins. Michael's neighbour in Surrey made every summer afternoon noxious with the
60 sound of his motor mower. Negotiations got nowhere so Michael bought an electric hedge trimmer and plied it right where the neighbour's wife liked to sunbathe. Neighbour opened up with a
65 chain saw. Michael lit bonfires full of wet leaves when the wind was westerly. Neighbour left his car engine running with the exhaust pointing through the fence. Michael served an ultimatum:
70 either an end to hostilities or he would sow a plantation of ground elder right along his side of the hedge. Legal, but a lethal threat to neighbour's well-tended acre and a half. Mowing now takes place
75 on weekday evenings and the weekends are silent.
There are two main areas where the law has a role: in boundary disputes where the title deeds are not clear and in
80 cases of nuisance from noise or fumes or some other persistent interference in someone's peaceful enjoyment of their home. The remedies available in case of nuisance are either an injunction –
85 a court order to stop it – or damages in compensation for the victim's suffering.
There is only one thing worse than having to take your neighbour to court,
90 and that is letting your fury build up so long that you lose your temper and end up in the dock yourself like Mrs Edith Holmes of Huntingdon who was driven mad by her neighbour's incessant
95 hammering, drilling and other DIY activities between 7.30 and 11.30 every night. She ended up throwing a brick through his done-it-himself double glazing and had to plead guilty to criminal
100 damage. A merciful magistrate gave her a conditional discharge and allowed only £35 of her neighbour's £70.41 claim for compensation. The neighbour, he said, was an expert and could do his own
105 repairs.
But judges and ten-foot walls and conciliation and bribery can only do so much. In this one vital area of living you are entirely at the mercy of luck, which
110 may deal you a curse or a blessing regardless of any attempts to arrange things otherwise.

from 'What can be done if the people next door breed maggots...'   by Liz Forgan in the Guardian

1 What, in general terms, did the writer appreciate about the Italian restaurant owners as neighbours?
2 Explain how neighbours live in 'compulsory intimacy' (line 13) and say what is unusual about the phrase.
3 What is the writer's advice about conversation with neighbours?
4 Explain what is meant by 'a tiny breach in the wall of platitudes' (line 16–17).
5 Explain the distinction between 'sympathetic chats' and 'face to face confrontation' (line 37–38)
6 What does Joan find worrying about her neighbours' behaviour?
7 What does the writer mean by 'the side which is prepared to go nuclear wins' (line 56–57)?
8 Which phrase in paragraph 5 sums up the development between Michael and his neighbour?
9 What was the purpose of Michael's bonfire?
10 What can you deduce about 'ground elder' (line 71) and its effect?
11 Explain the alternative to an injunction in cases of nuisance.
12 What does the magistrate's judgement suggest about his attitude to her action?
13 Summarise, in a paragraph of 50–100 words, the various ways in which bad neighbours can affect your life, as mentioned by the writer. (See STUDY BOX – Summary Writing on page 127.)

STUDY BOX
Sue vs Prosecute
eg *There are three basic responses . . . surrender, retaliate or* **sue**. (Text 2)

sue means to start a legal case against someone, usually in order to claim money from them for loss or injury. An ordinary member of the public can **sue** a person or a company (usually through a solicitor).

eg *If the shop refuses to give me my money back, I'll* **sue** *the owner.*

prosecute means to bring legal action against someone in a court of law for a criminal offence. In this case, the Public Prosecutor **prosecutes** the offender on behalf of the state or the public.

eg *Shoplifters will be* **prosecuted**.

▶ Focus on grammar · Modal verbs 1

Modal verbs like *can, may* and *should* are like other auxiliary verbs in that they cannot be used alone but only in combination with another verb. They are followed by the infinitive without *to*.

Unlike other auxiliaries, their form does not change. They do not take an *s* in the 3rd person singular and they do not use *do* to form questions and negatives.

Modal verbs also differ from other auxiliaries in that they express a particular *mood*:

eg *He may go to Cardiff.* (possibiity)
You may come in now. (permission)
You must sign the form. (obligation)
He must be ill. (probability)

Permission Look at this example from Text 1:

Hence the elementary principle: anything *may* be said

Put the following requests for permission in order of politeness/formality by writing **1** by the most casual, **2** by the next most casual and so on to **7** for the most formal.

May I use *your 'phone?*
Do you think I could use *your 'phone?*
Could I use *your 'phone?*
Can I use *your 'phone?*
Is it alright if I use *your 'phone?*
Might I use *your 'phone?*
I wonder if I might use *your 'phone?*

Notes **1** In requests for permission

  a *Can* and *could* are widely used. *Could* is more polite than *can* and a request can be made even more tactful by lengthening it:

    eg *Could I possibly . . .*
    I wonder if I could . . .
    I wonder if I could possibly . . .

  b *May* is more polite still and *might* sounds very formal.

  2 In replies to requests for permission:

  a Positive replies – *can* is the most usual answer although *may* can be used in a more formal context. *Might* cannot be used.

  b Negative replies – *can't* is the most usual form. *May not* is also possible in answer to a question with *may*

    Note: Past permission is usually expressed by *could* or *couldn't*

Probability Look at these examples from Texts 1 and 2:

Those who miss their first apprenticeship *may* care to enrol in the second.
This *can* be perilous for the neophyte.

A quarrel *may* last for years.

There *must* be pleasure in feuding with neighbours.

she feared . . . that the child of the family *might* be at risk.

Put the following statements in order of probability by writing **1** by the most certain, **2** by the next most probable, and so on.

That *could be* the postman now.
That *must be* the postman now.
That *might be* the postman now.
That'll be the postman now.
That *may be* the postman now.

If you disagreed with the statements above (because there was only one knock and the postman usually knocks twice), how would you contradict each one?

eg *No, that* couldn't be *the postman . . .*

Imagine that you have just been told that someone knocked on the door five minutes ago. How would you express *past* probability in each case?

Notes **1** *Will/won't* – express a confident assumption about the present:

eg *You'll be exhausted after all that gardening! Come and sit down.*
He won't be working at the moment. Give him a ring.

or, less frequently, about the past:

eg *He'll have received my letter last week.*

2 *Must* – expresses a similarly confident conclusion. The negative is *can't* (not *mustn't*).

eg *You must have been extremely proud of your son.*
He can't possibly be serious!
You can't have been listening to a word I've said!

3 *May might* and *could* suggest possibility rather than probability. *May* is the strongest possibility of the three. As in **1** and **2** above, past possibility is expressed with the perfect infinitive without 'to'.

eg *You* | *might*
may | *have left your wallet on the bus.*
could |

Note: could have and *might have* are also used to express a reproach:

eg *I've been waiting all evening. You* | *could*
might | *have phoned me!*

Exercise Rewrite the following sentences, replacing the words in blue with the correct form of one of the modal verbs from the sections on *Permission* or *Probability*. Make any other changes necessary. Try to reproduce the meaning of the original sentence as accurately as possible.
a You can try 'phoning but *it's possible that* the car has been sold by now. (Begin: 'The car . . .')
b He asked if he *would be allowed to* write in ballpoint pen during the exam.
c If you've been out of the country, you *obviously* haven't heard about the robbery.
d *I just don't believe that* the line has been engaged all this time. *Maybe* there's a fault on it. (Begin: 'The line . . .')
e Don't start worrying. *It's possible that* he took a later plane.
f Where *would there be a chance of* finding a flat to rent?
g I'm sorry to trouble you but I was wondering if *there was any possibility* of my using your 'phone for a moment. My car's broken down.
h I've forgotten to return the key of the safe. *I'm sure* people have been looking everywhere for it.
i *It's possible* that you won't even have to show a pass to get in.
j She's *unlikely to* have left without warning anyone.

"Computer dating sent me."

▶ Focus on writing 1 · Discussion (essay form)

Write a balanced discussion on the theme:

> 'Good fences make good neighbours'
> (*About 350 words*)

Preparation

1 What does the statement mean to you? A simple explanation in your own words will help to clarify the issue in your mind. Is there a literal example to illustrate the quotation?
2 In terms of next-door or near neighbours, what kind of 'fences' can there be – concrete or abstract? And what are the characteristics of the 'good' neighbour that they create?
3 What are the counter arguments? How can 'fences' inhibit a good relationship with your neighbour or prevent your neighbour from being as 'good' as he would like to be, perhaps?
4 Can you generalise to other relationships – social, work, or emotional? What kind of 'fences' might be appropriate and what do they protect? Again, what are the counter arguments?

Planning

1 Plan an opening paragraph that will crystallise your approach. It may be a clear statement of your interpretation of the quotation; it may be a personal anecdote which illustrates the point; it may be an expression of reservation or even dissent.
    Whichever you choose, your opening paragraph should stimulate your reader and lead logically into the body of the essay.
2 Plan the ideas to be dealt with in the succeeding paragraphs, bearing in mind the need for balance. Pay special attention also to the linking of clauses and sentences.
3 Plan a suitable conclusion which brings together the various strands of the essay and represents a satisfying resolution of the conflicting arguments.

Optional additional topic

> Friendship or love – which is the more important relationship?
> (*About 200 words*)

▶ Communication activity · Self assertion

Assertion training has gained increasing recognition in recent years. Its aim is to help people express themselves more effectively and appropriately.

The following three types of behaviour are identified:

1 **Non-assertive behaviour** – failing to express your feelings, needs, opinions, or preferences, or expressing them in an indirect or implicit way. For example, agreeing to activities you are not really interested in or failing to ask for a favour even though one is needed. Statements like 'I suppose we could go to the cinema' or 'I wish I knew someone who could help me repair my car' represent indirect or implicit statements in which the other person must infer what the needs and opinions of the speaker really are. One difficulty with this type of communication is that it is open to varying interpretations and is therefore easily misunderstood.

2 **Aggressive behaviour** – expressing your feelings or opinions but in a punishing, threatening, demanding or hostile manner. There is little or no consideration of the feelings or rights of the other person. In addition, the person who behaves aggressively assumes little responsibility for the consequences of his/her action.

    eg You'd *better* lend me £5.
       You are *going* with me whether you like it or not.

3 **Assertive behaviour** – expressing your feelings, needs, legitimate rights or opinions honestly and directly without being aggressive to others, without infringing on their rights and without expecting the other person to read your mind. Assertive behaviour is not designed primarily to enable an individual to obtain what he/she wants. Rather, its purpose is the clear, direct and inoffensive communication of one's needs, opinions and so on. To the extent that this is accomplished, the probability of achieving one's goals without denying the rights of others is increased.

Discrimination exercise

Work in pairs. For each of the following situations, decide whether each response is non-assertive, aggressive or assertive. (You may use each category more than once.) Discuss the reasons for your decisions and try saying the sentences out loud.

Situation 1
Your friend has just arrived an hour late for dinner. He/she did not telephone to let you know that he/she would be detained. You are annoyed and you say:

1a Come on in. Dinner's on the table.	assertive non-assertive aggressive
1b I've been waiting for an hour. I would have appreciated it if you could have 'phoned to say you would be late.	assertive non-assertive aggressive
1c You've got a lot of nerve coming late. That's the last time I'll invite you.	assertive non-assertive aggressive

Example assessment
1a Non-assertive, because you pretend that nothing has happened. You neither mention that your friend is late nor that you are displeased by his/her behaviour.
1b Assertive, because you tell your friend that he/she is late, that you've been waiting, and that you feel he/she should have let you know.
1c Aggressive because you put your friend down and threaten him/her.

Situation 2
A friend has just complimented you on your new suit. It's the first time you've worn it and you really like it.
You say:

2a Thank you.	assertive non-assertive aggressive
2b This? It's nothing special.	assertive non-assertive aggressive
2c Well . . . I picked it up at a sale . . . well . . .	assertive non-assertive aggressive

Situation 3
You are returning a faulty item to a department store. You bought a shirt/blouse. When you took it home, you found a flaw in the fabric. You do not want the item as it is. The assistant has just said that no one will ever notice it. You say:

3a Well, I'd still like to return it or exchange it. I don't want this one.	assertive non-assertive aggressive
3b Look, give me my money. I haven't got all day for you to waste my time.	assertive non-assertive aggressive
3c Well, are you sure no one will notice it?	assertive non-assertive aggressive

Situation 4

A colleague keeps giving you all his/her work to do. You've decided to put an end to this. Your colleague has just asked you to do some more of his/her work. You say:

4a I'm rather busy. But if you can't get it done, I suppose I can help you.	assertive non-assertive aggressive
4b Forget it. It's about time you did your own work. I'm not your slave, you know.	assertive non-assertive aggressive
4c No, Sue/Tom. I'm not going to do any more of your work. I'm tired of doing both my work and yours.	assertive non-assertive aggressive

Situation 5

A new person has just moved in next door. You really want to get to know them.

5a You smile as your neighbour walks by, but say nothing.	assertive non-assertive aggressive
5b You go next door and say, 'Hello. I'm Sue/Tom. I live next door. Welcome to the neighbourhood.'	assertive non-assertive aggressive
5c You watch your neighbour through the window.	assertive non-assertive aggressive

Now check your answers with the assessments on page 197.

Practice situations

Work with a partner. One of you should look at the notes for Role A below and the other should turn to the notes for Role B on page 197.

If your notes are marked with an **A**, you should try to express your feelings *assertively* and not give in too easily!

Role A

1 You want to buy a snack for lunch but you haven't got any money on you. Your friend has helped you out with small loans in the past, so you ask him or her. You speak first.

2 A few weeks ago you decided that you were definitely overweight. You have been on a strict diet since then and have managed to lose a little weight. You are now at a friend's house for a dinner party and he/she is insisting that you try everything and have second helpings. Your partner speaks first. (**A**)

3 You are a very experienced doctor and, in general, you don't believe in giving patients too much information about the drugs you prescribe. You feel that technical details only confuse or worry patients and in any case you're too busy to explain at length. You have just prescribed an antibiotic called TOXIDIN to a patient. You've never had any complaints about side-effects but you have read that it can cause headaches. Your partner speaks first.

4 At 4.00 pm a friend asks if he/she could borrow your car to pick up a package at the post office. You agreed provided your friend was back by 5.30 pm because you need to be at a meeting at 6.00 pm. It's 6.15 pm and your friend has just returned. You are quite annoyed. Your partner speaks first. (**A**)

5 You borrowed a friend's record recently. Unfortunately, your hand slipped while you were putting it on the turntable and the record was scratched slightly. You know that your friend is very fussy about his records and he's sure to notice. You speak first.

▶ Focus on listening

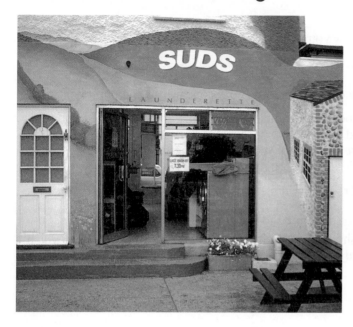

You are going to hear part of a radio programme. Choose the correct answers for each question.

1 The interior of the launderette can best be described as
   a warm and cheerful.
   b harshly-lit and draughty.
   c modern and well-designed.
   d crowded and uncomfortable.

2 The reason Mrs White gives for coming to the launderette is that
   a she needs a rest from her housework.
   b she has a large amount of washing to do.
   c she can't afford a washing machine.
   d she finds the companionship consoling.

3 May and Burnie's position is that of
   a part-time supervisors.
   b full-time supervisors.
   c temporary supervisors.
   d owner-supervisors.

4 One of the attendant's duties is to
   a replace faulty machines.
   b prevent children from using the machines.
   c make sure the machines are used correctly.
   d clean the machines regularly.

5 When they bring their washing to the launderette, some customers also
   a talk freely about their problems.
   b bring their clothes for mending.
   c ask for advice about their cleaning.
   d help the attendants with their work.

6 From the evidence in the programme, May and Burnie may be said to
   a enjoy gossiping about their neighbours.
   b show a concern for the community.
   c organise their customers' lives.
   d disapprove of their customers' ways of life.

▶ Focus on writing 2 · Narrative descriptive

> Describe your closest friend and how your friendship came about.
> (*About 250 words*)

Notes

1 The descriptive part of the essay clearly concerns both appearance and personality.

   a It's best not to attempt to be too comprehensive about appearance – it is far more effective to capture your friend's distinctive personal features. In other words, a particular expression in the eyes, a tone of voice or a characteristic laugh may reveal more than height, build, complexion and length of hair.

   b When describing someone's personality, it's often helpful to give concrete examples to illustrate a point.

2 The narrative part of the essay should be a lively account of the circumstances in which you met and the factors which led to the development of your friendship.

▶ Focus on register

Extract A

Lights, cameras, action . . .

Starting a film club gets people together and indulges all tastes from Laurel and Hardy to Rock Hudson. With enough members your own film shows will be cheaper than a cinema outing and much friendlier: the members can get involved in choosing programmes; keen cooks could sell home-baked snacks during the interval.

WHAT YOU NEED
First find premises, such as a school, church hall, library, or arts centre, with at least two clearly marked exits if you ex-pect audiences of more than 60. You'll probably need a 16mm projector (with another projector so that you can show the 40-minute reels without a break, or a long play attach-ment). A wide range of films, of all ages, come in this size. You'll need an experienced projectionist – ask who usually operates the projector you've arranged to borrow.

Extract B

Babysitter solutions

If finding – or affording – a babysitter is putting a damper on your social life, the remedy could be here.
Contact local playschemes, school PTAs, and women's groups to find out how other parents in your area cope.
Start a babysitting circle providing free babysitting for each other. Give everyone the same number of tokens to start with, to pay and be paid for their services.
Encourage newcomers to your neighbourhood to join, and have a monthly get-together where the children can get used to the other mothers. Americans organise 'pyjama parties' for their children at one person's house, so that a group of parents can have an evening out. Advertise for babysitters on college notice boards and in nurses' homes.

Extract C

Out and about

Develop your local knowledge by discovering the workings of community institutions.

Watch the legal system in real life from the public gallery of the court. If you're going in a group, ask a legal adviser to your local Citizens Advice Bureau to explain the technicalities to you one evening beforehand.

Organise a group tour behind the scenes at your nearest theatre, and meet the director or some of the cast.

See a newspaper going to press – most of them run tours. Contact the editorial office.

1 The style of the three extracts is predominantly
   a formal.
   b slangy.
   c chatty.
   d humorous.

2 The advice given in the three passages seems to be aimed at
   a increasing educational opportunities locally.
   b encouraging the reader to join local societies.
   c suggesting ways of raising money locally.
   d improving the social life of the community.

3 In order to start a film club it is necessary to
   a purchase the appropriate equipment.
   b join the British Federation of Film Societies.
   c enrol at least sixty members.
   d arrange to use a suitable venue.

4 Extract B is aimed at
   a people who are available to look after children in the evening.
   b parents who have difficulty in arranging supervision for their children.
   c people who have only recently moved into the local community.
   d parents who want their children to mix with other youngsters.

5 Extract C recommends
   a doing research into the organisation of local establishments.
   b getting legal advice before taking a group to court.
   c taking advantage of visits to local places of interest.
   d finding out about excursions arranged by the local newspaper.

LANGUAGE CHECK
Dependent Prepositions 3: Adjective + Preposition

Here is a list of 16 adjectives, some of which have been used in the texts in this unit. Write in the preposition which follows them.

Check your answers with your teacher or in the dictionary so that you have an accurate reference list for the future.

capable . . .	**ignorant** . . .
compared . . . (2 possibilities)	**keen** . . .
contrary . . .	**regardless** . . .
convinced . . .	**responsible** . . .
deprived . . .	**satisfied** . . .
familiar . . .	**subject** . . .
fed up . . .	**surprised** . . . (2 possibilities)
guilty . . .	**suspicious** . . . (2 possibilities)

▶Vocabulary practice

Review   Choose the word or phrase which best completes each sentence.

1 The job requires a(n) .... for hard work in difficult conditions.

   A ability   B skill   C faculty   D capacity

2 He left the meeting early on the unlikely .... that he had a sick friend to visit.

   A claim   B excuse   C pretext   D motive

3 The theft of my father's camera cast rather a .... on the holiday.

   A blight   B curse   C misfortune   D misery

4 I'm afraid I can't tell you what he said. It would be a .... of confidence.

   A rupture   B break   C rift   D breach

5 A statement will be made after the police have finished .... the evidence.

   A straining   B sifting   C shredding   D sieving

6 Anticipating renewed rioting, the authorities erected .... to block off certain streets.

   A barrages   B barricades   C ditches   D dykes

7 She took up so many hobbies when she retired that she had hardly any time ....

   A on her hands   B in hand   C at her hand   D at hand

8 He was a hardened criminal without a scrap of .... for his crimes.

   A pity   B reproach   C remorse   D penance

9 In the hands of a reckless driver a car becomes a .... weapon.

   A lethal   B fatal   C mortal   D venal

10 He was caught using forged bank notes to pay for goods and charged with ....

   A deception   B fraud   C embezzlement   D theft

11 I can lend you five pounds to help you .... until you've had time to go to the bank.

   A by   B up   C on   D out

12 You should be grateful to have opportunities which were .... to me at your age.

   A refused   B declined   C denied   D restricted

13 Working with the mentally handicapped requires considerable .... of patience and understanding.

   A means   B resources   C stocks   D provisions

14 The book took me the .... part of a year to write.

A most B greatest C best D largest

15 The air-sea search operation is continuing although hopes of finding survivors are ....

A dimming B fading C dissolving D reducing

16 If you .... in arriving late, I shall have to report you to the Manager.

A persist B persevere C insist D prevail

17 I'm not by .... a particularly ambitious man.

A inclination B habit C character D tendency

18 After the robbery, the shop installed a sophisticated alarm system as an insurance .... further losses.

A for B from C against D towards

19 If you reprimand him, he'll probably .... by behaving even worse in future.

A retort B resist C recompense D retaliate

20 After the church service, several people .... outside to chat.

A loitered B lagged C lingered D lapsed

21 I'm afraid I had to have .... to a dictionary in order to complete the translation.

A application B avail C resort D recourse

22 I was in no way prepared for the .... of criticism my play received.

A onslaught B onset C offensive D assault

23 The doctor prescribed tablets to help .... the pain.

A lighten B calm C relieve D rid

24 .... the regular written work, you will be required to submit a long essay.

A Apart from B Beside C In addition D Beyond

25 .... the difficulty of the task, I shall be lucky to complete it by May.

A Regarding B Given C Presuming D Accepted

The adjective suffix '-some' Look at the following pairs of words with similar meanings and pick out the *nine* which take the suffix *-some* to form an adjective. What spelling changes will there be, if any?

argument/quarrel	problem/trouble	loathe/hate	annoy/irk
reverence/awe	meddle/interfere	weary/tire	dread/fear

How do the remaining words form adjectives?

Give an adjective formed with '-some' which means:

a heavy and awkward to carry ....

b good for the health ....

c heavy and hard to bear (eg responsibility) ....

71

Verbs ending in 'ate' Give a verb ending in *-ate* for each of the following meanings. The first four come from the text *Neighbours*. The first letter is given to help you.

a make very angry   i...............

b pay back ill-treatment by ill-treatment   r...............

c increase in intensity or magnitude   e...............

d make up for loss or injury   c...............

e prove the truth of   s...............

f move up and down (eg temperature)   f...............

g make movements of hands and arms while speaking   g...............

h leave unoccupied   v...............

i handle, operate with skill   m...............

j invent in order to deceive   f...............

▶ Grammar practice

1 Fill each of the numbered blanks in the following passage with *one* suitable word.

Men have lived in groups and societies .... (1) all times and in all places, as .... (2) as we know. They do not seem .... (3) to survive as human beings .... (4) they live in .... (5) cooperation with one .... (6). The most basic of .... (7) human groups is the family in .... (8) various forms. The most important reason for this is the simple .... (9) that human beings take many years to .... (10). In .... (11) they are the most helpless of all earthly creatures. For several years after .... (12), a child has to be .... (13), clothed and protected day and night. In all societies such duties normally fall .... (14) a family group of some .... (15).

Men .... (16) groups for countless .... (17) reasons. For instance, it is .... (18) by cooperating that they are able to .... (19) their environment and defend .... (20).

from 'The Family' by Richard Cootes, Longman

2 Finish each of the following sentences in such a way that it means exactly the same as the sentence printed before it.

a I felt that it had been a mistake to write the letter.
   I regretted ever...

b Although it rained torrentially all day, we all enjoyed the excursion.
   Despite...

c I went down with 'flu as soon as I had recovered from bronchitis.
   No sooner...

d The Manager is not to be disturbed.
   On no account...

e She said she thought I was a liar.
   She accused...

f If we don't hear from you within seven days, the order will be cancelled.
   Unless...

g They are relaying the news by satellite.
   The news...

h However friendly he seems, he's not to be trusted.
   Friendly...

i If you didn't contribute generously, we couldn't continue our work.
   But for...

j He always wants to borrow money when he telephones.
   Whenever...

UNIT 5 Health

▶ Lead-in

The table below lists a number of risks which we may run in our day-to-day lives. These risks are *not in the correct order* and do not match the figures on the right hand side.

Working with a partner, try to estimate which of the voluntary risks is most likely to prove fatal in a ten-year period. Write it in next to number 1 at the top of the right hand column. Continue by writing the next most dangerous risk by number 2, and so on. Work through the involuntary risks in the same way.

The risks of being killed per person per 10-year period	
voluntary risks	
a car driving	1 (1 in 25) ....
b car racing	2 (1 in 50) ....
c drinking (1 bottle of wine/day)	3 (1 in 80) ....
d motor cycling	4 (1 in 600) ....
e rock climbing	5 (1 in 700) ....
f smoking (20 cigarettes/day)	6 (1 in 5000) ....
involuntary risks	
a atomic power station (at 1 km)	1 (1 in 500) ....
b being run over	2 (1 in 1250) ....
c falling aircraft	3 (1 in 1700) ....
d influenza	4 (1 in a million) ....
e leukemia	4 (1 in a million) ....
f lightning	6 (1 in 5 million) ....

Now compare your completed tables with those of other pairs. Are there any significant differences in your results?

Finally, check your answers with the table on page 198. Are there any surprises?

▶ Text 1 · Why do we still dice with death?

Read through the passage and answer these questions.

1 Why is it important to understand how people make 'health decisions'?

2 What is surprising about people's behaviour, in his opinion?

3 What kind of information about health risks do people rely on most?

If asked, 'What are health decisions?', most of us would answer in terms of hospitals, doctors and pills. Yet we are all making a whole range of deci-
5 sions about our health which go beyond this limited area; for example, whether or not to smoke, exercise, drive a motorbike, drink alcohol regularly. The ways we reach
10 decisions and form attitudes about our health are only just beginning to be understood.

The main paradox is why people consistently do things which are
15 known to be very hazardous. Two good examples of this are smoking and not wearing seat belts: addiction helps keep smokers smoking; and whether to wear a seat belt is only
20 partly affected by safety considerations. Taken together, both these examples underline elements of how people reach decisions about their health. Understanding this process is
25 crucial. We can then more effectively change public attitudes to hazardous, voluntary activities like smoking.

Smokers run double the risk of contracting heart disease, several
30 times the risk of suffering from chronic bronchitis and at least 25 times the risk of lung cancer, as compared to non-smokers. Despite extensive press campaigns (es-
35 pecially in the past 20 years), which have regularly told smokers and car drivers the grave risks they are running, the number of smokers and seat belt wearers has remained much the
40 same. Although the number of deaths from road accidents and smoking are well publicised, they have aroused little public interest.

If we give smokers the real figures,
45 will it alter their views on the dangers of smoking? Unfortunately not. Many of the 'real figures' are in the form of probabilistic estimates, and evidence shows that people are very
50 bad at processing and understanding this kind of information. Giving people information like that contained in Table 1 should alter their behaviour, but it is unlikely to.

55 The kind of information that tends to be relied on both by the smoker and seat belt non-wearer is anecdotal, based on personal experiences. All smokers seem to have an Uncle Bill 60 or an Auntie Mabel who has been smoking cigarettes since they were twelve, lived to 90, and died because they fell down the stairs. And if they don't have such an aunt or uncle, 65 they are certain to have heard of someone who has. Similarly, many motorists seem to have heard of people who would have been killed if they had been wearing seat belts.

70 Reliance on this kind of evidence and not being able to cope with 'probabilistic' data form the two main foundation stones of people's assessment of risk. A third is reliance on 75 press-publicised dangers and causes of death. American psychologists have shown that people overestimate the frequency (and therefore the danger) of the dramatic causes of 80 death (like aeroplane crashes) and underestimate the undramatic, unpublicised killers (like smoking) which actually take a greater toll of life.

85 What is needed is some way of changing people's evaluations and attitudes to the risks of certain activities like smoking. What can be done? The 'rational' approach of 90 giving people the 'facts and figures' seems ineffective. But the evidence shows that when people are *frightened*, they are more likely to change their estimates of the dangers in-95 volved in smoking or not wearing seat belts. Press and television can do this very cost-effectively. Programmes like *Dying for a Fag* (a Thames TV programme) vividly 100 showed the health hazards of smoking and may have increased the chances of people stopping smoking permanently.

So a mass-media approach may 105 work. But it needs to be carefully controlled. Overall, the new awareness of the problem of health decisions and behaviour is at least a more hopeful sign for the future.

from 'Why do we still dice with death?' by Robert Hallet in New Society

Complete these statements by choosing the answer which you think fits best.

1 The subject under discussion in this article is
   a why people persist in running health risks.
   b why people fail to make health decisions.
   c how people estimate the dangers of smoking.
   d how to use the mass media for health education.

2 The writer suggests that the main reason that people don't stop smoking is that
   a they tend to imitate friends and relations who smoke heavily.
   b they are unable to break the habit although they know the risks.
   c they are unaware of the degree of danger involved in smoking.
   d they don't accept the statistical evidence against smoking.

3 Publishing figures for health risks has been found to have little effect because people
   a found them difficult to interpret.
   b considered them to be exaggerated.
   c were too shocked to respond to them.
   d usually fail to read such reports.

4 A reason given for using the mass media to publicise health risks is that they
   a are known to be successful in changing people's habits.
   b can reach the widest cross-section of the population.
   c are the only really effective means of frightening people.
   d are an economical way to influence large numbers of people.

5 The most optimistic aspect of this article is the fact that
   a the media are having an increasing effect in health education.
   b attention is being paid to how people assess health risks.
   c people are becoming more concerned about their own health.
   d precise figures are now available to underline health risks.

▶Focus on grammar 1 · Review of conditional 3

Type 3 conditionals show how a *result* in the past or present depends on a *condition* in the past. Since we cannot change that condition or its result, type 3 conditionals are sometimes known as impossible conditionals.

Type 3a
(past result)

Look at these examples from Text 1:

many motorists seem to have heard of people who *would have been killed if they had been wearing their seat belts*

Form

IF	past perfect simple or continuous	perfect conditional simple or continuous

Complete these examples:

If you hadn't lost the car keys, we would have been . . .
I wouldn't have washed the car if I'd known it was going to . . .

Type 3b
(present result)

IF	past perfect simple or continuous	present conditional simple or continuous

Complete these examples:

He'd be playing in the team today if he hadn't gone down with an attack of ....
If she had kept those shares instead of selling them, she'd be ....

Exercise 1

Complete these examples of types 3a and 3b conditionals. Try to make interesting and natural-sounding sentences.

a If we had lost the map, . . .

b He would have been absolutely furious if . . .

c You wouldn't have cramp in your leg if you . . .

d If I hadn't seen the police car in time, . . .

e Would you have resigned from your job if . . .

f If we had listened to his advice, . . .

Points to
remember

1 **Order of clauses and punctuation:** the same rules apply to type 3 conditionals as to types 1 and 2. See Focus on grammar Unit 3 p. 44 and 45.

2 **Might and could:** using *might* or *could* + perfect infinitive to replace the past conditional suggests that the result is *probable* rather than certain.

eg *I might have got* the job *if I hadn't been late* for the interview.

3 **Inversion:** the subject and verb in conditional clauses can be inverted. The effect is more formal.

eg *Had I known* your intention, *I would* certainly *have tried* to stop you.

Exercise 2

Revision of conditionals types 1, 2 and 3.

Put the verbs in the following sentences into the correct tenses.

a If the lights (not fuse), I (not mind) being alone that night.

b I (never keep) a large pet unless I (have) time to exercise it properly.

c Supposing we (never meet) all those years ago, who do you think you (might marry)?

d He (not have) any difficulty in finding the cottage provided that he (arrive) before dusk.

e If I (not watch) television, I (certainly hear) the burglar alarm go off.

f We (not be refused) credit if we (always pay) our bills on time in the past.

g Where you (be) now if you (not have) financial backing from your family from the start?

h What you (do) about the blackmail attempt last year if you (be) me?

i Medical evidence suggests that most people (enjoy) better health if they (eat) less refined sugar.

j If it (not be) for the quick thinking of a neighbour, the fire (might spread) to other floors.

▶ Text 2 · Hypochondriacs arise!

How many hypochondriacs are there? Can anybody in the great social science industry tell me? Even to the nearest ten thousand?

I doubt it, and I think I know why. The trouble about being a hypochondriac (and I speak from a lifetime of practice) is that you feel silly.

5 My rational mind tells me that, just because the cut on my finger has been throbbing for two days, I am unlikely to die of gangrene; but in a hypochondriacal mood I can see the gangrene creeping up my arm as my finger turns black. My hypochondria is fed, in constant doses, by half the scientific knowledge I need, and twice the imagination. I know enough anatomy to identify the twitch in my chest as the first spasm of coronary 10 thrombosis, and to point to my duodenum with the authority of a second-year medical student.

Of course, like many hypochondriacs, I enjoy (not exactly the word) sound health. My fat medical file contains very little of substance, though there is a fine selection of negative barium meal tests. In fact, the only spell I ever had in hospital took place when 15 I actually had something. What I thought was a cold turned out to be pneumonia. So much for my diagnostic accuracy.

Hypochondria lies between the rational self which says, 'Nonsense, you're fine,' and the deeply pessimistic self, which fingers a swelling discovered under the jaw as you shave and converts it into the first lump of a fatal cancer of the lymph gland.

20 These feelings are embarrassing enough but they are made worse by the brisk treatment I get from the many overt anti-hypochondriacs about: people like wives or editors, who say, 'Get up! There's nothing wrong with you', or 'Never seen you looking better, old boy', when the first stages of a brain tumour have begun to paralyse my left arm.

25 Such persons know nothing. They are capable of astonishing acts of self-forgetfulness. They walk about with lips so chapped that a penny could fit in the cracks. They go so far as to forget to take medicine prescribed for them. For these creatures of the light, the world is a simple place. You are either well or sick and that's that, categories which admit of no confusion. 'If you are ill,' anti-hypochondriacs say, 'you ought to go to bed 30 and stop moping.' They remind me of the story told of the economist, Keynes, and his Russian ballerina wife, staring silently into the fire. Keynes asked, 'What are you thinking, my dear?' She replied, 'Nothing.' and he said, 'I wish I could do that.'

There is not much comfort to be had from other hypochondriacs, either. I had lunch once with a distinguished writer whom I very much wanted to impress. He greeted me 35 with the words, 'Please excuse the condition of my nose.' During the next few minutes, fascinated but trying not to be caught staring, I established two things: first, that he had a small inflammation by his right nostril, and second, that he was a fellow-hypochondriac. The combination meant that I could have been three other people for all he cared. As we parted, he again apologised about his nose. I was furious.

from an article by Jonathan Steinberg in New Society

Now complete these statements by choosing the answer which you think fits best.

1 The author suggests that the exact number of hypochondriacs is not known because hypochondriacs
 a are not taken seriously by social scientists.
 b feel too embarrassed about their fears to admit them.
 c don't take their fears seriously enough to discuss them.
 d are aware that they represent a tiny minority.

2 The author describes how his own hypochondria can be set off by
 a reading articles in medical journals.
 b noticing unusual physical sensations.
 c studying his personal medical files.
 d asking for advice from student doctors.

3 The author's medical history suggests that
 a he has never had any serious illnesses.
 b his diagnoses have sometimes proved correct.
 c he has had very few medical examinations.
 d most of his fears have proved groundless.

4 Anti-hypochondriacs are described as people who
 a pay no attention to minor ailments.
 b don't accept that people get ill.
 c have little faith in the medical profession.
 d smile cheerfully however ill they are.

5 The author recognised a fellow-hypochondriac by the fact that
 a the conversation centred around the writer's health.
 b the writer was so sympathetic towards him.
 c a minor complaint so concerned the writer.
 d the writer seemed to want attention from more people.

STUDY BOX 1
Expressing Concession – Part 1.
Look at the following common mistakes. Can you say what is wrong, and why?

> *Although he hadn't any money, but he lived comfortably.*
> *They caught the bus even although they were late.*
> *Despite it was raining, we went ahead with the picnic.*
> *In spite her good exam results, she had trouble finding a job.*
> *I wasn't very optimistic. The news was however good.*

Check your answers with the notes below, and Expressing Concession Part 2 (p. 90).

But and **Yet** are both conjunctions used to introduce a statement which contrasts with what has been said previously. **Yet** is more emphatic.

> eg *So a mass media approach may work.* **But** *it needs to be carefully controlled.*
> *If asked, "What are health decisions?", most of us would answer in terms of hospitals, doctors and pills.* **Yet** *we are all making a whole range of decisions about our health which go beyond this limited area;*

(Al)though/even though are also conjunctions, used in a similar way. They introduce a statement which makes the main information in the sentence seem surprising.

> eg **Although** *the number of deaths from road accidents and smoking are well publicised, they have aroused little public interest.*

Though can be used as an adverb meaning 'however'. It's always used with commas.

> eg *I can't stay long. I'll have a coffee,* **though**.

▶ Focus on grammar 2 ·
Expressing wishes and regrets

Look at this example from Text 2:

I wish I could do that.

Since Keynes *can't* do it, he is referring to something which is unreal. The word *wish* is followed by the *past form* of the verb (in fact a rare use of the subjunctive in English).

Further examples:

I wish I had enough money to buy a car.
I wish you didn't smoke so much!

If Keynes had been referring to the past, with regret, *wish* would have been followed by the *past perfect*:

eg *I wish I had been able to do that.*

The same sequence of tenses occurs after 'If only', an expression with a similar meaning:

eg *If only I knew the answer!*
If only you had been there!

Note The use of the subjunctive form *were* instead of the normal past form *was* is preferable after the first person but rather formal after the third person:

eg *I wish I were you.*
If only he were with us now!

In both cases, *stress and intonation* are crucial to the meaning. Practise saying these:

I wish I could do that!
If only you had been there!

Exercise 1   Imagine you are the people in the cartoons. What would you say?

1

2

3

4

5

6

wish + would   This form can be used as an alternative to *wish/if only* + past when you are referring to a habitual action:

eg *I wish he would come to see us more often.*
If only you wouldn't drink so heavily.

This form *must* be used when you express a wish or regret about a specific action in the future:

eg *If only he would go home!*
I wish they would sell me their car.

Other expressions which take the past tense:

1 would rather   eg *I'd rather you came with me.*

2 as if/as though   eg *She speaks as if she knew the country well.*
As if you didn't know!

3 Suppose   eg *Just suppose someone saw us together.*
   Supposing   *Supposing you had been arrested!*

4 It's time   eg *It's about time you did some housework.*
   . . . about time
   . . . high time

Exercise 2   Complete the following:

a You .... I came with you to the hospital, ... you?

b .... you were offered the job in Australia, would you take it?

c I really think .... he faced up to his responsibilities.

d You could get a Grade A in Music .... you practised a bit more.

e There's no need to treat him .... he were a criminal!

f I wish you .... to what I'm trying to tell you.

g I've got to get up early tomorrow so it's high time ....

h He tells the story of that medieval battle as vividly as if ....

i What I've told you is confidential and I'd rather you ....

j You took quite a risk in coming here. Supposing ....

80

▶ Text 3 · Angels in hell

Think about these questions *before* you read the passage:

1 In what ways is a nurse expected to be 'an angel'?
2 What aspects of her work might lead to anxiety?

Now answer the same questions from information in the text.

There should still, it seems, be something of an angel about a nurse. A job which draws its tradition from the middle class ministering to the grateful poor, its hierarchy and
5 ferociously differentiated uniforms from the armed services, its sense of self-sacrificing vocation from the church, and which is staffed mostly by women, doesn't fit easily with the notion that those who do it are prey
10 to the usual human range of tragedies, depressions and muddles, let alone the particular stresses of their work.

Penny Crawley, senior counsellor at the Royal College of Nursing's CHAT (which
15 stands for Counselling Help and Advice Together), can guarantee a reaction of dismay if, while talking to nurses about her work, she mentions a visit to one of their colleagues in prison. Nurses do not commit
20 crimes, any more than they fall prey to mental or physical sickness.

Or if they do, they can't expect much support from colleagues who, after coping with pain all day, have little energy left for
25 their own. 'The minute a nurse becomes ill, the minute she stops being one of Us and starts being one of Them,' Penny Crawley has noticed, 'she's thrown out of the tribe. It's very hard, it seems, to relate to col-
30 league-patients.'

Yet the sources of unavoidable stress don't take much seeking, in a job which has to do with death and distress among both patients and relatives, which can trigger
35 your own fears and barely remembered unhappinesses, which has to do with mess and dirt and the most menial of tasks. It's over 20 years since Isobel Menzies wondered why, nevertheless, nurses should
40 show such high levels of worry, fear, guilt, depression, shame, embarrassment, strain, distrust, and disappointment, and detailed the ways in which hospitals set up social defence systems against anxiety which,
45 ironically, make matters worse, not better.

Her study of the ways hospitals cope by depersonalisation of patients and nurses, by concentration on mechanical tasks, by vagueness in definition of responsibility has
50 since become a classic.

Yet the evasions she noted still go on, and with them comes stress that is avoidable. There are still the wards where it simply isn't done for nurses to discuss their feel-
55 ings about the death of patients – which leaves them with a load of guilt and distress, and makes it harder for them to comfort relatives. There are still senior nurses who put their priority on keeping a ward tidy –
60 like the ones who interrupted conversations between nurses and unhappy patients to tell the nurse not to wear her cardigan, or sit on the bed, or to wash the tea things. And that leads to loss of job satisfaction. There is still
65 the organisational approach which substitutes rigid hierarchy for teaching personal responsibility and then leaves the learner nurse suddenly, and quite without preparation, in charge of a ward. There are still
70 the young nurses who find that if they are singled out, it is always for blame and never for praise.

Behaviour like that can contribute to a level of anxiety which, as the author of the
75 so far single study of stress among nurse-learners concluded, might produce 'frank inability and ineffective functioning'. And if they do little for nurses, they don't do much for patients either. Not surprising, perhaps,
80 that a recent study showed patients to feel that it was their fellow sufferers, not nurses at all who come nearest to understanding what is really worrying them. Not surprising, either, that where nurses are encour-
85 aged to give up that 'character armour' which insists that being professional means showing no feelings at all, not only do they do better in their exams, but their patients, freed to discuss their own feelings, get
90 better faster.

from an article in the Guardian by Ann Shearer

1 Explain in other words 'prey to' (lines 9–10).
2 Explain in other words 'let alone' (line 11).
3 Why is there a 'reaction of dismay' (lines 16–17) when Penny Crawley mentions a nurse in prison?
4 What does 'their own' (line 25) refer to?
5 Explain in your own words 'don't take much seeking' (line 32).
6 Why is it surprising to find that the 'social defence systems' (lines 43–44) still exist?
7 Explain in other words 'it simply isn't done for nurses to . . .' (lines 53–54).
8 What criticism could be made about the senior nurses' behaviour (lines 58–63)?
9 Why is the learner nurse 'quite without preparation' (lines 68–69) for being left in charge of a ward?
10 Explain in other words 'singled out' (line 71).
11 What is the effect of anxiety on learner-nurses in simple terms?
12 From the information in the passage, write a paragraph of 80–100 words describing the improvements which could be made in the nursing profession. (See STUDY BOX – Summary Writing on page 127.)

▶ Communication activity · Fitness project

Work *with a partner* to carry out this project. It is in three parts. Decide who will interview and who will be interviewed first. After you have finished the three parts, you can change roles if there is time.

The instructions are for the interviewer.

Part 1 **How active are you?**
Look at the table below with your partner. Ask your partner to think through a typical day and tell you about his/her activities according to how vigorous they are.

Fill in the table for *your partner*. If your partner's activity is the same as an example given, put a tick (√) next to it. If an activity is different, write it down on the right-hand side of the table.

You should spend about 5 minutes on Part 1.

Vigorous activity		
Our everyday activities can be divided into four grades according to how vigorous they are.		
Grade	**Examples**	**Your partner's activities**
A No conscious activity	Sleeping, lying down	
B Minimal activity	Sitting down, motorway driving	
C Light activity	Standing while doing something, eg shaving, washing-up. Moving around a bit, eg sweeping the floor, washing the car	
D Vigorous activity	Brisk walking, gardening, scrubbing floors, polishing furniture, washing clothes by hand, light manual work, climbing stairs, running, cycling, most sports, heavy manual labouring	

Now concentrate on your partner's *Grade D activities*.

Does he/she do *a total* of 30 or more minutes of Grade D activity each day? (It need not necessarily be done all at once.)

It's only Grade D activities that count. Doing more of a less vigorous activity doesn't have the same effect on the body. Vigorous activity gets the heart pumping fast and hard which it needs to do every day.

If your partner *does* do at least 30 minutes of Grade D activity each day, then he/she probably has all the exercise needed to keep physically fit.

If not, continue to Part 2 . . .

Part 2   What's in it for you?

Look at the following table with your partner and find out which benefits he/she would most like to gain from becoming more active. Put a tick (√) next to those benefits in the boxes.

Becoming more active can help you to:		
1 work harder for longer without tiring too quickly ☐	6 trim your figure by toning up your muscles ☐	
2 have more energy for everyday tasks ☐	7 lose some weight ☐	
3 improve muscle strength for lifting, pushing, etc ☐	8 keep your body feeling young ☐	
	9 ward off heart disease ☐	
4 bend down and stretch up for things more easily ☐	10 have feeling of well-being ☐	
	11 beat the stress in your working life ☐	
5 be more agile and graceful ☐	12 relax and feel refreshed ☐	
	13 meet people and socialise ☐	
	14 enjoy yourself ☐	

Now check the results:

Look at the *numbers* of the benefits which you ticked for your partner.

- Ticks between numbers *1 and 5* mean a concern with

A – Physical fitness and work capacity

Physical fitness has three elements:

Suppleness – the ability to move freely including bending, twisting and turning the head, body, arms and legs.

Strength – the power of the muscles to lift and push heavy objects easily.

Stamina – the ability to continue doing an activity which uses up a lot of energy without getting tired.

- Ticks between numbers *5 and 8* mean a concern with

B – Looks and figure

- Ticks between numbers *7 and 11* mean a concern with

C – General health and well-being

- Ticks between numbers *11 and 14* mean a concern with

D – Relaxation and social life

Remember which main area(s) your partner was concerned with and move on to Part 3.

*"For Heaven's sake ask him how he's getting
on with his body building course."*

Part 3   Which activity for you?

The chart opposite will help you to choose the best activity for your partner. The symbols show how good the activity is for helping to develop stamina, strength or suppleness. Three stars ★★★ means the activity is a very good one. One star ★ means the activity has little or no effect.

Now check the results of Part 2 to see which benefits your partner would like to get.

If **A** (Physical fitness and work capacity) or **C** (General health and well-being) was chosen, look down the three columns for stamina, suppleness and strength and put a tick (√) in *column 1* for those activities which score high for all three.

If **B** (Looks and figure) was chosen, you need an exercise which scores high for suppleness. Tick (√) suitable activities in *column 1*.

If **D** (Relaxation and social life) was chosen, you will need to put a tick (√) in *column 2* for those activities which appeal to your partner and have a social element.

In *column 3,* you should put a tick if your partner can *afford* to take up his/her chosen activities. Consider such things as:

- do you need to travel? If so, how much does it cost?

- do you need to buy equipment such as racquets and balls, or could you hire them?

- do you need to pay to use a court or swimming pool?

- do you need lessons?

Finally, in *column 4,* you need to consider whether your partner can fit the activity easily into his/her way of life. Tick those activities which would be suitable.

You will probably then be left with only one or two activities that your partner could take up. If you find that there is not even one left then either your partner doesn't really want to take up any kind of recreation or he/she has been too severe in his/her judgements. You could try going through the chart again. If there are several activities your partner would like to take up, he/she could either take them all up at once (if he/she has the time and energy and can afford it!) or aim to do a different activity each season.

	Stamina	Strength	Suppleness	1	2	3	4
1 Badminton	★★	★★	★★				
2 Billiards/Snooker	★	★	★				
3 Climbing stairs	★★	★★	★				
4 Cricket	★	★	★★				
5 Cycling	★★★	★★	★				
6 Dancing (Ballroom)	★★	★	★				
7 Dancing (Disco)	★★	★★	★★★				
8 Darts	★	★	★				
9 Digging in garden	★	★★★	★				
10 Driving	★	★	★				
11 Fishing	★	★	★				
12 Football (Soccer)	★★	★★	★★				
13 Golf	★	★	★★				
14 Keep-fit classes	★★	★★	★★★				
15 Housework	★	★★	★★				
15 Jogging on spot	★★	★	★				
17 Judo/Karate	★★	★★	★★★				
18 Mowing lawn	★	★★	★				
19 Rugby	★★	★★	★★				
20 Running	★★★	★★	★				
21 Squash	★★★	★★	★★				
22 Swimming	★★★	★★★	★★				
23 Table tennis	★	★	★★				
24 Tennis	★★	★★	★★				
25 Walking briskly (over 1 hour)	★★	★	★				
26 Washing/ polishing car	★	★★	★				

STUDY BOX 2
Phrasal Verbs 2

Look at these examples from this unit:

1 *Work with a partner to* **carry out** *this project.* (Communication Activity)
carry out means 'perform or complete a task'.

   NB **carry on** means 'continue' eg *Please* **carry on** *with your work.*

2 *... the ways in which hospitals* **set up** *social defence systems.* (Text 3)
set up means 'establish'.

   NB If you **set up house** or **home,** you begin living somewhere. If you **set up shop,** you start trading.

3 *... nurses are encouraged to* **give up** *that 'character armour'.* (Text 3)
give up means 'surrender'.

   NB **give up** can also mean 'stop doing something' eg *I wish I could* **give up** *smoking.*

85

▶ Focus on listening

You are going to hear the instructions for *six* exercises. As you listen, match the instructions for each exercise with one of the drawings below. Number them 1 to 6, in the order in which you hear them. Write the numbers in the boxes in the top right-hand corner of each drawing. Write × in the remaining boxes.

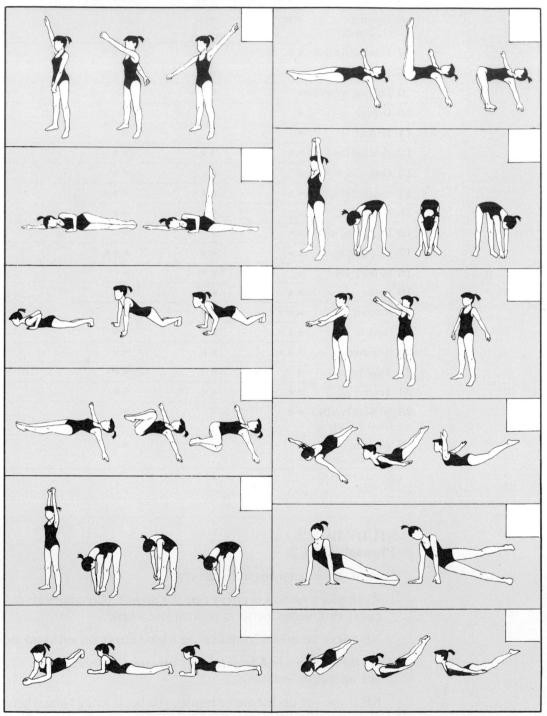

When you have finished and checked your answers, look at the drawings marked ×.

Choose one of them and describe the exercise to another student. See if your partner can identify the correct drawing.

Do the same for the other drawings, taking it in turns to describe and identify. (You could even try doing some of the exercises if there's enough room and you feel energetic!)

Useful language

Stand	upright erect up straight	Lie	face down on your back on your side		with your feet	apart astride together

with your arms	at your sides extended over your head stretched sideways (at shoulder level)	Raise Lower Bend Straighten	your legs arms body

Bend down Bob up/down	Tuck in Tuck . . . in

palm forearm upper arm elbow shoulder	toe heel shin knee thigh	hip waist

▶ Focus on writing 1 · Instructions

The following pictures illustrate six exercises which have been designed as a warm-up routine before jogging or running.

Write clear instructions for each exercise suitable for inclusion in a simple guide to fitness.

A reader should be able to understand your instructions without looking at the pictures, so be precise about starting positions, parts of the body and movements. The figures in brackets tell you how long a position should be held or how often a movement should be repeated.

Number each exercise and start with a verb in the imperative. The one on this page has been started for you.

Warming up for a run

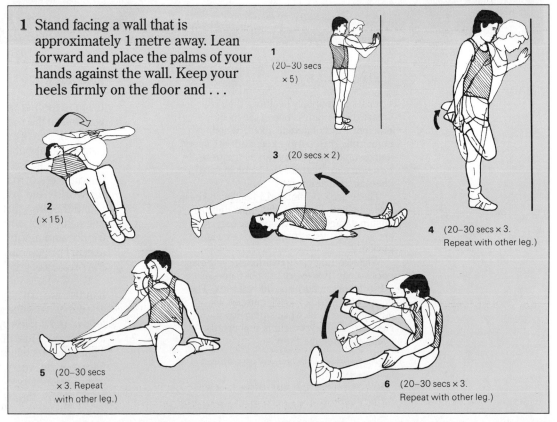

1 Stand facing a wall that is approximately 1 metre away. Lean forward and place the palms of your hands against the wall. Keep your heels firmly on the floor and . . .

1 (20–30 secs × 5)

2 (× 15)

3 (20 secs × 2)

4 (20–30 secs × 3. Repeat with other leg.)

5 (20–30 secs × 3. Repeat with other leg.)

6 (20–30 secs × 3. Repeat with other leg.)

▶Focus on register

Extract 1

Cyclists are not only healthy – they're smart. Bike riding is one of the most efficient ways of getting about. When comparing the energy expended with speed and distance covered, even the rustiest two-wheeler outstrips the hummingbird[1], cheetah[2] and jumbo jet.

There are an estimated 14 million bikes in Britain – with 5 million of them gathering dust in garages. A pity, because bicycles are so versatile; as transport or for simple pleasure.

While getting you to work, a bicycle also gets you fit. For every half hour's pedalling, a 150 lb person burns up 300 calories. The heart, lungs, back and leg muscles are strengthened – all while sitting down. Because the bodyweight is supported, cycling is effective exercise.

[1] a small bird whose wings beat very fast and make a humming sound
[2] an African animal of the large cat family; the fastest mammal on land.

Extract 2

If you're feeling rather under the weather at the moment, a trifle sluggish, here's an opportunity to do something about it. A regular stint on our super Fitness Cycle will make all the difference, make you feel on top of the world. And you don't have to ride round the draughty streets at some unearthly hour when you know your friends and neighbours will not be about. For you may do the necessary in the privacy of your own home.

The Cycle is full size, the seat and handlebars are adjustable. It's tough enough to take the weight of a hefty fellow and it folds up neatly and slimly to be stored. Just think of the benefits. Your muscles will be toned up – not filled out, no worry about that. Your arms and legs become firmer, so does your tummy, thighs and hips.

Extract 3

I have been experiencing cramp pains in my thighs. I returned to cycling about two years ago, after a lay-off of approximately fifteen or sixteen years. After breaking myself in gradually, I started commuting to the City by bike, a journey of about twelve miles each way, usually every other day.

Last September the cramps first occurred, then again in February this year, both times when walking, having been off the bike for two or three days. These pains made walking very painful and, at times, difficult.

I have a lightweight bike, am forty years old and my general health, I consider, is very good.

Extract 4

Cycling, like any regular exercise, makes you fitter – and even half an hour a day slowly but inexorably slims you, even if you don't or won't diet. But the doubters say that for town cyclists the health benefits are outweighed by the damage caused by the polluted air of the cities. As the cyclists pedal briskly, inhaling more deeply than, say, a motorist, the damage will be that much more. Or so the argument goes. An article by Dr R. Williams in *The British Medical Journal* dispels the theory. He measured the concentration of carbon monoxide in the bloodstream; on a calm day the percentage was a trivial 0.5. People living in the Outer Hebrides have shown as much.

Look at Extracts 1, 2 and 4 and find words or phrases which mean the same as:

a clever (1)	....	*i* period of work (2) ....
b used up (1)	....	*j* inconvenient (2) ....
c bicycle (1)	....	*k* big, strong, heavy (2) ....
d does better than (1)	....	*l* less important than (4) ....
e having many uses (1)	....	*m* quickly (4) ....
f not very well (2)	....	*n* breathing in (4) ....
g rather (2)	....	*o* disproves (4) ....
h slow-moving (2)	....	*p* unimportant (4) ....

Now complete these statements by choosing the answer which fits best.

1 Extract 1 points out that, as a form of transport, the bicycle is extremely
  a fast.
  b strongly built.
  c economical of energy.
  d up-to-the minute in fashion.

2 Extract 2 is aimed at the type of reader who
  a is dissatisfied with normal bicycles.
  b has never ridden a normal bicycle.
  c is too overweight to ride a normal bicycle.
  d would not want to be seen on a normal bicycle.

3 Extracts 3 and 4 are both concerned with
  a the effects of pollution on cyclists.
  b common complaints suffered by cyclists.
  c fears about the possible bad effects of cycling.
  d the overall health benefits of vigorous cycling.

4 The extract which contains the most colloquial use of language is
  a Extract 1.
  b Extract 2.
  c Extract 3.
  d Extract 4.

5 The extract which recognises that many people overlook the advantages of their bicycle is
  a Extract 1.
  b Extract 2.
  c Extract 3.
  d Extract 4.

▶ Focus on writing 2

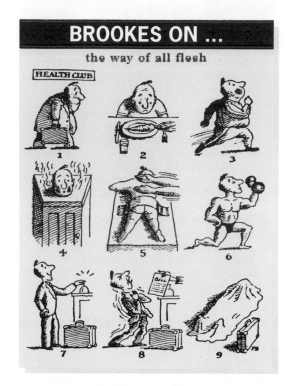

Write a balanced discussion on *one* of the following themes:

a New fashions in diets and exercise are more concerned with commercial profit than with health and fitness.

b Good health is the most important thing in life.
(*350 words*)

Remember the importance of *planning* and note the following points before you start.

1 Note down all the points which you want to include, with concrete examples where appropriate.

2 Decide how to organise your ideas logically in paragraphs.

3 Devise an effective introduction and conclusion.

STUDY BOX 2
Expressing Concession Part 2

Despite and **in spite of** are prepositions and are followed by nouns (or gerunds).

eg **Despite** *extensive press campaigns . . . the number of smokers . . . has remained the same*.

They cannot be followed by a clause. To introduce a clause, use:

despite/in spite of **the fact that** (*it was raining*) . . .

However and **nevertheless** are adverbs and are used when adding a comment which contrasts with what has been said before. **However** is always separated from the rest of the sentence by commas. **Nevertheless** is followed by a comma when it begins a sentence.

eg *That's one good reason. It is not,* **however,** *the only one.*
He had not slept that night. **Nevertheless,** *he seemed as energetic as ever.*

▶ Vocabulary practice

Review   Choose the word or phrase which best completes each sentence.

1 He still suffers from a rare tropical disease which he .... while in Africa.

   A infected   B complained   C gained   D contracted

2 I was proud to be .... out for special praise for my performance.

   A selected   B singled   C separated   D distinguished

3 There's no point in telephoning him. He's certain .... by now.

   A to leave   B to have left   C left   D having left

4 If you don't stop smoking, you .... this risk of developing chronic bronchitis.

   A bear   B suffer   C make   D run

5 I think you'll find that the inconvenience of the diet is .... by the benefits.

   A outranked   B overthrown   C overbalanced   D outweighed

6 We started off walking .... but had slowed to a snail's pace after an hour.

   A heartily   B briskly   C sharply   D crisply

7 That song .... me of my youth.

   A recalls   B remembers   C reminds   D recollects

8 Giving up smoking is just one of the ways to .... heart disease.

   A push off   B put off   C ward off   D throw off

9 We might just as well have stayed at home .... the enjoyment we had.

   A on account of   B as far as   C for all   D concerning

10 Don't stick your elbows out when you eat, ... them in by your sides.

   A tuck   B bend   C place   D turn

11 The windows don't fit very well and it makes the room awfully ....

   A airy   B draughty   C breezy   D ventilated

12 She gave up nursing training when she found she had no .... for looking after the sick.

   A vocation   B mission   C service   D ambition

13 There's no point in .... about all day. Cheer up and try to find a new job!

   A moping   B mourning   C brooding   D sulking

14 He was so .... in answer to my questions that I knew he had something to hide.

A effusive   B elusive   C allusive   D evasive

15 There is no .... for hard work and perseverance if you want to succeed.

A alternative   B substitute   C equivalent   D imitation

16 He looks much older. His financial worries seem to have taken a terrible .... on his health.

A burden   B toll   C strain   D tax

17 I haven't got the time to do my own work .... help you with yours.

A leaving aside   B not counting   C let alone   D apart from

18 You'll feel better after you've taken a .... of cough medicine.

A ration   B helping   C dose   D portion

19 There's a small hard .... on my wrist. I think I'd better see the doctor.

A swelling   B lump   C bruise   D rash

20 People in financial difficulties sometimes fall .... to unscrupulous money lenders.

A prey   B fool   C scapegoat   D sacrifice

21 What the company needs is a .... actor who can take on a variety of roles.

A variable   B changeable   C versatile   D diverse

22 With their modern, lightweight boat, they soon .... the older vessels in the race.

A outstripped   B caught up   C overran   D exceeded

23 If you .... too much of your energy on the climb, you'll have none left for the descent.

A spend   B lose   C expend   D invest

24 I've got such a .... headache that I can't concentrate on the lecture.

A beating   B drumming   C hammering   D throbbing

25 The rules are clearly stated and admit .... no confusion.

A to   B for   C of   D from

Common expressions for describing ill health and injuries

Symptoms

Choose words from the group below to complete the sentences.

runny	swollen	dizzy	feverish
sore	seedy	queasy	rash

1 When I stand up the room seems to be going round. I feel really ....

2 I'm not in pain but the glands in my neck seem to be ....

3 I've got a .... nose. I suppose it's a cold coming on.

4 I've come out in a .... all over my chest and arms. I think I may be allergic to cats.

5 It's like being sea-sick. I feel .... whenever I move about.

6 It's hard to describe. I just feel generally .... Can you prescribe a tonic?

7 My throat's awfully .... I hope it's not another bout of tonsillitis.

8 I haven't taken her temperature yet but her face is flushed and she seems

....

Injuries

Complete the sentences using words from the group below used as verbs or nouns, as appropriate.

bruise	scald	blister	scratch
graze	gash	sprain	fracture

1 He fell on the pavement and .... his knee. I've washed and dressed it but it isn't serious.

2 The lid of the kettle wasn't on properly and I .... my arm in the steam.

3 My feet are all .... after my attempt at the marathon yesterday.

4 He landed awkwardly after the high jump and .... his ankle. He's lucky it's not broken.

5 That's not a cut – it's just a .... Don't make such a fuss!

6 I caught my leg on the drawer of the filing cabinet and it gave me quite a nasty

....

7 The X-ray showed that I had .... several ribs in the accident.

8 She fell down the stairs and was lucky to get away with a few ....

▶ Grammar practice

1 Fill each of the numbered blanks in the following passage with *one* suitable word.

The worry about salt is that it may .... (1) high blood pressure. Chemically, salt .... (2) of sodium and chloride ions, both of .... (3) are common in the human .... (4) and are important for many physiological and biochemical .... (5). We not only need salt, we are salt, but too .... (6) may still be bad for us. Although the idea of a .... (7) between salt and high blood pressure .... (8) back to 2000 BC, there is still no scientific .... (9) as to whether this is so or not. One reason for this .... (10) to agree is that individual salt intake............................ (11) enormously from day to day, and so reliable measures of intake are hard to come .... (12).

Those who believe that salt does .... (13) to high blood pressure .... (14) to the high incidence of high blood pressure in countries that eat a very .... (15) diet. In Japan, for instance, where salted fish is an important part of the diet, high blood pressure and .... (16) complications are common, ... (17) among some Amazonian and African tribes, which have a low intake of salt, they are almost .... (18).

But .... (19) there is this neat relation between salt intake and the incidence of high blood pressure between countries, it doesn't seem to apply .... (20) those countries themselves. Studies, for instance, of couples who have a similar salt intake don't show any consistency in how often they develop high blood pressure.

from an article in the Observer Magazine by Dr Richard Smith

2 For each of the following sentences, write a new sentence as similar as possible in meaning to the original sentence, but using the words given: these words must *not be altered* in any way.

    EXAMPLE: She stopped asking for advice
               gave

    ANSWER: She *gave up* asking for advice.

a I don't think he's likely to telephone this late at night.
   doubt

b I'm sorry, I thought you were somebody else.
   took

c Any correspondence from the London office must be dealt with before other matters
   priority

d I advise you not to believe what you read in the papers about me.
   reliance

e Surely it was dangerous for you to hitch-hike all that way alone?
   risk

f There's a chance that my secretary took the order book away.
   may

g I'm trying to work out how much these dollars are worth in pounds.
   convert

h He didn't take any part in the conversation.
   contribute

i Let me know as soon as you have any news.
   minute

j This dispute is likely to lead to a strike.
   result

UNIT 6 Crime and Punishment

▶ Lead-in · Quiz

Work with a partner to discuss the following questions and choose answers.

1 What is the age of criminal responsibility in England and Wales (ie the age at which a person can be charged with a criminal offence)?

    a 8 years old   *b* 10 years old   *c* 12 years old   *d* 14 years old

2 The criminal statistics of England and Wales distinguish between *indictable* and *non-indictable* offences, which correspond approximately to serious and less serious crimes. Non-indictable crimes are tried only at the level of magistrates' courts, while indictable offences may be tried by jury in a higher court.

    What is the most common type of indictable offence recorded by the police?

    a Car crime   *d* Violent crime
    b Other theft   *e* Fraud and forgery
    c Burglary   *f* Criminal damage

3 At what age is a person most likely to be found guilty of or cautioned for an indictable offence?

    a 14 and under 17   *b* 17 and under 21   *c* 21 and over

4 Which one of the following crimes known to the police in England and Wales involves the greatest total value of property stolen?

    a Burglary   *d* Theft of motor vehicles
    b Theft from another person   *e* Shop-lifting
    c Theft by an employee

5 Who among the following is *least* likely to kill you?

    a A friend or acquaintance   *b* A present or former spouse or lover
    c Another member of your family   *d* A stranger

6 If you commit a murder, which of the following methods are you most likely to use?

    a Shooting   *b* Hitting or kicking   *c* Sharp instrument   *d* Strangulation   *e* Other

7 What is the average age of judges in England and Wales?

    a 50   *b* 60   *c* 70

8 What is the most frequently used punishment for indictable offences?

    a Probation   *b* Prison   *c* Fine

9 How likely is a man over 21 to be found guilty of an indictable offence than a woman over 21?

a As likely   *b* Twice as likely   *c* More than four times as likely

10 True or false?

More women than men are found guilty of shoplifting.

Now check your answers with the key on page 198.

▶Text 1 · Hoisting

Read through the passage and answer these questions.

1 What is hoisting?
2 How did the writer acquire his information about hoisting?
3 What did he learn about techniques of hoisting?

'I just couldn't do it. I don't know what it is. It's not embarrassment. No, that's not it. You see, you're putting your head in a noose; that's what it seems to
5 me.' Derek, an armed robber with a long record of bank jobs, was talking about hoisting (shop-lifting). 'No, I just couldn't do it. I mean just going in there.' He paused to try to find a more
10 exact way of fixing his antipathy. 'I tell you what. It's too blatant for my liking.'

It seemed a funny way to put it. Pushing a couple of ties in your pocket at a shop was hardly the last word in
15 extroversion, and even a bit on the discreet side when compared to all that firing of shotguns and vaulting over counters which made up the typical bank raid.
20 But my ideas of shop-lifting were still bound up with teenage memories of nicking packets of chewing gum from the local newsagents. A lot of guilt and not much loot. After a few conversa-
25 tions with professional hoisters, I re-alised that 'blatant' was just about right.

Nobody took a couple of ties: they took the whole rack. The first member of the gang would walk in nice and
30 purposefully. Their job was to set up the goods: perhaps put an elastic band round the ends of a few dozen silk scarves; move the valuable pieces of jewellery nearer the edge of the count-
35 er; slide the ties on the rack into a compact bunch. Then, while somebody else diverts the assistant or provides some sort of masking, the third member lifts the lot.
40 If the walk to the door is a little long, then there may be someone else to take over for the last stretch. No one is in possession for more than a few sec-onds, and there's always a couple of
45 spare bodies to obstruct anyone who seems to be getting too near the carrier. Store detectives who move forward with well-founded suspicions may still find themselves clutching empty air.
50 Store detectives watch for three main give-aways: any sort of loitering which looks different from the usual hanging around and dithering that characterises the real customer; any covert contact
55 between individuals who've shown no other sign of knowing each other; any over-friendliness towards sales staff which might be acting as a distraction. 'There's one other little angle,' said one
60 detective. 'I often pop round the back stairs; that's where you'll occasionally find one of them; trying to relax and get themselves in the right mood before starting the next job.'

from an article by Laurie Taylor in New Society

Now complete these statements by choosing the answer which you think fits best.

1 The bank robber wouldn't consider shop-lifting because

    a it was beneath his dignity.
    b the penalties were too high.
    c it wasn't challenging enough.
    d the risks were too great.

2 The writer's experience led him to think that most shop-lifters

    a were in their teens.
    b stole modest amounts.
    c used violent methods.
    d stole for excitement.

3 The role of the first member of the gang is to

    a convince the staff he's a serious shopper.
    b remove the goods from the shelves.
    c establish the easiest goods to steal.
    d smooth the path for his accomplice.

4 Professional shop-lifters avoid being caught in the act by

    a passing goods from one to another.
    b hiding behind ordinary shoppers.
    c racing for the nearest exit.
    d concealing goods in ordinary bags.

5 Potential shop-lifters may be identified when they

    a seem unable to decide what to buy.
    b openly signal to apparent strangers.
    c are unusually chatty to assistants.
    d set off towards emergency exits.

▶ Focus on grammar 1 · Gerunds

Look at the following examples from Text 1:

> *Pushing* a couple of ties in your pocket at a shop was hardly the last word in extroversion.

The *-ing* form looks like a present participle but is used like a noun. It is, in fact, a verbal noun, or gerund. Compare the following example of a present participle:

> When I saw him he was pushing ties in his pocket.

As a verbal noun, a gerund can take a possessive as the following example from Text 1 shows:

> It's too blatant for *my liking*.

Exercise 1 Which of the following *-ing* forms are gerunds and which are present participles?

a We were just discussing the matter when you arrived.

b Finding suitable premises was more difficult than we anticipated.

c I'm afraid I must object to your smoking in here.

d Crossing the park this morning, I saw a rabbit.

e The job involved his travelling considerable distances.

f The man reading the newspaper didn't see us waving.

Verbs used with gerunds

1 Gerunds are always used after certain verbs. The most common of these verbs are:

admit	finish	put off
anticipate	involve (= entail)	recall (= remember)
appreciate	keep on (= persist in)	recommend
avoid	mention	report
cannot help	mind (= object to)	resent
consider	miss	resist
deny	postpone	risk
dislike	practise	stop (prevent)
enjoy	prevent	stop (cease)*
give up	propose	suggest

The verbs in blue can also be used with a 'that' clause.

eg He admitted taking the money.
   He admitted that he had taken the money.

*See also Special Uses in *Focus on grammar 3* in this unit.

2 Some verbs can be used with either a gerund or an infinitive without any change of meaning. Examples are: begin continue start

3 Some verbs can be used with either the gerund or infinitive but there is a difference of meaning. Examples are: *remember forget stop*. These are dealt with in *Focus on grammar 3* in this unit.

4 The gerund is also used after prepositions. This includes *to* when it is used as a preposition rather than as part of the infinitive.
   eg We're looking forward to welcoming you as a student.

5 Certain phrases are always followed by the gerund. Examples are: it's no good it's no use it's not worth

Exercise 2 Complete the following sentences using one of the verbs from the list above.

a I know it's none of my business but I .... wondering where he gets all his money from.

b I don't .... your going at all but you'd better see if your father has any objections.

c If you can't .... smoking, at least you could cut down a bit!

d He categorically .... stealing the radio.

e Do you .... reading an item in the newspaper about teenage criminals recently?

f Now I'm living on my own, I really .... having someone to chat to.

g I've .... going to the dentist for as long as I could but now I've no choice.

h Apparently someone has .... hearing strange noises from a warehouse and the police have decided to search the building.

i The scheme will .... demolishing some of the Victorian buildings in the town centre.

j Have you .... borrowing money from the bank as a way of financing your holiday?

k The shoes seemed such a bargain that I couldn't .... buying them.

l If you insist on taking your case to court you .... losing everything.

m He seems to .... my being here for some reason. It's making me feel most uncomfortable.

n Wasn't there anything you could do to .... him going?

o We .... running into heavy traffic around London so we left plenty of time for the journey.

Further points to remember

1 *need + Gerund* — this construction has a passive meaning:

    eg My car badly needs servicing. (+ badly needs to be serviced)

2 *The Perfect Gerund* can be used to express past actions:

    eg I admitted to having made a mistake.

Exercise 3   Complete the following sentences using verbs in the *gerund* form and any other necessary words.

a Don't ever attempt to mend a fuse before .... the electricity at the mains.

b I have no intention .... any unnecessary risks.

c It's no use .... to dissuade me. My mind is made up!

d I blame myself for .... the fire brigade sooner.

e At the police station he was charged .... money under false pretences.

f He clearly wasn't used .... orders from a woman.

g His parents thoroughly disapprove .... his studies in order to take a job abroad.

h He congratulated me .... to represent the university in the national championship.

i I'm very disappointed .... the opportunity to see you when you were in town.

j We all tried to discourage her .... for the job as a waitress.

k It's not worth .... any special preparations for their visit until you know for sure they're coming.

l She lost her temper and accused him .... in her affairs.

m Well, thank you for calling. I'll look forward .... from you again in the near future.

n The college specialises .... overseas students feel at home.

o I think we would all benefit .... to a healthier diet.

"And how long have you been convinced you're a telephone box?"

▶ Text 2 · Computer hacking – high-tech crime

Read the following article to find out:

1 What computer hacking is.

2 Why the hackers do what they do.

3 How seriously companies are taking the problem.

You can rob a bank without leaving the house these days. Who needs stocking masks, guns and getaway cars? If you're a computer whizz-kid, you could grab your first million armed with nothing more dangerous than a personal computer (PC), a telephone and a modem to connect them.

All you have to do is dial into the networks that link the computers in large organisations together, type in a couple of passwords and you can rummage about in the information that's stored there to your heart's content.

Fortunately it isn't always quite as easy as it sounds. But, as more and more information is processed and stored on computer, whether it's details of your bank account or the number of tins of baked beans in the stockroom at the supermarket, computer crime seems set to grow.

A couple of months ago a newspaper reported that five British banks were being held to ransom by a gang of hackers who had managed to break into their computer. The hackers were demanding money in return for revealing exactly how they did it. In cases like this, banks may consider paying just so they can protect themselves better in the future.

No one knows exactly how much money is stolen by keyboard criminals – banks and other companies tend to be very secretive if it happens to them. It doesn't exactly fill customers with confidence if they think their bank account can be accessed by anyone with a PC! Some experts believe that only around a tenth of all computer crimes are actually reported. Insurance company Hogg Robinson estimate that computer frauds cost British companies an incredible £400 million a year.

Most computer crimes are 'inside jobs', where staff with access to the company's computers fiddle with the records. A comparatively small amount are committed by the more glamorous – and headline-grabbing – hackers.

The true hacker, it seems, doesn't do it for financial gain. The thrill appears to be, not in getting rich, but in beating the system. Two of Britain's most notorious hackers are Nicholas 'Mad Hacker' Whiteley and Edward Singh. The renegade pair have been the scourge of organisations with insecure computers for years, seemingly competing for the title of Britain's best hacker.

Whiteley's hacking days came to an abrupt halt in June, when the 21-year-old was sent to prison for four months for damaging computer discs. Edward Singh first came to public attention after claiming that he had hacked into American and British government and military computers.

'It has never been my intention to steal anything,' said Singh. 'I really see myself as a highly skilled software engineer.' His mission seems to be to prove just how insecure their systems are.

As with everything else, hackers start young in the States. A 12-year-old boy in Detroit was accused of entering a company's credit rating computer and distributing the numbers he found there. His mother told reporters that he spent up to 14 hours on his computer during the weekend. 'He didn't bother me,' she said. 'I figured, computers, that's the thing of the day.'

Last month, two New York teenagers, one aged 14 and one aged 17, were charged with breaking into a computer system owned by a company that publishes computer magazines. They are alleged to have changed polite recorded greetings to rude messages, added bomb threats and wiped advertisers' orders. Customers linked into the system only to be told that 'Daffy Duck is not available'! The company estimates that the tampering has cost $2.4 million.

Prevention is probably easier than detection, and many companies now spend lots of time and money devising programmes using passwords and codes. Of course, all this is no use at all if computer users tell each other their password, stick it on their screen so they don't forget it or use passwords like 'password'. It all happens.

There are plenty of software companies who specialise in writing software that make computers hacker-proof. One company in the States set out to prove that its system can defeat hackers by asking over 2,000 of them to try to hack in. The hackers were given two weeks to discover the secret message stored on two PCs in offices in New York and San Francisco. The message reads: 'The persistent hunter who wins his prize sooner or later becomes the hunted.' You'll be relieved – or perhaps disappointed – to learn that not one hacker managed it.

Find words or phrases in the text which mean the same as:

Paras 1 – 6
a expert (especially at a young age) ....
b search through ....
c as much as you want ....
d be called up on a computer screen ....
e make small changes to/interfere with ....

Paras 7 – 11
f rebellious/lawless ....
g caused a lot of trouble to ....
h aim in life ....
i removed completely ....
j interfering with (without permission) ....

Now complete these statements by choosing the answer which you think fits best.

1 Banks may pay computer criminals
   a to give back information they have stolen.
   b to explain what their technique is.
   c not to commit the same crime again.
   d not to pass on information they have stolen.

2 Companies don't always report computer crime because they
   a think it would create bad publicity.
   b don't expect the criminals to be caught.
   c don't want the police to investigate.
   d think the criminals are members of their staff.

3 The computer hackers' motive seems to be
   a to win a competition.
   b to make a lot of money.
   c to overcome a challenge.
   d to appear in the newspapers.

4 The mother of the 12-year-old hacker in Detroit
   a had been worried about the time her son spent at his computer.
   b thought her son's interest in his computer was normal.
   c had been involved in her son's criminal activity.
   d had tried to prevent her son's criminal activity.

5 What was the result of one software company's attempt to prove that its security systems were effective?
   a It was a complete success.
   b It was a partial success.
   c It was a failure.
   d The results were inconclusive.

STUDY BOX 1
Accuse of/Charge with

accuse (*somebody*) **of** (*doing*) something means you say that someone has done something wrong or bad.
   eg *A 12-year-old boy in Detroit was* **accused of** *entering a company's credit rating computer . . .* (Text 2)
charge (*somebody*) **with** (*doing*) something means to accuse someone formally of having done something illegal.
   eg *. . . two New York teenagers . . . were* **charged with** *breaking into a computer system . . .* (Text 2)
   He was taken to the police station and **charged with** *murder.*

▶ Focus on grammar 2 · The infinitive

1 The full infinitive

The full infinitive is used:

a to express purpose:

    eg The hackers were given two weeks *to discover* the secret message ... (Text 2)
       It has never been my intention *to steal* anything ... (Text 2)

b after certain verbs (eg hope, expect, want, manage, tend etc):

    eg Banks and other companies tend *to be* very secretive ... (Text 2)

c after the objects of certain verbs (eg want, ask, tell, advise etc):

    eg I advise you *to pay* the greatest attention to what I'm going to say.

d after certain auxiliary and defective verbs (eg be, have, ought, used, need etc):

    eg Do you really need *to be met* at the station?

e after adjectives:

    eg You'll be relieved – or perhaps disappointed - *to learn* ... (Text 2)

f as grammatical subject:

    eg *To travel* hopefully is better than *to arrive*

g after too/enough:

    eg This plate is far too hot *to touch*
       He wasn't experienced enough *to handle* the job.

2 The plain infinitive

The plain infinitive is used:

a after certain modal auxiliaries and modal 'dare' and 'need':

    eg How dare you *speak* to me like that?
       ... their bank account can *be accessed* by anyone with a PC! (Text 2)

b after the objects of certain verbs (eg make, let):

    eg He let me *persuade* him to join us.

c after the following expressions: would rather/sooner ... (than); had better; Why not ...

    eg You'd better *be telling* the truth!
       I'd rather *leave* now, if that's all right.
       Why not *take* a few day's holiday?

Exercise 1

Complete the following article by putting the verbs in brackets into the correct form: gerund, plain infinitive or full infinitive (active or passive).

Offenders sent to island in the sun

Thirteen young offenders from London are being sent (spend) a year on a Caribbean island in an experiment aimed at (combat) crime and broken families.

The young people – aged 15–17 – are (train) in Denmark for six years before (go) to the West Indian island of St Vincent (live) in a small communal farm at the foot of a volcano.

The school is run by a Danish co-operative which specialises in (provide) challenges for difficult young people (build) up their confidence with adults.

The two London boroughs whose social services departments are responsible for (introduce) the scheme say they are sending the young people so they can (learn) (face) up to challenges which they have no opportunity of (meet) on the streets of the capital.

All the young people have been in the care of the authority for some time and need (receive) their parents' permission before (allow) to leave. They are (accompany) and (supervise) by social workers.

Other London boroughs are showing an interest in (adopt) the scheme, particularly as it works out cheaper than (keep) young offenders in homes in London.

from an article in the Guardian by David Hencke

Exercise 2   Finish each of the following sentences so that it means the same as the sentence above it. In each case, use a gerund, plain infinitive or full infinitive.

1 It's high time we were leaving!

We'd better ....

2 I never expected such congestion on the roads.

I never expected the roads ....

3 She concealed her nervousness from us.

She didn't let us ....

4 I'm on duty from 6 pm till midnight.

My job involves ....

5 You've got a nerve, implying that it was all my fault.

How dare you ....

6 Is it really necessary for me to type the application?

Does the application ....

7 It was good of you to vote for me. I really appreciated it.

I really appreciated ....

8 You seem to do nothing but complain. I've had enough of it.

I'm fed up ....

STUDY BOX 2
Phrasal Verbs 3

Look at these examples from this unit:
1   … *a gang of hackers who had managed to* **break into** *their computer.* (Text 2)
break into means 'enter by force'.
2   *Anyone trying to get in* **sets off** *a 97 decibel siren.* (Listening)
set off means 'make something start working'.
NB **set off** can also mean 'start a journey' eg *We* **set off** *for London at dawn.*
3   *If you attempt to . . .* **cut off** *the power supply . . .* (Listening)
cut off means 'disconnect'

▶ Focus on writing 1 · Narrative/descriptive essay

Describe a day in the life of a policeman or a prisoner. (*About 350 words.*)

Look at the notes below first.

Notes   **1** Although the topic may *seem* relatively straightforward, it will need the same degree of planning as all essay writing at this level. Without careful planning, it could easily become a rambling and inconsequential account.

2 The first choice is whether to write in the first or third person. The first is likely to lead to the most vivid account but there *are* other options. You could, for example write from the viewpoint of a reporter who has arranged to spend a day with the person in question. Consider the advantages and disadvantages of the two possibilities before deciding.

3 'Describe' is a keyword. More important than the actual events of the day are your *reactions* to them. They should come to life for the reader and this will depend on your ability to describe them effectively and from your chosen viewpoint. Humour and/or irony may well prove useful.

4 The introduction and conclusion should provide a perspective on the day's activities.

▶ Communication activity · Alibi

Situation

Flash and Grab

Thieves broke into Brown's Camera Centre in Baldwin Street last night and stole photographic equipment worth £1,500. Police say the thieves appeared to know exactly what they were looking for. They took only the two most expensive cameras and some accessories and left the rest of the shop virtually undisturbed.

Procedure
Groups of four to eight are needed for this activity. In each group there should be two suspects and two or more police inspectors, divided into two sets. Role B – the suspects – is on page 198.

When suspects and police inspectors have read their instructions and prepared for the role play, each set of police inspectors should interview one of the suspects for about 10 minutes. When this time is over, the other suspects should be interviewed.

Role A
Police
inspectors
You know that the thieves who broke into the shop were able to get in easily through a window with a faulty catch. The shop owner strongly suspects a former employee of his who left because of a disagreement over pay. This employee would have known about the faulty catch and would also have known enough about the stock to be able to pick out the most valuable items. He also had a possible motive.

You have contacted the employee who says he/she spent the whole evening with a friend who lives in the same house. You have also spoken to the two suspects' neighbours. A woman who lives on the ground floor says she was woken at about 12.30 am when her dog started barking. When she looked out, she saw the two coming in and she thinks one of them was carrying a large bag.

You have decided to interview each of the suspects in turn about their activities between 8.00 pm and 12.30 am that night. You want to see how far their stories correspond. Plan the kind of questions you should ask in order to test the truth of their stories. Save the question about the 'large bag' until last.

Finally, you will have to decide whether to charge the suspects with the theft.

LANGUAGE CHECK
Dependent Prepositions 4: Verb + Preposition

Here is a list of 16 verbs, some of which have been used in the texts in this unit. Write in the preposition which follows them.

Check your answers with your teacher or in the dictionary so that you have an accurate reference list for the future.

benefit . . .	**differ** . . .
charge somebody . . . (*a crime*)	**disapprove** . . .
cheat *somebody* . . . *something*	**plead guilty** . . .
compliment *somebody* . . .	**prevent** *somebody/something* . . .
concentrate . . .	**rob** *somebody* . . .
confess . . .	**specialise** . . .
convince *somebody* . . . *something*	**suspect** *somebody* . . .
deprive *somebody* . . .	**threaten** *somebody* . . .

▶ Focus on listening

You are going to hear part of a radio programme on security devices. As you listen, you should complete the table below by filling in the number of the picture which illustrates each device discussed, the type of power used, the volume in decibels and the price. If a piece of information is not heard, put an ✕ in the appropriate space.

Note not all the pictures are described.

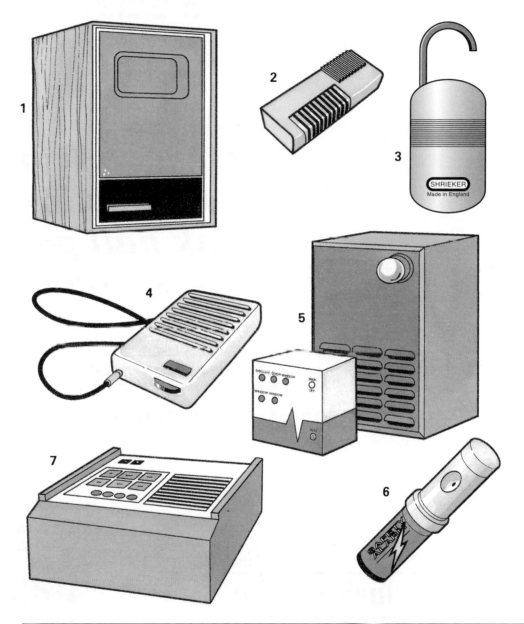

DEVICE	NUMBER	POWER: M – Mains B – Battery	VOLUME in decibels	PRICE
ultra-sonic burglar alarm			85	
do-it-yourself burglar alarm				£138
infra-red burglar alarm	1			
portable door alarm				
personal attack/door alarm				
personal attack alarm		B		

▶ Focus on register

1 Look at the following headlines. Discuss with your neighbour what crimes they might describe.

A
Yard check on 'sale' of A-level papers

B
Gem vanishes from auction in pink nail polish switch

C
Chips were downfall of computer conman

D
Luggage tags invitation to burglars

E
Sneeze traps a bungling burglar

2 Now look at the extracts from the reports which followed the headlines. Can you match the headlines to the reports?

1 late at night in a rowing boat, intending to break into an Islington record warehouse and steal a haul of LPs but climbed into the wrong building. . . . . .

2   He was caught because he became homesick for Yorkshire and wanted to "taste some real fish and chips." . . . . .

3   Crooks mingle with trippers at Heathrow and Gatwick and note where they live. They watch travellers fly out then . . . . .

4   It appeared that despite tight security, the 9.58 carat diamond was stolen during a series of pre-sale examinations in a specially-lighted . . . . .

5   About 5,500 pupils who sat A-level French yesterday in London and at schools in the South-east may be asked to re- . . . . .

Read the reports below and on the next page:

1

Vincent Pattison's attempted burglary went badly wrong. He paddled across Regent's Canal late at night in a rowing boat, intending to break into an Islington record warehouse and steal a haul of LPs but climbed into the wrong building, Clerkenwell Court was told yesterday.

A police car crew were alerted by the noise as he tried to sledgehammer his way through a wall to the record firm. The boat sank as he jumped aboard and he had to swim to the opposite bank, the court was told.

Finally, Pattison, 23, of Tolmers Square, Euston, hid in a nearby block of flat but was arrested within minutes when he sneezed. Pattison, who admitted taking and rowing a boat and attempted burglary, was given a two-year unconditional discharge.

2

A YOUTH of 17 who found a flaw in the Barclays Bank computer system travelled the country living in style on the proceeds of crime, said Mr SIMON EVANS, prosecuting at the Old Bailey yesterday.

He was caught because he became homesick for Yorkshire and wanted to "taste some real fish and chips."

CHRISTOPHER HEARD, an unemployed van boy, drove to Thirsk in a Pontiac Firebird which he had bought with £2,500 of his "ill-gotten gains," said Mr Evans.

As he lounged against the car, munching cod and chips, he was arrested by a policeman who suspected he had taken the car unlawfully.

Inquiries revealed that Heard, a computer games fanatic, was wanted by police throughout the country for cheque frauds.

3

HOLIDAYMAKERS passing through airports issue open invitations to burglars by putting their name and address on luggage, say police.

Crooks mingle with trippers at Heathrow and Gatwick and note where they live. They watch travellers fly out and then drive round to these addresses with a van and clean them out.

Police believe the luggage tag ruse could be a major reason behind the soaring increase in summer burglaries

4

A "POTENTIALLY FLAWLESS" $600,000 (£390,000) pink diamond was stolen from Sotheby Parke Bernet's New York galleries shortly before auction and replaced by one worth about 5,000 (£3,200) and coated with pink nail polish, it was learned yesterday.

The "big switch" was being investigated by police and FBI agents.

It appeared that despite tight security, the 9·58-carat diamond was stolen during a series of pre-sale examinations in a specially-lighted viewing booth.

Carefully screened clients were allowed to examine the diamond and other jewels in a 300-piece jewellery collection that was up for auction. The room was filled with Sotheby's employees and armed guards and monitored by videotape cameras.

Potential bidder

The theft was discovered after a potential bidder had asked to examine a diamond ring that was being exhibited in the case holding the diamond. As a Sotheby's employee reached for the ring she noticed a flaw in the diamond and that its pink colour appeared to be painted on.

5

Scotland Yard was last night investigating the removal of A-level examination papers from the University of London Exam Centre, and allegations that stolen papers were being sold for £100 each.

About 3,500 pupils who sat A-level French yesterday in London and at schools in the South-east may be asked to re-sit the examination with a new paper, and a history A-level test scheduled for next Thursday may be cancelled, depending on the outcome of police investigations.

Police were called in by *The Standard*, the London evening newspaper, after it had been handed the papers by a man who said he worked in the university.

The newspaper said its informant, whose name has not been given to the police or university authorities, did not ask for any payment for the documents. He was "seething with indignation" about the lax security which made it so easy for him to remove them.

1 In this report the criminal was arrested for a crime which he had not committed.

    1   2   4   5

2 These reports concern poor security.

    1 and 5   2 and 4   3 and 4   3 and 5

3 In this report a theft was committed without criminal intentions.

    1   2   4   5

4 This criminal's hobby may have helped him to exploit a weakness in a system.

    1   2   4   5

5 The person who detected this crime was particularly sharp-sighted.

    1   2   4   5

▶ Focus on grammar 3 · Gerund or infinitive

Some verbs can take either the gerund or infinitive. Cover the right hand part of the page and look at the examples on the left. See if you can explain the difference in meaning between the examples *a* with the gerund, and *b* with the infinitive. Check your explanations against those on the right of the page.

1 Remember and **forget**

a Do you remember seeing this man before?
I'll never forget arriving in Venice by ship the first time.

These verbs take a gerund when they refer to an action which occurred *beforehand*.

b Remember to put out all the lights before you leave.
I'm afraid you forgot to sign the cheque.

They take an infinitive when they refer to an action which comes *afterwards*.

2 Regret and **dread**

a Do you regret not having gone to university?
I'm dreading going to the dentist's.

These verbs take the gerund when they refer to the past or likely future.

b I dread to think what might have happened if you'd tried to drive the car.
I regret to tell you that your application has not been successful.

In addition, *dread* takes the infinitive 'to think' and *regret* the infinitives 'to say', 'to tell' and 'to inform'.

3 Like, love, hate and **prefer**

a I simply love getting unexpected invitations.
I don't like cooking all that much.
Do you prefer typing your letters to writing them by hand?

These verbs may take either a gerund or an infinitive when they mean 'to enjoy' or 'take pleasure in'. (Negative sentences, however, usually take a gerund.)

b Would you like to have a look round?
I don't like to bother you when you're busy, but . . .
He likes to arrive in plenty of time for his appointments.

When they mean 'want' or 'wish', they take the infinitive.
When *prefer* is used in a comparison, the gerund is always used.

4 Try

(You've locked yourself out . . .)
a Try ringing the doorbell. Someone may be in.

b Try to climb in through the window.

When this verb takes the gerund, the meaning is '*experiment*'. (You will have no difficulty in ringing the bell but the action may or may not be successful in enabling you to enter.)
When the infinitive is used, the meaning is '*attempt*'. (You may or may not be successful in climbing through the window.)

5 Mean

a Are you sure the job won't mean moving to another area?

With the gerund, the verb means 'involve'.

b He means to get at the truth, however long it takes.

With the infinitive, the verb means 'intend'.

6 Need and **want**

a The hedge needs trimming
The piano wants tuning

With the gerund, these verbs mean 'be in need of'.

b We'll need to borrow a substantial sum of money to repair the roof.
You want to ask John. He's the financial expert.
Do you want to discuss the matter?

With the infinitive, *need* means 'have a need' while *want* can mean 'should/ought to' (informally) or 'wish'.

7 Go on

a They went on talking about the contract all evening.

With a gerund, this verb means 'continue an action'.

b After describing the arrangements for our accommodation, he went on to give us some useful tips for living abroad.

With an infinitive, the verb means 'introduce a new action'.

8 Stop

a If you would stop crying for a moment, I might find out what's wrong.

With a gerund, the verb means 'cease'.

b He stopped to look at the map and then walked on.

With an infinitive, it means to interrupt one action in order to perform another.

Exercise Complete the following dialogue by putting the verbs in brackets into the correct form, gerund or infinitive, as required.

A You complain about feeling lonely but you've only yourself to blame, you know. You don't even try (make) new friends. Why don't you join a club of some sort and stop (feel) so sorry for yourself?

B Look, John, I know you mean (be) kind but I'd prefer (do) things my own way. I've tried (join) clubs in the past but I absolutely hate (have) to meet a lot of new people and I used to dread (go) to meetings so much that I stopped (attend) altogether after a few weeks, I regret (say).

A But if you don't go on (attend), how can you expect to make friends? You need (persevere) more. Friendship doesn't just happen. It means (spend) time with people and (share) experiences with them. If you only stopped (think) about it for a moment, you'd see I was right.

B But I've so little time for a social life. There's always work that needs (do) in the house and then there's the novel I'm writing. I dread (think) what will happen if that's not finished by the deadline. And that's not all …

A OK, OK, before you go on (give) me any more reasons why you can't go out, let me make a final suggestion. Do you remember (meet) an American friend of mine at my house recently? Well, he's trying (make) up a party to go to the theatre to see 'Private Lives' next week. He told me not to forget (invite) you. I know you prefer (go) to concerts to (see) plays, on the whole, but this production has had rave notices and I'm sure you'd enjoy it. What do you say?

B Yes, I'd love (come). If you could give me your friend's number. I'll remember (ring) him and thank him.

▶ Focus on writing 2 · Discussion

'The concept of prison as society's punishment of the offender is both barbaric and ineffective.'

Give your views on the purpose of prison and say whether certain crimes could be better dealt with in other ways, in your opinion. *(About 350 words.)*

▶ Vocabulary practice

Review Choose the word or phrase which best completes each sentence.

1 I've tried .... with the controls but I still can't get a picture on the screen.

A fidgeting **B** adjusting **C** fiddling **D** tampering

2 The tent was very complicated to erect but simple enough to ....

A dismantle **B** dismount **C** disconnect **D** detach

3 I had a good chance of getting the job but I'm afraid I .... the interview by saying all the wrong things.

A fumbled **B** gambled **C** bungled **D** stumbled

4 The crime was .... in the middle of a busy street, in full view of people returning home from work.

A achieved **B** committed **C** performed **D** practised

5 As a trusted employee, she had .... to highly confidential information.

A admission **B** entrance **C** contact **D** access

6 A good friend is one who will .... you when you're in trouble.

A stand for **B** stand up to **C** stand by **D** stand over

7 I'm hopeless at making decisions. I even .... for ages over which toothpaste to buy.

A totter   **B** dodder   **C** dither   **D** falter

8 The electronic anti-theft device was far from easy to .... in my car.

A implant   **B** install   **C** insert   **D** immerse

9 You may think him rather on the quiet .... when you first meet him, but he can be extremely witty.

A hand   **B** side   **C** level   **D** part

10 As he was caught in .... of an offensive weapon, he was immediately a suspect.

A possession   **B** ownership   **C** handling   **D** control

11 His football career .... to an abrupt halt after he was injured.

A went   **B** came   **C** brought   **D** dropped

12 The meat was beautifully cooked, I agree, but the vegetables were a bit too salty for my ....

A appetite   **B** desire   **C** liking   **D** favour

13 The safe deposit box .... a high-pitched sound when it was moved.

A ejected   **B** expelled   **C** emitted   **D** exuded

14 The gang is .... to have caused thousands of pounds worth of damage to computer equipment.

A alleged   **B** claimed   **C** announced   **D** blamed

15 Traffic is being .... from the High Street while the water main is under repair.

A averted   **B** perverted   **C** diverted   **D** subverted

16 Thieves got away with a .... of jewellery worth hundreds of pounds.

A catch   **B** haul   **C** snatch   **D** loot

17 If he hadn't shown such a .... disregard for company regulations by smoking while on duty, he wouldn't have been dismissed.

A callous   **B** blatant   **C** dire   **D** abject

18 When I pointed out that there was a small .... in one of the glasses, the shop gave me a 10% reduction on the set.

A blot   **B** smear   **C** smudge   **D** flaw

19 While you pedal away on the exercise bicycle, a machine will be .... your breathing and heart rate.

A reviewing   **B** screening   **C** surveying   **D** monitoring

20 He was .... of forgery and sentenced to two years in prison.

A charged   **B** convicted   **C** accused   **D** confirmed

21 All the .... from the jumble sale will be given to charity.

A expenses   B Income   C proceeds   D rewards

22 I hate .... formal examinations. I find it so difficult to organise my thoughts in a limited time.

A passing   B making   C writing   D sitting

23 The inspector reported that office staff were rather .... in their attention to security.

A lenient   B lax   C loose   D limp

24 I'd say let's meet on Saturday but I'm none .... sure what's happening at the weekend.

A so   B very   C that   D too

25 When I left the office I was .... with indignation at the treatment I had received.

A seething   B overflowing   C stewing   D spinning

Phrasal verbs: GET

Match the following phrasal verbs with their meanings:

1	get at	*a*	recover from
2	get away with	*b*	avoid
3	get by	*c*	suggest/imply
4	get down	*d*	find time for
5	get on	*e*	make contact with
6	get out of	*f*	persuade
7	get over	*g*	depress
8	get round	*h*	escape punishment
9	get round to	*i*	be on friendly terms
10	get through	*j*	manage/survive

Check your answers by looking at page 198.

Now choose the appropriate phrasal verb to complete the following sentences:

1 I've been so busy that I just haven't .... answering you letter, I'm afraid.

2 Frankly, I don't know how he .... on the small amount he earns.

3 He nearly always managed to .... doing the heavy work by pretending he had a bad back.

4 Considering how little they've got in common, it's surprising how well they .... together.

5 How's your mother? Has she .... her operation yet?

6 Did you 'phone your solicitor?   No I couldn't ...., the line was engaged.

7 The job itself is well paid and interesting, but commuting to the City every day really .... me ....

8 It's no use trying to .... him with charm. Once he's made up his mind he never changes it.

9 I can't see quite what you're .... Could you be a bit more specific?

10 So, he's finally been arrested for tax fraud. I'm surprised he managed to .... it for so long.

▶ Grammar practice

1 Fill each of the numbered blanks in the passage with one suitable word.

When is a thief not a thief?

The impression that more women shoplift than men may be .... (1)
to publicity. As a recent report on shoplifting .... (2) out: 'Every
week, newspapers ......:.................... (3) the conviction of some middle-aged
woman of blameless .... (4) who has stolen, for quite unexplained
motives, some objects of .... (5) value which she could easily have
.... (6) to buy. Most psychiatrists have at some
.... (7) seen patients who were .... (8) of this
sort of theft.

   This .... (9) the question of .... (10) the
middle class have a better chance of getting .... (11) shop-lifting
charges than the working class. The shops insist that they are ....
(12) solely with whether customers have .... (13) for the goods:
their accent, class or ability to browbeat, is .... (14). But,
.... (15) charged, the middle class are undoubtedly in a better
.... (16). They are more likely to have, or call in, a solicitor; and
they are financially .... (17) to risk paying legal costs. The solicitor –
or friends or relations – may .... (18) a psychological assessment.
And a 'respectable' first-time .... (19), backed by a psychological
explanation of a momentary aberration, and defended by a solicitor, surely goes into the
dock with more chance of acquittal than someone .... (20) these
attributes.

from an article by Joy Melville in New Society

2 Fill each of the blanks with a suitable word or phrase:

a I'm a bit short of money. I'd .... bank on my way home.

b What's the matter? You look as .... ghost!

c Only if you enclose a stamped addressed envelope, ... you our
catalogue.

d I hope you don't mind .... on you unexpectedly like this. I just
happened to be passing.

e That seems rather a harsh punishment for so .... offence.

f He really .... in with that disguise. I didn't recognise him at all!

g She must .... her way. Otherwise she would be here by now.

h If you .... the piano all on your own you wouldn't have strained your
back.

i Strange as .... she's never been away from her native village.

j He's not used .... orders from people. He's always been his own
boss.

UNIT 7 Learning and Teaching

▶ Lead-in

1 How much does picture 1 remind you of your own schooldays? What are the similarities? And the differences?

2 Did you ever work in groups, as in picture 2? What sort of work can be done in this way? What are the advantages? And the disadvantages? How is the role of the teacher different from that in picture 1?

3 What's happening in picture 3? What might have led up to this situation? Did you ever have the same experience at school? How did you feel? What alternatives are there?

What makes a good teacher?

Look at the following ideas and say which ones are important, in your opinion.

A good teacher:
- knows his/her subject very well
- gives interesting lessons
- makes sure the classroom is tidy and attractive
- always prepares his/her lessons.

Now *work with a partner* to add at least *four* more characteristics of a good teacher.

▶ Text 1 · The teenage teachers

Read the following passage and answer these questions:

1 Who are the teachers?

2 Who are the pupils?

3 What is the reason behind the scheme?

4 How successful is it?

The best way to learn is to teach. This is the message emerging from experiments in several schools in which teenage pupils who have problems at school themselves
5 are tutoring younger children – with remarkable results for both sides.

According to American research, pupil-tutoring wins 'hands down' over computerised instruction and American
10 teachers say that no other recent innovation has proved so consistently successful.

Now the idea is spreading in Britain. Throughout this term, a group of 14-year-olds at Trinity comprehensive in
15 Leamington Spa have been spending an hour a week helping children at a nearby primary school with their reading. The younger children read aloud to their tutors (who are supervised by university
20 students of education) and then play word games with them.

All the 14-year-olds have some of their own lessons in a special unit for children who have difficulties at school. Though
25 their intelligence is around average, most of them have fallen behind on reading, writing and maths and, in some cases, this has led to truancy or bad behaviour in class.

30 Jean Bond, who is running the special unit while on sabbatical from Warwick University's education department, says that the main benefit of tutoring is that it improves the adolescents' self-esteem.
35 'The younger children come rushing up every time and welcome them. It makes the tutors feel important whereas, in normal school lessons, they often feel inadequate. Everyone benefits. The older
40 children need practice in reading but, if they had to do it in their own classes, they would say it was kids' stuff and be worried about losing face. The younger children get individual attention from very

45 patient people. The tutors are struggling at school themselves so, when the younger ones can't learn, they know exactly why.'

The tutors agree. 'When I was little, I 50 used to skive and say I couldn't do things when I really could,' says Mark Greger. 'The boy I've been teaching does the same. He says he can't read a page of his book so I tell him that, if he does do it, 55 we can play a game. That works.'

The younger children speak warmly of their new teachers. 'He doesn't shout like other teachers,' says eight-year-old Jenny of her tutor, Cliff McFarlane who, among 60 his own teachers, has a reputation for being a handful. Yet Cliff sees himself as a tough teacher. 'If they get a word wrong,' he says, 'I keep them at it until they get it right.'

65 Jean Bond, who describes pupil tutoring as an 'educational conjuring trick', has run two previous experiments. In one, six persistent truants, aged 15 upwards, tutored 12 slow-learning infants in 70 reading and maths. None of the six played truant from any of the tutoring sessions. 'The degree of concentration they showed while working with their tutees was remarkable for pupils who had 75 previously shown little ability to concentrate on anything related to school work for any period of time,' says Bond. The tutors became 'reliable, conscientious caring individuals'.

80 Their own reading, previously mechanical and monotonous, became far more expressive as a result of reading stories aloud to infants. Their view of education, which they had previously dismissed as 85 'crap' and 'a waste of time', was transformed. They became firmly resolved to teach their own children to read before starting school because, as one of them put it, 'if they go for a job and they can't 90 write, they're not going to employ you, are they?' The tutors also became more sympathetic to their own teachers' difficulties, because they were frustrated themselves when the infants 'mucked 95 about'.

In the seven weeks of the experiment, concludes Bond, 'these pupils received more recognition, reward and feelings of worth than they had previously experi-100 enced in many years of formal schooling.' And the infants, according to their own teachers, showed measurable gains in reading skills by the end of the scheme.

from an article by Peter Wilby in the Sunday Times

Now complete these statements by choosing the answer which you think fits best.

1 The majority of the tutors in the Trinity experiment are pupils who
 a cause discipline problems for their teachers.
 b frequently stay away from school.
 c are below standard in basic skills.
 d are unable to read or write.

2 According to the writer, the tutors wouldn't normally practise reading in class because
 a they would find it humiliating.
 b they wouldn't be able to concentrate.
 c their teachers wouldn't consider it necessary.
 d their teachers would get impatient with them.

3 The main reason that the tutors make such successful teachers seems to be that
 a they enjoy being the centre of attention.
 b they can relate to their pupils' problems.
 c they are never strict with their pupils.
 d their pupils enjoy playing games with them.

4 Pupil tutoring is described as 'an educational conjuring trick' because
 a no one understands why it works so well.
 b it has caught the attention of the media.
 c educational authorities are suspicious of it.
 d it is a simple idea with extraordinary results.

5 The most significant result of the experiments so far carried out seems to have been that the tutors
 a learnt to overcome their fear of reading aloud.
 b improved their pupils' ability to concentrate.
 c benefited from an increase in their self-respect.
 d came to see the importance of the writing skill.

▶ Focus on grammar 1 ·
Defining and non-defining relative clauses

Look at the two sentences which follow. Both have the same words but the meanings are different. Can you say in what way?

The position of sales manager went to the man who was 40.

The position of sales manager went to the man, who was 40.

In the first sentence, there were several men who applied for the position and the successful applicant was the man aged 40. The information in the relative clause is therefore essential to the meaning of the sentence. This is an example of a *defining relative clause*

In the second sentence, there was only one man among those who applied for the position and he was successful. The fact that he was 40 is additional information and not essential to the meaning. This is an example of a *non-defining relative clause.*

Here are two more examples. Can you say what the difference in meaning is here?

The students who had missed the bus started the test late.

The students, who had missed the bus, started the test late.

In the first sentence, *some* of the students started the test late because they had missed the bus (unlike the others). In the second sentence, *all* the students started the test late. The fact that they had missed the bus is additional information.

Look at these examples of relative clauses from Text 1 and say whether they are *defining* or *non-defining*:

a ... teenage pupils *who have problems at school themselves* are tutoring younger children.

b The younger children read to their tutors (*who are supervised by university students of education*) ...

c All the 14-year-olds have some of their lessons in a special unit for children *who have fallen behind on reading, writing and maths* ...

d Jean Bond, *who is running the special unit while on sabbatical from Warwick University's education department,* says ...

e The boy *I've been teaching* does the same.

f ... says 8-year-old Jenny of her tutor, Cliff McFarlane, *who,* among his own teachers, *has the reputation of being a bit of a handful*

g Jean Bond, *who describes pupil tutoring as an 'educational conjuring trick',* has run two previous experiments.

h The degree of concentration they showed ... was remarkable for pupils *who had previously shown little ability to concentrate on anything related to schoolwork* ...

i Their view of education, *which they had previously dismissed as 'crap' and 'a waste of time',* was transformed.

The examples from the text illustrate some of the important points about the *form* of the two kinds of relative clause.

Defining relative clauses

1 *Commas* are not used to separate the relative clause from the rest of the sentence.

2 *that* can be used instead of *who* or *which*

eg The man that you wanted to see is on the 'phone.
It's a problem that has taxed many brains.

3 Where the relative pronoun is the object, it can be omitted, as in sentence *e*.

eg The car she wanted has been sold.

4 *who* and *which* are never used as object pronouns after *superlatives, time expressions* or *indefinite pronouns*. They are either omitted or replaced by *that*

> eg This is the most expensive present (that) I ever intended to buy.
> I met him on the day (that) I was due to leave.
> Choose a seat anywhere (that) you want.

5 The possessive pronoun for both people and things is *whose*

> eg He didn't seem like a man whose friends had all deserted him.
> We stayed in a hotel whose only recommendation was its cheapness.

Non-defining relative clauses

1 The non-defining relative clause must be separated from the rest of the sentence by *commas*, as in sentence *d* (or occasionally by brackets as in sentence *b*).

2 *that* cannot be used to replace *who which whom*

3 The relative pronoun cannot be omitted.

Exercise 1 Say which type of relative clause each of the following pairs of sentences contains and what the difference in meaning is:

a A I took my jacket to the dry cleaner's, which had a two hour service.

B I took my jacket to the dry cleaner's which had a two hour service.

b A Commuters who had heard about the derailment arranged alternative transport home.

B Commuters, who had heard about the derailment, arranged alternative transport home.

c A The cars, whose owners had double-parked, were towed away by the police.

B The cars whose owners had double-parked were towed away by the police.

Exercise 2 In the following sentences, omit the relative pronoun or replace it with *that* where possible:

a The book which you borrowed from me is long overdue at the library.

b We called at a pub which is said to be the oldest in England.

c They eventually decided to part with their old car, which had given them so many years of loyal service.

d You should make sure that the travel agency which you deal with is a member of ABTA.

e I asked to speak to the manager, who turned out to have left the company.

Exercise 3 Join the following sentences using relative pronouns. Remember to put commas where necessary.

a Toledo is a very fine city to visit.
It gets extremely hot in summer.

b You lent me a tent.
It was damaged in a storm.
You heard about the storm on the news.

c The woman lives next door.
She bought an Old English Sheepdog.
It barks all night.

d The price of petrol is going up again.
It rose only last month.

e We rented a cottage from a man.
He has written a novel.
The novel has become a bestseller.

f I asked you to type some letters for me.
The letters are full of careless errors.

g The zoo's most famous giant panda has died.
Its name was Chi Chi.

h I told you about a record.
The record will be released next week.
It has been produced by a completely new method.

▶Text 2 · An education for life?

Read through the passage and answer these questions:

1 What are the two traditional reasons for education?
2 What changes might occur in future?
3 What might make it difficult for us to adjust to any changes?
4 What evidence does the writer give to suggest that we will succeed in adjusting?

There is a problem that will touch us all – men, women and children – in the not too distant future, a problem that resolves itself into a question: what is education
5 for? At the moment most of us can answer that fairly practically and without too much soul-searching. On the lowest level education is for enabling us to cope in an adult world where money must be added
10 up, tax forms filled in, numbers looked up in telephone directories, maps read, curtains measured and street signs understood. On the next level it is for getting some kind of job that will pay a living
15 wage.

But we are already peering into a future so different from anything we would now recognise as familiar that the last of these two educational aims may become as
20 obsolete as a dodo. Basic skills (reading, writing and arithmetic) will continue to be necessary but these, after all, can be taught to children in from one to two years during their childhood. But educa-
25 tion with a view to working for a living, at least in the sense of earning daily bread, may well be on its way out right now for the majority of us. Then the question 'what is education for?' becomes much
30 more complex. Because what the future proclaims is: an education is an education is an education.

In other words, our grandchildren may well spend their lives learning as, today,
35 we spend our lives working. This does not simply involve a straightforward substitution of activity but a complete transformation of motive. We work for things basically unconnected with that work –
40 usually money, prestige, success, security. We will learn for learning's sake alone: a rose is a rose because it *is* and not what we can get out of it. Nor need any cynic doubt that we shall not wish to work
45 without there being any obvious end in view. Already, adult education classes are overcrowded – one friend of mine teaching French literature says she could have had 10 pupils for every one she has.
50 Nevertheless, we still live in a very competitive society and most of us will need to reshuffle the furniture of our minds in order to gear our children towards a future in which outer rewards –
55 keeping up with the Joneses – become

less relevant than inner and more individual spurs. The existence of competition has always meant doing things because they win us some essentially unconnected
60 advantage but the aim of the future must be to integrate the doing with its own reward, like virtue.

Oddly enough it is in America, that citadel of competitiveness, that the first
65 experiments in this change of mind are taking place. In that New World, there are already organisations set up to examine ways in which competitiveness can be replaced by other inner-directed forms of
70 rewards and pleasures. Take one interesting example in a Foundation whose aim is to transform competitive sport. A tug-of-war, as we all know, consists of one team pitting its strength against another
75 team. The aim is to tug the opposing team over a line and, by doing so, win.

In the brand-new non-competitive version, things are very different. There are still two teams on either end of a rope but
80 now the aim is not to win but to *maintain* the struggle. As the two teams tug, any individual on either team who senses a coming victory must let go the winning end of the rope and rush over to lend his
85 weight to the other side, thus redressing the balance, and keeping the tug-of-war going as long as possible. If you actually imagine doing this, the startling fact that emerges is that the new game offers *more*
90 possibilities of individual judgement and skill just because victory is not the aim and the tug-of-war is ended only by defeat of those judgements and skills. What's more, I think most people would
95 get more pleasure out of the neo-tug than the old winners-take-all concept.

So could it be for learning. Most of us, at some time or another, have glimpsed one of the real inner pleasures of educa-
100 tion – a sort of one-person chase after an elusive goal that pits You only against You or, at the very most, against the discoveries of the greatest minds of other generations. On a more humble level,
105 most of us have already got some pleasurable hobby that we enjoy for its own sake and become expert in for that enjoyment. In my own stumbling efforts, since last year, to learn the piano, I have seen the
110 future and it works.

from an article by Jill Tweedie in the Guardian

Look at paragraphs 1–5 and find words or phrases which mean the same as:

a can be converted (1) ....

b deep examination of the mind (1) ....

c manage (1) ....

d out-of-date (2) ....

e rearrange (4) ....

f our ideas (4) ....

g prepare . . . for (4) ....

h competing socially (4) ....

i motives (4) ....

j combine (4) ....

k setting . . . against (5) ....

Now complete these statements by choosing the answer which you think fits best.

1 In the future envisaged by the writer,
  a there would be no need to deal with money.
  b there would be no need to communicate in writing.
  c there would be few employment prospects.
  d there would be few educational prospects.

2 According to the writer, the most difficult adjustment for us to make will be
  a getting used to having more free time.
  b working without the hope of material reward.
  c seeing education as being its own reward.
  d learning essentially impractical subjects.

3 Our duty towards our children will be to
  a prepare them to set their own goals.
  b encourage them to be more ambitious.
  c improve their chances of employment.
  d teach them basic moral values in life.

4 According to the writer, future learning will resemble the new-style tug-of-war in that
  a there will be no possibility of failing.
  b the object will be to avoid winning.
  c it will depend on operating as a team.
  d it will involve a personal challenge.

5 The reason for the writer's optimistic conclusion is that she has
  a discovered how satisfying learning can be.
  b shown a new talent for playing the piano.
  c found how easy it is to develop a new skill.
  d taken up a hobby for the first time.

▶ Focus on writing 1 · Report based on statistics

Write a short report outlining the main findings of a national opinion survey on the British educational system. The results are shown in the tables below and on p. 121

Children

Teachers

Parents

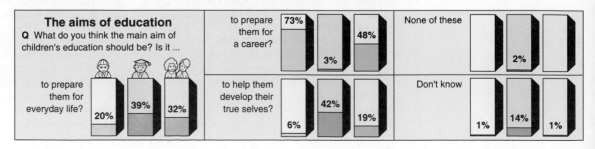

The aims of education
Q What do you think the main aim of children's education should be? Is it ...

to prepare them for everyday life? 20% 39% 32%

to prepare them for a career? 73% 48% 3%

to help them develop their true selves? 6% 42% 19%

None of these 2%

Don't know 1% 14% 1%

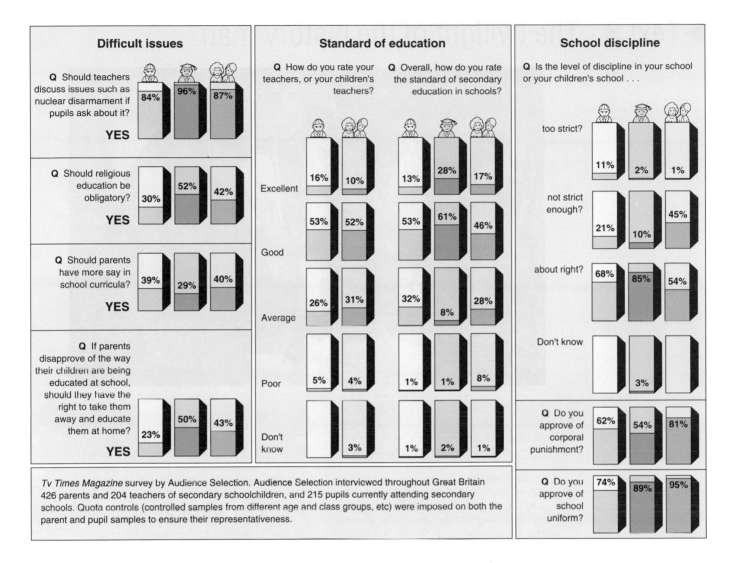

Difficult issues

Q Should teachers discuss issues such as nuclear disarmament if pupils ask about it?
YES — 84% 96% 87%

Q Should religious education be obligatory?
YES — 30% 52% 42%

Q Should parents have more say in school curricula?
YES — 39% 29% 40%

Q If parents disapprove of the way their children are being educated at school, should they have the right to take them away and educate them at home?
YES — 23% 50% 43%

Standard of education

Q How do you rate your teachers, or your children's teachers?
Q Overall, how do you rate the standard of secondary education in schools?

	Q1		Q2		
Excellent	16%	10%	13%	28%	17%
Good	53%	52%	53%	61%	46%
Average	26%	31%	32%	8%	28%
Poor	5%	4%	1%	1%	8%
Don't know		3%	1%	2%	1%

School discipline

Q Is the level of discipline in your school or your children's school . . .

too strict?	11%	2%	1%
not strict enough?	21%	10%	45%
about right?	68%	85%	54%
Don't know		3%	

Q Do you approve of corporal punishment? — 62% 54% 81%

Q Do you approve of school uniform? — 74% 89% 95%

Tv Times Magazine survey by Audience Selection. Audience Selection interviewed throughout Great Britain 426 parents and 204 teachers of secondary schoolchildren, and 215 pupils currently attending secondary schools. Quota controls (controlled samples from different age and class groups, etc) were imposed on both the parent and pupil samples to ensure their representativeness.

Notes

1 The function of a report of this kind is to *organise* the facts so that the most important findings become clear to the reader. The function is not to systematically reproduce every detail of the statistics since the diagram does that in a more accessible way.

2 It may be appropriate to express a reaction to a finding, eg 'It comes as something of a surprise to find . . .' 'Predictably . . .' and, in some cases, (such as the popularity of school uniform), to suggest a reason for a result.

3 The choice of expression for reporting results should be the one which makes the clearest impression. For example, 73% may be expressed approximately as 'three out of four'; 48% as 'almost half' and 3% as 'only three in every hundred'.

Varying the choice of expression and the sentence structure will help prevent the report from becoming monotonous.

4 The introduction should state clearly how the findings were arrived at. This information can be found at the foot of the tables.

The different issues should be dealt with in order of importance and linked together logically. For example, the results of the section on the aims of education might be appropriately followed by those from the section on the standards of education.

Don't forget a brief conclusion.

Begin your report as follows:

In a survey carried out by Audience Selection, on behalf of *TV Times Magazine*, 426 parents, 204 teachers and 215 secondary school pupils . . .

▶Text 3 · The twilight of the history man

"SORRY we're late – car keys again."

"Oh that's all right, I think we've a few more still to come yet."

There are few moments of tension at the
5 evening class in local history, and the entry of the late-comers is not one of them. For although a late arriver to the karate class down the corridor is doubtless set upon by other members of the group, it is all smiles
10 and embarrassment in Room 3. Far from swinging a fist at the miscreant student, medieval style, the Local History Man simply hands him a sheet with the town subsidy figures for 1523 on it. But perhaps
15 this is punishment enough.

Having delivered his leaflets around the class, the tutor then has to begin dangling the carrots. A good number of his students, having already worked a 12-hour day, soon
20 develop a keen resentment towards their evening class. Unless they are promised plenty of coffee breaks and periods when they can contemplate quietly to themselves, then large sections of his class might start to
25 make things awkward for him. The arrogant man with the pipe, for example, is a known authority on the area for the 1520s. If roused from his ruminations, this man could explode all the tutor's "qualified
30 estimates" and "considered opinions" at the drop of a fact or figure, thus finally putting paid to the Local History Man's already dwindling self-confidence.

Indeed, the tutor might easily feel temp-
35 ted to turn the whole evening into one of coffee and relaxation therapy, were it not for the presence of Sheila, Len, old Gilbert with his ripped jacket, and perhaps two or three others. These people are the devoted
40 ones. They never miss a lesson, have read all the recommended books and articles, and hang on the tutor's every word. On arrival, Len usually thrusts yet another fifty-year old Ordnance Survey map into the
45 tutor's hands and eagerly awaits comment, Sheila regularly threatens to bring in her husband's collection of local fossils, and Gilbert records the events of the evening on his huge reel to reel tape-recorder. And if
50 the tutor should bring in any old and musty documents himself, they gather around him like small children around Santa Claus, drooling over the prospect of a night of statistical analysis amongst the fungus.

55 "Lunatic fringe" or not, such characters keep the evening class going, prodding and pushing the tutor along in the quest for further enlightenment. While the others march off to the coffee room for half an
60 hour, the tutor will hear the latest saga of Gilbert's family tree and the possible link with Oliver Cromwell, after which Sheila pushes the tutor for an exact date, for the proposed field-trip. Len, not to be outdone,
65 then produces a copy of a 1953 newspaper with the Queen's coronation in it.

The tutor tends not to press the field-trip idea (mentioned in rash moment) too hard. He is not sure that his students will take at
70 all kindly to the idea of a Saturday search for medieval strip-farming, and if the luna-tic fringe would only let him, he would probably prefer to forget all about it. The date is generally put off until the end of the
75 course, when, with any luck, the more obstreperous element in the class will have ceased attending completely.

The trip, however, is doomed to go ahead. A surprisingly large number of the
80 class turns up for the morning coach jour-

ney, many of whom are doubtless willing to experience an alternative to the sober confines of the classroom. The driver is encouraged to stop off at a selection of 85 hostelries en route, and consequently, by the time they reach the proposed working area, enthusiasm is boundless. So much so, indeed, that they recklessly set off in all directions as soon as they are out of the 90 coach, leaving the tutor by the roadside looking around anxiously for the approach of a furious farmer. Suddenly, he feels a tap on his shoulder. He freezes. But it is Len, triumphantly holding a pointed piece of flint 95 in his hand.

by Stephen Petty in the Guardian

Look at the first two paragraphs and find words or phrases which mean the same as:

a attacked (1)   ....
b rather than (1)   ....
c guilty (1)   ....
d bitter (2)   ....
e difficult (2)   ....
f accepted expert (2)   ....
g awoken (2)   ....
h deep thought (2)   ....
i destroying (2)   ....
j becoming gradually smaller (2)   ....

1 How does the writer picture the arrival of a late-comer in the karate class?
2 Why does the writer see the sheet handed to the late-comer as 'punishment enough' (lines 12–15)?
3 Explain what the writer means by the phrase 'dangling the carrots' (lines 17–18).
4 Explain how 'the arrogant man with the pipe' could make things awkward for the tutor.
5 Give an alternative expression for the phrase 'putting paid to' (line 32).
6 Explain 'They . . . hang on the tutor's every word.' (line 42).
7 What is suggested by the writer's use of the word 'threatens' (line 46)?
8 Explain in your own words how the tutor's 'devoted students' react when he brings in old documents.
9 What do you understand by the phrase 'lunatic fringe' (line 55)?
10 Why is the date of the field trip generally postponed?
11 What reason does the writer suggest for the surprising number of participants in the field trip?
12 Why does the writer describe the group's behaviour as reckless when they leave the coach? What reason could there be for this recklessness?
13 Imagine that you are the tutor of this class and that you will not be able to continue teaching it next year. Using the information in the passage, write a paragraph of guidance (50–100 words) to the teacher who will succeed you. (See STUDY BOX – Summary Writing on page 127.)

LANGUAGE CHECK
Dependent Prepositions 5: Adjective + Preposition

Here is a list of 16 words or phrases, some of which have been used in the texts in this unit. Write in the preposition which follows them.

Check your answers with your teacher or in the dictionary so that you have an accurate reference list for the future.

according . . .	**expert** . . . (*2 possibilities*)
aimed . . .	**far** . . . (*something/somebody*)
aware . . .	**ignorant** . . .
capable . . .	**interested** . . .
confined . . .	**peculiar** . . .
content . . . (*something*)	**preferable** . . .
critical . . .	**proud** . . .
envious . . .	**sympathetic** . . .

▶ Focus on grammar 2 ·
–ing forms in place of clauses of time and reason

Look at these examples from Text 3:

    a *Having delivered his leaflets around the class*, the tutor then has to begin dangling the carrots.

    b A good number of students, *having already worked a 12-hour day*, soon develop a keen resentment towards their evening class.

The first example could be rewritten:

    'When he has delivered his leaflets around the class, the tutor . . .'

The *–ing* form therefore replaces a clause of *time* Look at these further examples and say how they could be rewritten:

    c Walking through the public gardens today, I noticed that vandals had damaged the benches.

    d Having been given your home number by your secretary, I tried to find a telephone box which was empty.

The second example could be rewritten:

    'As they have already worked a 12-hour day, a good number of students . . .'

The *–ing* form here replaces a clause of *reason*. Look at these further examples and say how they could be rewritten:

    e Being frightened of spiders, I never go down to the cellar if I can help it.

    f The car having broken down, all we could do was hitch a lift to the nearest town.

Exercise 1   Rewrite the following sentences, replacing the clauses of time or reason with an *–ing* form:

    a I saw that she was on the verge of tears so I changed the subject hurriedly.

    b He arrived rather late because he had been held up in the rush hour traffic.

    c The weather was unsettled so we decided not to venture very far from the hotel.

    d I heard about the hijack on the news and phoned the airline immediately to see if my brother was on the passenger list.

    e When the luggage had been unloaded, we all disappeared to our rooms to unpack.

    f I wasn't given the flight number so it was rather difficult to find out when the plane would arrive.

    g As the car approached the final bend, it skidded on the oily surface and spun out of control.

    h Once contracts have been exchanged, you will be free to move into the house.

    i As I was unwilling to offer any more for the painting, I had to let it go to a higher bidder.

    j He set off as soon as he had received his last minute instructions.

Note   The *–ing* form automatically refers to the subject of the sentence unless it has its own subject as in sentence *c*, *e* and *h* in exercise 1.

    Careless writing can produce unintentionally absurd sentences such as:

    Having a degree in education, the child was quite easy for me to tutor

where it appears that the child is the one with the qualification!

Exercise 2   Say what is wrong with the following sentences and rewrite them so that the intended meaning is clear:

    a Wearing a striped T-shirt, we thought he was rather casually dressed for an interview.

    b Having been designed as a racing bike, I found it very smooth and easy to handle.

    c Not looking where he was going, the car almost hit him as he was crossing the road.

    d The letter presented no particular problems to translate, having learnt German at school.

    e Not being starving hungry, the huge helping of paella was more than I could manage.

▶ Communication activity · Which evening class?

Local educational authorities in Britain offer a wide range of part-time classes to adults who want to study in their spare time. These classes are put on in schools and colleges at very modest fees and are open to anyone who wants to join.

In this activity you should work *in pairs*: one taking Role A, the student; and the other, Role B, the Adult Education supervisor (see page 198).

Role A You have decided that *this* year you are definitely going to attend an evening class. You would like the challenge of learning something new and preferably useful, and the opportunity to make new friends.

Listed below are the evening classes which are being offered at your local technical college with your preliminary notes on them.

Points to bear in mind:

1 You want the class to be of some practical use.

2 You finish work at 5.30 pm and although it only takes about 10 minutes to get to the college, you would like to have time to eat something before starting the class.

3 You don't know how long each course lasts or how much the fees are. You can only afford to pay up to £15 at the moment. If it's possible to pay term by term, you could afford a more expensive course.

4 You have a limited budget and don't want to spend too much on books or materials.

Think about the questions you will need to ask before deciding on which course you're going to enrol for. *Remember to keep an open mind.* Sometimes the most unpromising-sounding courses turn out to be fascinating!

✳1 Pottery — *sounds interesting and useful, but do you have to pay for what you make?*

2 Landscape painting — *doesn't appeal*

3 Antiques appreciation — *I haven't got any antiques!*

✳4 Basic computing — *This would impress the boss!*

5 Beginners' Russian — *Can't see it being much use*

? 6 Personality development — *what on earth is this?*

7 Shorthand — *boring!*

8 Chess for beginners — *ditto!*

? 9 Soft furnishings — *what does this involve?*

✳10 Car care — *might save a fortune on servicing the car!*

▶ Focus on writing 2 · Instructions

Choose *one* of the following activities and write clear, step-by-step instructions for someone who has never attempted it before.

a riding a bicycle (or horse)
b making an omelette
c changing the wheel of a car
d swimming
e using a tape recorder to make a recording

Notes

1 To do this, you must put yourself in the position of the absolute beginner. Take nothing for granted. At each stage, think how your instruction could be misinterpreted (and what could be the result!) and try to prevent such problems by making your instructions crystal clear.

2 Instructions can either be written on separate lines or as a paragraph. Decide which will be the clearest and most appropriate for the task. In both cases you should provide a heading.

a If you decide on separate lines, number each one and start with a verb in the imperative (eg ....?). Keep sentences fairly short. It may be better to break up a complicated instruction into several shorter ones.

b If you decide on a paragraph, you will need to make use of time adverbials to mark the sequence of events (eg ....?). Vary the language of instruction so that you don't have all imperatives or all 'you must's.

▶ Focus on listening

You are going to hear a radio interview with a 'mature' student. Listen and answer the following questions.

1 This programme is part of a series on

a how to go about choosing a career.
b the educational system in Britain.
c degree courses at British universities.
d educational opportunities for adults.

2 Steve left school at 16 because

a he got disappointing exam results.
b he wanted to be like everyone else.
c he wanted to be independent.
d he wasn't given the chance to stay on.

3 He felt that the philosophy part of his course

a wasn't explained clearly.
b wasn't very interesting.
c was simplified too much.
d was completely irrelevant.

4 He thinks he did badly in his exam because

a he hadn't done enough revision.
b he didn't have the right attitude.
c he didn't have enough time.
d he couldn't organise his ideas.

5 He would hesitate about doing an ordinary degree course because

    a the fees would be too expensive.
    b he would need to economise.
    c it might be too demanding.
    d he might feel he was too old.

6 Expenses

Item	Cost
Fees	
	£87
Books	

7 Hours of study per week

Recommended	Actual

8 Times of Open University television programmes

Thursday	Sunday
– am	8.55–9.20 am

STUDY BOX 1
How to write a summary – SIMPLE!

Study the text: read it first fairly quickly to get a sense of the general meaning. Then read more carefully, following the writer's argument and noticing what is fact and what is opinion, what is general statement and what is particular example. It is often helpful to summarise each paragraph in a few words at this stage.

Identify the key points: check the instructions for the summary – some parts of the text may be completely irrelevant. Go through the text again and mark the places where important information is given – by underlining, highlighting with a coloured pen or simply making a mark in the margin.

Make notes: write down the key points you've identified in note form *in your own words*. If you use the original words you may have difficulty in fitting all the necessary information into the word limit. It is also especially important in an exam because the examiner needs to know you *understand* what you've written.

Put points in order: look at the list of points you've made and see if there are any which go together. Then decide the best order to put the points in – this may be different from the order in which they appeared in the original text. Number the points in this order.

Leave out unnecessary detail: eg lists, anecdotes, figures of speech.

▼

FIRST DRAFT

Edit your first draft: check the spelling and grammar; count the number of words. If you have many fewer than the limit, you've probably left out something important so check the original text again. If you have more than the limit, look for ways of combining points in one sentence, or of "losing" words here and there.

▼

FINAL DRAFT

▶ Focus on register

Extract 1   Aimed at non-computer specialists and teachers of 8–16 year olds, the awareness pack will help to introduce a very wide range of microcomputer uses. Through a series of carefully structured activities, everything from setting up the microcomputer to simple programming is introduced.

A series of case studies shows how the microcomputer has been successfully used in classrooms all over the UK. There are also two projects covering a wide range of methods and content to work through and, if appropriate, to use with pupils.

For the 380Z edition, before ordering, please check that your microcomputer has one or two 5¼ inch double-sided disc drives and at least 32K of memory.

Extract 2   The image of wild-eyed school teachers who have caught the home computer bug beavering away in their attics writing programs – sets of instructions for the microcomputer to follow – is not so very far from the truth. Just as the purchase of micro depends on the traditional British exercise of voluntary initiative, so the development of programs is often being left to enthusiastic teachers.

There is disagreement about whether this is a good thing. One thing, however, is clear: teachers, particularly in primary schools, have little choice, thanks to the dearth of suitable programs caused by the speed with which the Micros in Schools scheme has been introduced. The ground was simply not prepared in advance.

Extract 3   Faced with a machine they know little about, teachers could be tempted to opt for simple 'practise and drill' programs, mainly produced for an eager market of anxious parents, and for space invader type games which, according to Croydon's adviser for computers in primary schools, Ms Heather Govier, may keep children happy but teach them little.

'Eighty per cent of the programs available are garbage,' the Inner London Education Authority's computer adviser, Mr Derek Esterson, said. 'They're real education dinosaurs.'

Now complete these statements by choosing the answer which you think fits best.

1 Extract 1 probably comes from

a an advertisement for computers.
b a catalogue of educational materials.
c a general introduction to computers.
d a handbook for computer programmers.

2 The image described at the beginning of Extract 2 suggests teachers who

a have become fanatical about computers.
b are terrified of using new technology.
c have become ill through using computers.
d hate changing their old teaching methods.

3 Extracts 2 and 3 both suggest that teachers

   a are reluctant to use computers in class.
   b are using computers badly in class.
   c are not being provided with suitable programs.
   d are not being allowed to choose good programs.

4 The first type of program mentioned in Extract 3 is designed

   a to teach adults.
   b to entertain adults.
   c to teach children.
   d to entertain children.

5 The problem about the materials described in Extract 3 is that they

   a are extremely expensive.
   b are completely out of date.
   c take up a great deal of space.
   d are very complicated to use.

▶ Focus on writing 3 · Discussion

Write a balanced discussion on *one* of the following topics:

a Should parents who wish to educate their children themselves, at home, be free to do so? What are the arguments for and against?

b How well did your education prepare you for life in today's world? What differences in the range of subjects or methods of teaching do you wish there had been, and why?

(*About 350 words*)

STUDY BOX 2
Phrasal Verbs 4

Look at these examples of phrasal verbs from this unit:

1 *The late arriver to the karate class is . . .* **set upon** *by other members of the group.* (Text 3)
   set (up)on means 'attack'

2 *He is not sure his students will* **take** *at all kindly* **to** *the idea of a Saturday search for medieval strip farming.* (Text 3)
   take to means 'react to' or 'like'.

3 *The date is generally* **put off** *until the end of the course.* (Text 3)
   put off means 'postpone', or 'delay till a later date'.

4 *We're looking at ways in which you can* **go about** *getting the qualifications which you may have missed out on at school.* (Listening)
   go about means 'start dealing with a task or problem'.

5 *Philosophy wasn't* **put across** *very well.* (Listening)
   put across means 'describe or explain something'.

6 *I think they'd* **send** *me* **up** *about it – start calling me 'the Professor' or something.* (Listening)
   send up is a colloquial expression and it means 'make fun of'.

▶ Vocabulary practice

Review Choose the word or phrase which best completes each sentence.

1 He thought that if he admitted he was afraid of swimming he would lose ....
   with his friends.

   A weight B nerve C face D regard

2 When the truth about the blackmail attempt finally ...., we were all astonished
   to hear who the culprit was.

   A evolved B emerged C arose D issued

3 The problem of finding a baby-sitter .... itself when my mother came to live
   with us.

   A arranged B composed C sorted D resolved

4 I took a course in shorthand and typing with a(n) .... to applying for a
   secretarial job.

   A intention B project C view D purpose

5 He's .... a bit with his history classes so I've arranged for him to have private
   tuition.

   A straining B struggling C fighting D dragging

6 You have managed to bungle every task I've given you so far. .... I am
   prepared to give you one last chance.

   A Notwithstanding B Regardless C Furthermore D Nevertheless

7 He spoke a few .... words in French and was applauded loudly.

   A stumbling B limping C fumbling D hobbling

8 He was a most effective speaker and his audience seemed to .... on his every
   word.

   A catch B hold C hang D cling

9 Numbers in the Latin evening class have .... rather badly. We may have to
   close it.

   A dwindled B deteriorated C reduced D lessened

10 I don't take .... to being disobeyed. That's a warning!

   A well B kindly C gently D nicely

11 Police blamed a small hooligan .... in the crowd for the violence which
   occurred.

   A portion B constituent C element D division

12 He kept .... him on the shoulder with his finger whenever he wanted to make
   a point.

   A prodding B slapping C pelting D pinching

13 The most important .... that he was responsible for was the use of video in
   teaching.

   A novelty B innovation C reformation D introduction

14 I tried to explain why I had been delayed but he .... my excuse as pathetic.

   A ignored B disregarded C dismissed D refused

15 She's fallen rather .... with her schoolwork since she's been swimming competitively.

A below   B back   C down   D behind

16 I can't imagine why he's been missing classes and getting poor marks. He's normally so ....

A conscientious   B attentive   C laborious   D observant

17 We caught a momentary .... of Prince Charles as his car drove past.

A glance   B glimpse   C peep   D view

18 I've been trying to contact you for days but you seem to be very ....

A inaccessible   B exclusive   C evasive   D elusive

19 You've done more of the work than I have recently so I'll give up my day off in order to .... the balance.

A redress   B compensate   C offset   D repair

20 The introduction of diesel engines sadly made the old steam trains ....

A archaic   B extinct   C derelict   D obsolete

21 When I .... promised to put you up, I didn't expect you to stay for a month!

A wildly   B rashly   C recklessly   D riskily

22 I'd give up my job .... if only I could find a better one.

A on the spur of the moment   B at the drop of a hat   C on the dot   D at one swoop

23 She had .... another rejection letter today. That makes thirty so far!

A still   B but   C again   D yet

24 Our plans to start our own business seem .... to failure!

A doomed   B fated   C compelled   D designed

25 My decision to leave university after a year is one I now .... regret.

A painfully   B harshly   C heavily   D keenly

Colloquial expressions using animal names as verbs

The schoolteachers in Extract 2 of Focus on register were described as: 'beavering away in their attics writing programs'

Beavers are small wild animals which use their sharp teeth to cut down tree branches and construct dams across rivers. They are supposed to be very industrious so the meaning of the phrasal verb 'to beaver away' becomes clear – 'to work hard'.

A number of other animals receive the same treatment. Below is a list of the most common expressions involving animals.

Think about each animal and its characteristics. This should help you to complete the sentences which follow.

beaver	monkey	hog	hare	beetle
swan	fox	worm	wolf	dog

1 I called out to him but he .... off in the opposite direction, at top speed.
2 Can't you stop .... about and be serious for a minute. This is no time for playing the fool.
3 He must have been starving. He .... a huge plate of stew and then asked for a second helping.
4 You've been .... that newspaper all morning. There *are* other people who'd like to read it, you know.

131

5 I've been .... away at the typewriter all day and I've nearly finished Chapter 2.

6 Since he joined the company he seems to have .... his way into the boss's favour by some very clever tactics.

7 Bad luck seems to have .... me throughout my career.

8 She was .... about doing the housework when I called in. Somehow she always seems so busy!

9 Wouldn't it be nice if we all had the time and money to .... off to France for a weekend?

10 This last clue in the crossword completely .... me. I can't imagine what the answer is.

▶Grammar practice

1 Fill each of the numbered blanks in the passage with one suitable word.

When Roger Bannister first ran the mile in .... (1) than four minutes on May 6, 1954, he broke a barrier which .... (2) now been crossed hundreds of times. Similarly, in other athletic .... (3) the limits of the possible continue to be pushed back as record .... (4) record is broken.

In a less spectacular .... (5), everyday skills such as riding bicycles .... (6) to have become easier to .... (7) up, with many children learning younger and faster than their grandparents .... (8). And recent studies have .... (9) that average performance in intelligence tests is also .... (10). .... (11) the war, the average IQ score of American children has been rising .... (12) about 1 point .... (13) three years, and .... (14) faster increases have .... (15) in Japan.

There are many possible .... (16) for these effects, such as better nutrition, improved teaching methods, ... (17) availability of facilities and so on. But there may be an important underlying factor which has so far been .... (18), namely an inherent tendency for past experience to .... (19) present performance through a kind of collective memory .... (20) which everyone has potential access.

from an article by Rupert Sheldrake in the Guardian

2 Finish each of the following sentences in such a way that it means exactly the same as the sentence printed before it.

a I would prefer you to wear something more formal to work.
   I'd rather . . .
b This is the worst coffee I have ever drunk.
   Never . . .
c I'm not friendly with him; in fact, I hardly even know him.
   Far from . . .
d Without your sound advice, I would never have made such a good investment.
   If it hadn't . . .
e Don't press the alarm button unless there's a real emergency.
   The alarm button . . .
f I'd better be getting home now.
   It's time . . .
g Someone stole my handbag while we were playing tennis.
   During . . .
h The train journey from Bristol to London took only 90 minutes.
   It was . . .
i If I have plenty of warning I'll willingly baby-sit for you.
   Provided you . . .
j As he grew older, he became more and more forgetful.
   The . . .

UNIT 8 The media

▶ ## Lead-in

1 Which of the above media provides most of your

   a international information? ....
   b national information? ....
   c local information? ....
   d entertainment? ....

2 If you had to rely on only *one* of the media, which would you choose? Why?

3 How do these media differ in their treatment of news?

4 In what ways can the media show subjectivity in their coverage of the news?

   Working with a partner list the effects of television on children under two headings: Positive and Negative.

▶ Text 1 · Illusions of power?

On 4th March 1887, William Randolph Hearst stalked into the offices of his father's ailing *San Francisco Examiner* and announced to the staff that he intended to 'startle, amaze and stupefy the world'. He then proceeded to do just that. Over the next half century his newspapers were in every sense amazing. They made and destroyed
5 reputations, often with impressive disregard for the truth. They exposed corruption, while at the same time buying politicians. They created stars; they even declared a war. Within a few years of becoming proprietor, Hearst turned his papers into vehicles through which he could successfully run for Congress and even put himself forward for the presidency of the United States. Though he never actually occupied the White
10 House nor achieved the mass popularity which he craved, he came within an ace of the 1904 Democratic presidential nomination, buying and cajoling his way to 263 votes before losing to the colourless but safe Judge Parker.

    Hearst's papers remained successful. They usually gained in circulation and some of them even made money – though the *Examiner* lost a fortune (his father's) while he
15 was editing it. But as long as the money lasted, the money did not matter. And the circulation was important only for the power, however specious, which he felt it represented. The glamour of newspaper ownership never left him, but the futility of the power ultimately corroded his personality. Shy, desperately unsure of himself in public, he finally died in an agony of loneliness – a loneliness etched on the minds of
20 millions by Orson Welles's film portrait of him in *Citizen Kane*.

Just as newspaper owners must never underestimate the nature of their power, so newspaper readers should never underestimate the lure of its glamour. Ninety years after Hearst took over the *Examiner*, I was sitting in the *Daily Express* building waiting for the new proprietor, Victor Matthews, to arrive to complete his purchase and tell his
25 expectant executives what was going to happen to them. He was a veteran of many industrial take-overs. But on this occasion he was clearly delighted to be welcomed by a bevy of reporters and a television crew. They delayed his arrival while they interviewed him on his views on politics and his ambitions as a proprietor, and even requested him to drive round the block to arrive again for better television effect. Mr
30 Matthews was a building contractor by trade and had been offered few chances to give his views on the world before. Attempting to adopt what he felt was the argot of such occasions, he murmured something about 'believing in Britain and helping make her great again'. The phrase seemed to go down well. He used it many times that day and afterwards. Overnight the glamour of newspapers had magically transformed him
35 into a public figure. Within weeks Matthews was letting it be known that he would appreciate an invitation to meet the prime minister at Downing Street. The flattery of newspaper proprietors has long been a favourite sport of premiers and an invitation duly came.

The incident was merely a modern pastiche of an aura which has motivated
40 proprietors throughout newspaper history. It has often been remarked that men acquire newspapers for many reasons, but rarely for the business of running them and making themselves rich. From the earliest times, the access papers have afforded to public life has been a major factor. That access has, on a few occasions, been converted into real political power. But for the most part it has been an illusion.
45 Ownership has been a ticket to the front stalls of public affairs, but not to the stage itself. Owners who have disobeyed this rule have had to retreat to their seats, bruised and disillusioned.

from 'Newspapers; the power and the money' by Simon Jenkins

Now complete these statements choosing the answer which you think fits best.

1 In achieving their success, Hearst's newspapers

    a lost a great deal of money.
    b employed politicians on their staff.
    c used some corrupt methods.
    d concentrated on political issues.

2 We find from the article that Hearst resembled other newspaper proprietors in that he

    a was more influential than leading politicians.
    b was disappointed in his ambition to make money.
    c failed to become a popular public figure.
    d was attracted by the power of the position.

3 According to the writer, Victor Matthews was pleased by his reception even though

    a this was not the first newspaper he had bought.
    b he had not wanted to be the centre of attention.
    c he had gained control of companies before then.
    d he was used to being interviewed about his views.

4 The writer suggests that he repeated his comment many times because

    a it seemed to please his audience.
    b it made him feel important.
    c he wanted to convince his audience.
    d he was a strongly patriotic man.

5 The article warns newspaper proprietors not to

    a expect to make a large profit.
    b seek an active role in public life.
    c look for the support of politicians.
    d imagine that they have any power.

▶ Text 2 · A medium of no importance

Grown-ups, as any child will tell you, are monstrous hypocrites, especially when it comes to television. It is to take their minds off their own telly-addiction that adults are so keen to hear and talk about the latest report on the effects of programmes on children. Surely all that nonsense they watch must be desensitising them, making them vicious, shallow, acquisitive, less responsible and generally sloppy about life and death? But no, not a scrap of convincing evidence from the sociologists and experts in the psyches of children.

The nation has lived with the box for more than 30 years now and has passed from total infatuation – revived temporarily by the advent of colour – to the present casual obsession which is not unlike that of the well-adjusted alcoholic. And now the important and pleasant truth is breaking, to the horror of programme makers and their detractors alike, that television really does not affect much at all. This is tough on those diligent professionals who produce excellent work; but since – as everyone agrees – awful pro-grammes far outnumber the good, it is a relief to know the former cannot do much harm. Television cannot even make impressionable children less pleasant.

Television turns out to be no great transformer of minds or society. We are not, *en masse*, as it was once predicted we would be, fantastically well-informed about other cultures or about the origins of life on earth. People do not remember much from television documentary beyond how *good* it was. Only those who knew something about the subject in the first place retain the information.

Documentaries are not what most people want to watch anyway. Television is at its most popular when it celebrates its own present. Its ideal subjects are those that need not be remembered and can be instantly re-placed, where what matters most is what is happening *now* and what is going to happen *next*. Sport, news, panel games, cop shows, long-running soap operas, situation comedies – these occupy us only for as long as they are on. However good or bad it is,

a night's viewing is wonderfully
60 forgettable. It's a little sleep, it's Entertainment; our morals, and for that
matter, our brutality, remain intact.

The box is further neutralised by
the sheer quantity people watch. The
65 more of it you see, the less any single
bit of it matters. Of course, some
programmes are infinitely better than
others. There are gifted people working in television. But seen from a
70 remoter perspective – say, four hours a
night viewing for three months – the
quality of individual programmes
means as much as the quality of each
car in the rush-hour traffic.

75 For the heavy viewer, TV has only
two meaningful states – on and off.
What are the kids doing? Watching
TV. No need to ask what, the answer
is sufficient. Soon, I'll go up there and
80 turn it off. Like a lightbulb it will go
out and the children will do something
else.

It appears the nation's children
spend more time in front of their TVs
85 than in the classroom. Their heads are
full of TV – but that's *all*, just TV.
The violence they witness is TV
violence, sufficient to itself. It does not
brutalise them to the point where they
90 cannot grieve the loss of a pet, or be
shocked at some minor playground

violence. Children, like everyone else,
know the difference between TV and
life. TV knows its place. It imparts
95 nothing but itself; it has its own rules,
its own language, its own priorities. It
is because this little glowing, chattering screen barely resembles life at all
that it remains so usefully ineffectual.
100 To stare at a brick wall would waste
time in a similar way. The difference is
that the brick wall would let you know
you were wasting your time.

Whatever the TV/video industry
105 might now say, television will never
have the impact on civilisation that the
invention of the written word has had.
The book – this little hinged thing – is
cheap, portable, virtually unbreak-
110 able, endlessly reusable, has instant
replay facilities and in slow motion if
you want it, needs no power lines,
batteries or aerials, works in planes
and train tunnels, can be stored inde-
115 finitely without much deterioriation, is
less amenable to censorship and cen-
tralised control, can be written and
manufactured by relatively un-
privileged individuals or groups, and –
120 most sophisticated of all – dozens of
different ones can be going at the same
time, in the same room *without a
sound*.

from an article by Ian McEwan in the Observer, London

To check your *general* understanding of the text, answer the following questions *briefly*.

Para 1
1 Does the writer think television is harmful to children? Why/Why not?

Para 2
2 Has the nation become more or less keen on television since it was first introduced?
What development had an effect on the popularity of television?

Para 3
3 How successful is television as an educator, according to the writer?

Para 4
4 Why do most people watch television, according to the writer?

Para 5/6
5 What effect does quantity of viewing have on people?

Para 7
6 Why are children not affected by television violence, according to the writer?

Para 8
7 In *one* word, what is the advantage of the book over television?

137

Now look again at paragraphs 1–4 and find words or phrases in the passage which mean the same as:

a extremely shocking (1) ....
b showing a desire to hurt (1) ....
c careless or muddled (1) ....
d absolutely none (1) ....
e television (slang) (2) ....
f arrival/introduction (2) ....
g becoming known (2) ....
h critics (2) ....
i hardworking (2) ....
j easily influenced (2) ....
k cruel and violent behaviour (4) ....
l complete, not damaged or changed (4) ....

1 Explain in your own words why adults are described as 'hypocrites' (line 2).
2 Explain in your own words how people reacted to television when it first became available.
3 In what way are television viewers today like 'well-adjusted alcoholics' (lines 21–22)?
4 What is 'a relief' (line 31) to the writer?
5 How is watching television like 'a little sleep' (line 60)?
6 Explain the phrase 'remain intact' (line 62).
7 Explain what the writer means by 'The box is further neutralised . . .' (line 63).
8 What is suggested about the heavy viewer's attitude to the programmes he and his children watch?
9 What does 'brutalise' (line 89) mean?
10 What does the word 'chattering' (line 97) suggest about television?
11 What point is the writer making about books in the final paragraph?
12 In a paragraph of 50–100 words explain why television is seen as 'a medium of no importance'. (see STUDY BOX – Summary Writing on page 127.)

STUDY BOX
Phrasal Verbs 5

Look at these examples from this unit:

1 *The phrase seemed to* **go down** *well.* (Text 1)
   go down means 'get a reaction (from)' or 'be accepted (by)'

   NB **go off** can mean 'to succeed' eg *The trip* **went off** *very well.*

2 *Sociologists are beginning to fall into disrepute for failing to* **come up with** *the desired results.* (Text 2)
   come up with means 'produce'.

   NB **come across** means 'find by chance' eg *I* **came across** *a fascinating book in a bookshop today.*

3 *TV* **turns out** *to be no great transformer of minds or society.* (Text 2)
   turn out (to be) means 'be revealed' or 'happen to be (in the end)'.

   NB **turn out** can also mean 'to produce' eg *We* **turn out** *1,500 engines a day at this factory.*

▶ Focus on grammar 1 ·
Expressing future time: review

There is no standardised future *tense* in English although there is a future *form*. The way we choose to talk about the future reflects our *attitude* towards it, that is, how likely we think an event is, how much control over a future event we have and so on.

Cover the right-hand side of the page. Look at the examples on the left-hand side and say for each group what attitude towards the future they express. Check your answers at the end of each main section.

Going to   **1**   *a*   We're going to hire a mini bus for the trip. What are you going to do about the money you owe?

expresses *personal intention*, usually *premeditated*, ie the action has already been considered and some preparations may have been made.

b   Look at that black sky! There's going to be a storm before long.
It's going to be hard to change his mind. (He's very stubborn.)

expresses a sense of *probability* based on present evidence
ie what you can see or what you know.

Future simple   **2**   *a*   I'll be 36 next birthday.
The meeting will be over by 5.
You won't have any trouble finding a job.

states *future fact* or *prediction*.

b   Mary's leaving now.
So am I. I'll give her a lift home.

expresses a *sudden* (ie unpremeditated) *decision*. Compare the difference in meaning of:
Mary's leaving now.
So am I. I'm going to give her a lift home.

c   Shall I give you a hand?
Will you open the door for me?

expresses an *offer* or *request*.

d   Next time you come near the house I'll set my dog on you!
I'll give a reward to anyone who finds my wallet.

expresses a *threat* or *promise*.

e   I suppose you'll be pretty busy for a week or so.
I doubt if you'll be able to read my writing.
Do you think you'll have time to go to the bank?
It'll probably arrive tomorrow.

expresses *opinion*, *speculation* and *assumption* about the future with verbs like 'think', 'suppose', 'expect' and also with 'probably'.

f   There's an official-looking letter for you.
Oh, that'll be from the tax office.

Have you seen Robert?
He'll be at lunch now.

expresses *strong probability*.
= must be from the tax office.

Future continuous   **3**   *a*   This time tomorrow we'll be crossing the Channel.
Don't call tomorrow. I'll be entertaining friends.

indicates an *action which will be in progress at a future time point*.

b   The BBC will be showing highlights from the match this evening.

indicates an anticipated *action which will happen as a matter of course.*

c   Will you be bringing your girlfriend to the party?

expresses a *request for information* rather than a request for action. Compare the difference in meaning in: 'Will you bring your girlfriend . . .?'

d   What's Helen doing?
She'll be typing those letters you dictated.

expresses a sense of *strong probability* about a present or future action.

139

Future perfect 4
(simple and
continuous)

a I'll have run out of money by the end of the month.
There's no point in phoning. She'll have left by now.

indicates *an action which will have occurred before a future time point*.

b You'll have seen my letter in today's *Times*, I assume.
Are these John's glasses?
Oh dear! He'll have been looking everywhere for them.

expresses *strong probability*.

Exercise Use one of the five future forms above to complete the following sentences.

a I've decided what to do about my financial problems. I (sell) my car and buy a bike!

b He seems to think about nothing but work, morning, noon and night. If he's not careful he (have) a nervous breakdown.

c I expect you (hear) the news about the takeover. It's been featured heavily in the local press.

d (You/take) the train to London? If so, don't forget to keep your ticket. You'll need it if you want to claim travel expenses.

e If you have any further queries, give me a ring and I (do) my best to answer them.

f If there aren't any tickets left when we reach the front of the queue, we (wait) all this time for nothing.

g (You/take) a tape recorder along to the meeting, please. Then we (can) make a transcript of the proceedings for those of us who can't attend.

h She looks awfully pale suddenly. You don't think she (faint) do you?

i Stop pestering me or I (call) the police.

j 'There's someone in Reception asking for you.'
'Oh, that (be) the reporter I agreed to talk to.'

k The company (publish) a series of novels by little-known women authors early next year.

l He's risen to Deputy Director in a very short space of time and no doubt, in due course, he (become) Director.

m 'Isn't that the Chancellor of the Exchequer coming out of Broadcasting House?'
'Yes, he (give) an interview on his budget proposals.'

n How much longer (we/must) put up with antiquated equipment and Dickensian working conditions?

o Don't expect me to be the life and soul of the party tomorrow night. Remember I (move) furniture all day!

p What (you/do) about the damage to your car? Is there any chance that the other driver (admit) responsibility?

q I very much doubt if you (can) persuade the disciplinary committee to reverse their decision.

r You (not/have) dinner at 8 o'clock tomorrow evening if I call in then, ... you?

s 'Mr Brown, there's a gentleman outside who's insisting on speaking to the manager. He (not/go) away.'
'Thank you Miss Bowen, I (deal) with him.'

t If I telephone you after the weekend, (you/have) enough time to have reached a decision?

▶ Communication activity · Radio interviews

Meet the people is a weekly programme on local radio in which ordinary people are interviewed about their lives and opinions. Each week there is a different theme and people are invited who have had experiences related to the particular theme.

Possible themes for the next programme are:

FEAR	'my most frightening experience'
TURNING POINTS	'the day that changed my life'
ACHIEVEMENTS	'the proudest moment of my life'
DISASTERS	'the worst holiday of my life'
LEISURE	'why my hobby is important to me'

There are three *roles*: Interviewer   *Equipment*: one or more tape-
Assistant   recorders if possible
Guest   (but not essential).

Procedure **1** Interviewers work together to prepare for the interviews. (See notes on page 142).

meanwhile

Assistants conduct preliminary interviews with guests to establish basic facts. Their notes will be handed to the interviewers. (See notes on page 142).

Note

If the class doesn't divide evenly into threes, it will be necessary for one or two assistants to interview more than one guest.

2 Practice interviews take place.

while

Assistants observe and offer comments and advice

3 Real interviews take place.

while

Assistants operate tape-recorder(s) if used *or* observe a different interview in progress.

4 (*Optional*) Recordings are played back *or* assistants report back. Discussion of success of interviews.

5 (*If time*) Change roles and repeat procedure.

Notes for guests

1 First decide which topic you have something to say about. Make notes, if you like, to help you remember the details (but don't try to write out an account).

2 Answer the questions which the assistant puts to you.

3 Look on the interview as a friendly chat rather than a formal interview!

Notes for interviewers

A PREPARATION   Work out (and make notes on):

– a short but realistic introduction to the programme, the theme and the guest.

– the kind of questions to ask. These should be 'leading' questions, designed to get your guest to explain or describe rather than just answer 'yes' or 'no'. For example:

not	'You're married to a doctor, aren't you?'
but	'What's it like being a doctor's wife?'
or	'What are the disadvantages to being a doctor's wife?'

– a suitable conclusion, thanking your guest and perhaps mentioning next week's theme.

– an appropriate time limit for the interview!

B INTERVIEWS

1 Read your assistant's notes.

2 Try to be relaxed and make your guest feel at ease!

3 Start with general questions and lead up to your guest's particular experience.

4 Remember to ask leading questions which prompt your guest to talk.

5 Really listen to the answers and be prepared to develop any interesting points.

6 Remember your time limit and stick to it!

Notes for assistants

1 Your job is to provide the interviewer with basic information about the guest. This should include:

name/age/nationality

married/single, children?

job/work experience etc

choice of theme to talk about

outline of particular experience

2 Prepare clear notes for the interviewer and give them to him/her before the programme.

3 Be prepared to observe the practice interviews and offer comments and advice (eg additional questions which could be asked).

4 Be prepared to operate recording equipment, if used. Otherwise, go and observe a different interview in progress.

5 Give the interviewer a warning one minute before the end of the time limit and clearly signal the end.

▶ Focus on listening

Some people are being shown round a television studio and you are going to hear part of their guide's commentary. Answer the questions below.

1 As you listen, label the diagram of the control room below. Write in the correct place on the diagram the appropriate number from the list of equipment and personnel.

1 Lighting control	*6* Producer
2 Make-up, wardrobe, design	*7* Production secretary
3 Microphone	*8* Sound control
4 Mixer's controls	*9* Technical manager
5 Preview monitor	*10* Transmission monitor

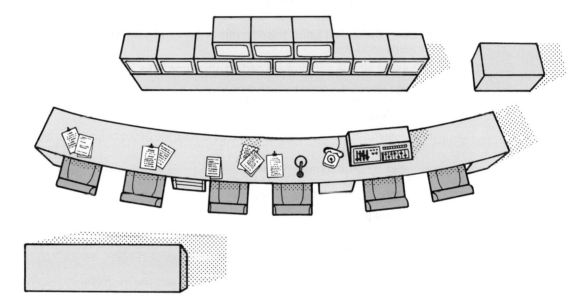

Now answer these questions.

2 The control room, unlike the studio floor,
a was dimly lit.
b was air-conditioned.
c had a hushed atmosphere
d had little equipment.

3 Individual directors are needed when a programme
a is longer than usual.
b is part of a regular series.
c involves several people.
d involves pre-recorded material.

4 Which member of the production team is described as having a most important role?
a The production secretary.
b The vision mixer.
c The technical manager.
d The sound engineer.

5 Which part of the studio did members of the tour group not see for themselves?
a The gallery.
b The lighting control room.
c The sound control room.
d The wardrobe department.

▶ Focus on grammar 2 · Present tenses used to express the future

1 Present continuous

> eg I'm seeing my bank manager tomorrow.
> What are you doing for Christmas?

Indicates a *pre-arranged future action*. Very similar in meaning and use to the 'going to' future but conveys less personal intention.

'I'm going to see my bank manager tomorrow' might suggest that the speaker had asked for the appointment while the use of the present continuous suggests simply that an arrangement has been made.

2 Present simple

> eg We arrive in Lisbon at 10.00 am.
> When do you break up for the summer holidays?

Indicates the *certain future*, based on the evidence of a fixed timetable or programme. The meaning is the same as 'due to'.

3 Present simple and present perfect after time links

> eg Destroy the document *as soon as* you've read it.
> *Once* you've tasted real champagne you'll never be satisfied with the imitation stuff.
> Give me a ring *as soon as* you get home.

The present simple or present perfect, rather than the future or future perfect, are used after the following time links:

after	as soon as	while
before	once	until
when	by the time	as

4 Is to/are to

> eg You're to go and see the Director at once!

Expresses an *instruction* or *order*.

Exercise Put the verbs in brackets into the correct tense to express the future:

a He (see) the news in the paper before he (get) your letter.

b You (report) to the police station once a week until your case (come up) in court.

c I (drive) to Heathrow tomorrow to try and film the President as he (step off) the plane.

d I (give) you my considered opinion just as soon as I (have) time to read through all the information.

e Tell the children they (not/go) outside to play till they (tidy) their room.

f We (do) the worst part of the journey once we (get) through London.

g The train (arrive) in Bristol at 11.00 and as my boyfriend (meet) me at the station, I (not/need) a taxi.

h You (do) anything special this weekend?
Well, my mother (come) on Saturday and after she (leave), I (try) to get some gardening done.

▶ Focus on writing · Discussion

The Charter of the British Broadcasting Corporation defines the role of broadcasting as providing 'information, education and entertainment'. Which of these elements is the most important in broadcasting? (*About 350 words*)

Notes 1 What areas do the three headings include/exclude? For example, does information include the weather forecast and theatre reviews as well as pure news?

2 Is there a clear dividing line between the categories? Where do they overlap?

3 What other considerations are there? eg quality.

LANGUAGE CHECK
Just

eg *Randolph Hearst . . . announced to the staff that he intended to 'startle, amaze and stupefy the world'. He then proceeded to do* **just** *that.* (Text 1)

Just is used in a wide variety of ways in English. Here is a list of its main meanings. (The definitions and examples below are taken from the *Collins COBUILD English Language Dictionary*.)

a recently/a short time ago	*f simply*
b soon	*g exactly*
c at the same time	*h easily*
d only	*i roughly*
e barely (nearly not)	*j fair/reasonable*

Decide what **just** means in the examples below.

1 That's just what I wanted to hear!
2 Stop feeling obliged to do things just because others expect them from you.
3 Let us be cautious in our actions, cautious but just.
4 I'm just coming . . .
5 The heat was just bearable.
6 She had only just moved in.
7 She was just about his age.
8 There's just no reason for him to be here.
9 The telephone rang just as I was about to serve up the dinner.
10 What a wonderful description. I can just smell the sea air . . .

▶ Focus on register

Britain's newspapers divide broadly into the quality press (*The Times, Daily Telegraph, Guardian, Independent, Financial Times*) and the popular press (*Daily Mirror, Sun, Star, Daily Express* etc). The treatment of news items can differ considerably in the two types of papers, particularly in emphasis. The style of headlines too, is often markedly different.

Popular headlines frequently use slang and punning references to an article's content while quality newspapers tend to provide more information in their headlines. Both types of newspaper, however, use common jargon words to save space (BID = attempt, BLAST = explosion, QUIT = leave or resign etc.).

1 The 10 headlines below refer to five news items. Work with a partner to find five pairs of headlines.

2 Discuss with your partner what the story behind the headlines might be.

3 Compare your ideas with other pairs of students.

4 Which words in the headlines enabled you to identify the subject?

5 Can you guess the meaning of any words which you are not familiar with?

(a) **'Shoplift slur' on Doris, 72**

(b) Locked up for taking lad's ball

(c) Fined for refusing car patient

(d) **ALL-OUT STRIKE**

(e) **Day the jailbirds came out in sympathy**

(f) 'Lazy' doc gets a rap

(g) **BEV HITS ROOF AT NO-GIRLS JOB BAN**

(h) Woman wins sex bias case

(i) *Pensioner is arrested in ball-back row*

(j) **Shop sued over Christmas card arrest**

Now read the articles on page 147 and 148 and try to decide which headline applies to which article. Then answer the questions which follow the articles.

A   The quality press

1A

POLICE appealed to Belgians yesterday to remove all garments from clothes lines to frustrate 31 criminals who escaped from prison in normal striped attire during a strike by warders.

Since it has been raining virtually non-stop in Belgium for the past several days, the escapees would probably have found clothes lines empty anyway. Recapturing them, however, was still not proving an easy matter.

Originally 38 men, some convicted of armed robbery, broke out of Tournai jail during Friday night, crawled through a tunnel, then scaled the prison wall with ropes. Seven were picked up yesterday by police. Helicopters and fast cars were searching for the rest, many of whom were thought to have made a dash for the French border.

The warders' strike was part of a national stoppage by public service workers which also slowed down Belgium's rail, air and travel ferry services. The strike is in protest against the government's austerity measures.

When the prison warders downed keys, the jail was manned by inexperienced policemen. It is still unclear how the prisoners managed to open their cell doors, or why two hours elapsed before the break-out was noticed. Soon after the escape, the striking warders went back to work.

The strike-bound nation's spirits soared as reports of the escape and news of the police chase was broadcast throughout the day. Finding the missing men was hampered by having to scrutinise the large number of people trying to thumb lifts because of the absence of public transport.

2A

A young woman's hopes of a career with an estate agents crumbled because they believed highly paid clients would only deal with men, an industrial tribunal in Manchester was told yesterday.

Beverley Jackson, aged 19, of Heaton Norris, Stockport, applied for an advertised vacancy as assistant to Mr Nicholas Rowcliffe, a partner of J. R. Bridgford and Sons, at the branch in the village of Prestbury, Cheshire.

Mr Rowcliffe replied: 'I thank you for your letter but I feel the position more suits a male applicant but I will keep your name on file, and thank you for replying.'

Miss Jackson, who has eight O levels, three A levels and has started a business studies course, told the tribunal the letter made her feel like a second class citizen.

Mr Rowcliffe said Prestbury had a strong concentration of men from the 'higher echelons of business and professional life' such as managing directors, airline pilots and barristers, who would not deal with women.

The job involved dealing with house sales of up to £300,000. 'It would be impractical from both the firm and clients' point of view to employ a woman assistant.

'It stems from the type of village and the type of people who live there. Many of them insist on talking to men on certain matters like finance and will not take advice from women. This is nothing to do with me; it is the clients.'

Miss Jackson's solicitor, Mr Jack Thornley, told the tribunal: 'I am not sure whether this is an insult to the people of Prestbury or whether Mr Rowcliffe is living in the Dark Ages.'

Miss Jackson said later: 'It was a matter of principle.'

3A

A pensioner was arrested and held in a cell for an hour after she refused to return a football kicked into her garden by a neighbour's son.

Mrs Sheila Jackson, 62, who has spent hundreds of pounds on her garden and opens it twice a year to the public to raise money for charity, was questioned about the alleged theft of the ball before being bailed.

She said yesterday that police accused her of wasting their time because she refused to accept a caution.

4A

A DOCTOR has been fined £200 for refusing to leave his surgery to see a sick patient, aged 67, who was too ill to leave his car and walk to the surgery.

A passer-by came to the assistance of the man and alerted the health centre receptionist. However, the doctor said that the patient should drive home where he would be visited after surgery.

The passer-by persisted, only to be told that the doctor could not make an examination in the street because of the noise from the traffic. Eventually the doctor asked the receptionist to order an ambulance for the sick man.

The Avon Family Practitioner Committee decided that the doctor, based at an Avon Health Centre, had offered no reasonable excuse for not seeing the sick man.

A spokesman said: 'Although the committee recognised that the doctor was holding a surgery and might have been unwilling to interrupt it, they felt he misjudged the situation and should have acted with more concern'.

5A

An elderly woman yesterday sued a department store which wrongly accused her of stealing a Christmas card.

Miss Doris White, aged 72, of Hampden Street, York, is claiming £3,000 damages from the family firm of W P Brown for alleged false imprisonment and wrongful arrest.

Her counsel, Mr Paul White, told the York County Court jury that Miss White was of impeccable character.

Miss White visited the store in Davygate, York, while Christmas shopping in December but did not buy anything. She was followed through the city by a store manager, who had been told that a customer saw her take a card and put it in her shopping bag.

He stopped her at a local newspaper office as she browsed through back issues.

Miss White said: 'This man – a total stranger – just snatched my bag while asking if he could look in it.'

She was taken back to the store and sat in a cubicle in full view of shoppers for 20 minutes, with an assistant on guard, until police arrived.

At the police station she was body-searched and nothing was found.

Her counsel said the company sent a 'veiled apology' but they persisted in the suggestion that she may have been stealing, he said.

The hearing continues today.

B The popular press

1B

WHILE warders were on strike, thirty-seven prisoners escaped from a Brussels jail, Belgian police said yesterday.

2B

BEVERLEY JACKSON had all the qualifications for a career with a top people's estate agents – except one. She wasn't a man.

The pretty 19-year-old's hopes crumbled when she was told only men could sell homes to stockbroker belt buyers.

But yesterday Beverley struck a blow for women's lib when an industrial tribunal awarded her £600 damages and costs against the estate agents.

Applied

The Manchester tribunal heard that Beverley, of Green Lane, Heaton Norris, Stockport, left school a year ago with eight O levels and three A levels.

She applied to the estate agents, J. H. Bridgford, for a job as a junior assistant.

A partner in the firm, Mr. Nicholas Rowcliffe, told her in a two-line letter: 'Sorry, we want a man.'

'I was livid,' said Beverley, who took her case to the Equal Opportunities Commission.

Mr. Rowcliffe, who runs Bridgford's office in Prestbury, Cheshire, where the average price of a house is £70,000, told the tribunal that executives and managing directors who live there would not deal with a woman.

'Prestbury is a unique village,' he said. 'I find my clients insist on taking advice from a man.

'They are living in quality houses and expect quality treatment. They are from the higher echelons and they just won't deal with women.'

Mr. Jack Thornley, for Beverley, asked the tribunal: 'Is there something in the water in Prestbury that makes people difficult and demanding?

'It seems a place of male chauvinists, and female chauvinists as well.'

3B

ANGRY NEIGHBOUR Sheila Jackson got locked up for theft – when she wouldn't give a little lad his ball back.

The law stepped in after a three-year vendetta between pensioner Sheila and the young family next door.

She said yesterday: 'About 40 balls have come over the fence in that time and I never give them back.

'The fence gets damaged and plants ruined. I love my garden and have spent hundreds on making it nice.

Horrible

'This was the first time they have actually asked for their ball back and when I said no they fetched a policeman.'

She was taken to the police station and spent an hour in the cells on suspicion of theft before being given a warning.

Helen Booth, 27, her neighbour in Codnor, Derbyshire said: 'My five-year-old son Anthony was in tears saying Mrs Jackson had been horrible to him.

'I was so mad that she could be so obnoxious to a little child that I phoned the police.

'But I can't believe it has gone this far, it's really petty.'

4B

A DOCTOR who refused to leave his surgery to see a seriously ill man in a car outside has been fined £200.

A secret health watchdog hearing said the unnamed doctor, based at an Avon health centre, gave no reasonable excuse for not seeing the 67-year-old man.

The doctor said he could not use a stethoscope because of traffic noise.

Headlines Remember that headlines don't *always* give an accurate indication of the content of an article. They may exaggerate the facts or provide a witty comment.

Now complete these statements by choosing the answer which you think fits best.

1 Headline (e) suggests that prisoners

    a were extremely co-operative.
    b planned an escape from jail.
    c supported a strike.
    d were released from jail.

2 Headline (g) suggests that a particular prohibition made a girl extremely

    a shocked.
    b embarrassed.
    c disappointed.
    d angry.

3 Headline (f) suggests that the doctor has been

  a criticised.
  b sued.
  c fined.
  d dismissed.

4 Headline (a) suggests that an accusation of shop-lifting has

  a made an elderly woman furious.
  b made an elderly woman confused.
  c damaged an elderly woman's reputation.
  d damaged an elderly woman's health.

Articles **5** In Extract 1A, we learn that public service workers are on strike because of

  a economic restrictions.
  b prison conditions.
  c low pay.
  d lack of promotion.

6 According to Extract 2A, Miss Jackson was considered unsuitable for the job because

  a she wasn't well-qualified enough.
  b she wasn't used to dealing with large sums of money.
  c she wouldn't be acceptable to the firm's clients.
  d she came from a working-class background.

7 According to Extract 3A, the police found Mrs Jackson

  a repentant.
  b uncooperative.
  c distressed.
  d shocked.

8 According to Extract 4A, the doctor was fined because

  a he had offered no excuse for his action.
  b his defence was unsatisfactory.
  c he was considered to have been lazy.
  d his diagnosis had been incorrect.

9 According to Extract 5A, Miss White's bag was taken from her as she was

  a walking along the street.
  b paying her newspaper bill.
  c looking round another store.
  d looking through old newspapers.

10 According to Mrs Booth in Extract 3B, she contacted the police because her neighbour

  a had stolen her son's ball.
  b had spoilt her son's game.
  c had upset her son.
  d had been offensive to her.

Comparing the different treatments **1** How much additional information do we gain by reading Extract 1A after 1B? Is this information worth having, in your opinion?

2 Extract 1A is slightly shorter than the original article while Extract 1B is complete. What does this suggest about attitudes to foreign news in the two sorts of newspapers?

3 Can you detect any difference in sympathy for the two parties in Extracts 3A and 3B and their headlines? If so, how does this come across?

4 What information present in Extract 4A is missing from Extract 4B? How much does this information strengthen the case against the doctor?

149

▶ Vocabulary practice

Review   Choose the word or phrase that best completes each sentence.

1 Why don't you have a night out? It would take your .... off your worries.

A thoughts   B heart   C head   D mind

2 I can't think why the police have detained him. There isn't a .... of evidence against him.

A speck   B scrap   C drop   D thread

3 As a .... prime minister, his views are treated with respect when he is interviewed.

A prior   B previous   C late   D former

4 He's an exceptionally .... violinist and has won several prizes in international competitions.

A gifted   B artful   C ingenious   D competent

5 You'd better pack those glasses extremely carefully if you want them to arrive ....

A entire   B intact   C whole   D complete

6 He realised that his fondness for her was turning into a foolish ....

A fascination   B infection   C infatuation   D affliction

7 Oh, it's you! You really .... me, jumping out of the shadows like that.

A struck   B amazed   C impressed   D startled

8 She was attracted by the .... of fashion modelling as a job and hadn't realised what hard work it was.

A charm   B splendour   C glamour   D grace

9 'A special feature of the room is the huge picture window which .... a splendid view of the Quantock hills.'

A allows   B affords   C enables   D presents

10 His jokes seemed to .... very well with his audience, if their laughter was any indication.

A go off   B go down   C go along   D go by

11 In an effort to increase his newspaper's ...., the editor introduced a weekly competition.

A propagation   B distribution   C circulation   D dispersion

12 He was .... a mile of the hotel when he ran out of petrol.

A within   B inside   C only   D hardly

13 The stuntman seemed to show a total disregard .... fear as he performed his daredevil tricks.

A of   B over   C for   D about

14 I did think of giving up my acting career at one time but the .... of the stage was too great.

A desire   B pressure   C love   D lure

15 She used her weekly column in the local newspaper as a .... for her political views.

A vehicle   B means   C vessel   D passage

16 What's done is done. It's .... wondering if you could have prevented it.

A helpless   B valueless   C futile   D antiquated

17 Having been a foreign correspondent all his working life, he's a .... traveller.

A veteran   B vintage   C customary   D antiquated

18 Police have .... to the public to come forward with any information which might help them in their enquiries.

A urged   B claimed   C appealed   D called

19 I think my fear of spiders must .... from a horror film which I saw as a child.

A lead   B rise   C start   D stem

20 If you'd like to take a seat in the waiting room till the doctor can see you, you'll find plenty of magazines to ....

A refer to   B browse through   C look over   D stare at

21 We decided to .... the coastguard when we realised that the yacht was several hours late in arriving.

A alert   B alarm   C arouse   D caution

22 The newspaper was ordered to pay him £1,500 .... for printing the libellous story about him.

A damages   B refund   C penalty   D restitution

23 My hopes of becoming a lawyer .... when I failed my 'A' levels.

A cracked   B crumbled   C crashed   D smashed

24 I should like to point out that two months have .... since you promised to come and repair my washing machine.

A expired   B lapsed   C transpired   D elapsed

25 Since we had only one day left, we decided to make an .... effort to finish the run in record time.

A all-in   B all-out   C overall   D all-round

Phrasal verbs: PUT

2 Match the following phrasal verbs with their meanings:

1	put about	*a*	discourage
2	put across	*b*	provide accommodation
3	put down to	*c*	postpone
4	put forward	*d*	tolerate
5	put off	*e*	pretend
6	put off	*f*	suggest
7	put on	*g*	communicate
8	put out	*h*	circulate information
9	put up	*i*	inconvenience
10	put up with	*j*	attribute to

Check your answers by looking at page 199.

Now choose the appropriate phrasal verb to complete the following sentences:

1 Don't let me .... you .... going to see it. I mean, the film does have its good points.

2 At the meeting someone .... the idea that there should be a student representative on the committee.

3 He did seem a bit short-tempered, I agree. I .... it .... to overwork.

4 I'm just not prepared to .... your inefficiency any longer. You're fired!

5 Thank you. I'd love to stay to dinner, as long as it won't .... you .... at all.

6 We'll just have to .... the meeting .... until everyone's back from holiday.

7 The part of the course I enjoyed least was philosophy. It wasn't .... very well by the lecturer.

8 If my sister can .... me .... it'll save the cost of a hotel room for the night.

9 She .... it .... that she was thinking of leaving the company and, as a result, she received several offers from rival organisations.

10 He didn't really hurt his leg, you know. He limped a bit, but he was only .... it .... to get our sympathy.

▶ Grammar practice

1 Fill each of the numbered blanks in the passage with one suitable word.

Publications that come out at regular .... (1) of more than one day are known .... (2) periodicals. The majority of periodicals .... (3) to press between a week and six weeks before publication and they are therefore .... (4) to print topical news stories and articles in a way that a book .... (5). This is one advantage that the periodical has .... (6) the book. .... (7) advantages are that periodicals are cheaper, they are easier to read, and their .... (8) is more varied.

Periodicals .... (9) from newspapers because they do not concentrate upon .... (10) the reader a summary of the immediate news. There are also physical .... (11). Most periodicals are .... (12) on better paper, they are smaller and are stapled or stitched .... (13) so that they last longer. The line between newspapers and periodicals is not clearly .... (14), however, because some weeklies that appear in newspaper .... (15) are really periodicals.

Great differences .... (16) between the various types of periodicals. They .... (17) for a wide variety of tastes and may be .... (18) with anything from the technical aspects of frying fish and chips to trends .... (19) present-day African literature. They .... (20) magazines of all types, trade and technical journals, reviews, children's magazines and comics.

from 'The Mass Media' by R. B. Heath

2 Finish each of the following sentences in such a way that it is as similar as possible in meaning to the original sentence. Use the words in italics which must *not* be altered in any way.

EXAMPLE: She stopped asking for advice.
gave

ANSWER: She gave up asking for advice.

a He is said to be a very hard bargainer.
reputation

b As I intended to expand my shop, I made an offer for the premises next door.
view

c Both children and adults will enjoy this game.
alike

d The prisoner was recaptured as he rushed towards the gate.
dash

e This particular wine is regarded as one of the finest in the world.
considered

f Since the company's methods were exposed in a newspaper, people have lost their good opinion of it.
disrepute

g What really depresses me is this continual wet weather.
gets

h We missed the bus because we had overslept.
consequence

i She passed the word around that she was looking for a flat.
known

j They continued to suggest that I was lying.
persisted

UNIT 9 Science and Technology

▶ Lead-in

1 Work with a partner to discuss the inventions below and decide:

a which *two* you think were the most important;

b which *one* is the least important.

1 Rover safety bicycle, 1885

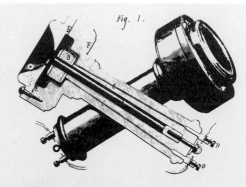

2 Bell's telephone, 1877

3 Edison's carbon-filament lamp, 1881

4 Daguerreotype outfit, 1847

5 First Lanchester car (converted to wheel-steering), 1896

6 Stephenson's *Rocket*, 1829

7 Bleriot landing at Dover after the first crossing of the English Channel, 1909

2 Consider those inventions which members of the class thought least important. If they hadn't been produced, what effect would that have on our lives today?

The inventions below were somewhat less influential than those on the previous page! Work with a partner to:

   a describe the appearance of the invention;

   b discuss what the invention is intended for.

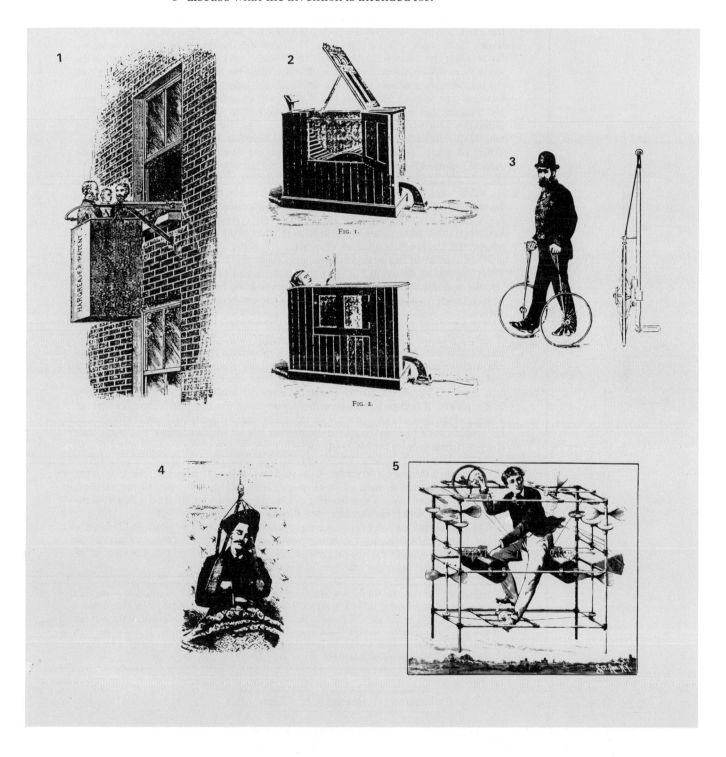

On the following page are headlines and extracts from the articles which originally announced the new inventions above.

Match the pictures to the appropriate headline and text.

A **A New Aerial Machine.**
B **Hargreaves' Patent Window Fire Escape Apparatus.**
C **Sitting while Asleep.**
D **The 'Sultan' Domestic Turkish Bath.**
E **New Method of Locomotion**

1 The action of propelling is that of skating on ice, and any forward figure that can be done on ice can be accomplished with ease by these machines. Each wheel is independent of the other, and backward travel is prevented by a mechanical action. An idea how to learn to ride them is given in the engraving. The balance is the first movement to be learnt. By pressing the thumbs on the brakes the wheels become fixed, by which means the learner can walk on them the same as on stilts. When the balance of walking is acquired, the learner may gradually let go the brake on one side for the wheel to move a little forward, then fix the brake on the wheel advanced, let go the brake on the opposite side, and advance that wheel a little in front of the other, always, however, taking care to brake the front wheel before advancing the hind one. By this means the action of the wheels moving under you is acquired, but it is advisable to go slowly to work at first. When the balance is lost it is best to jump off the machines and commence again, as the rider is not fixed in any way on the machine.

2 As will be seen from our engraving Fig. 1, which shows the bath open, it consists of a rectangular cabinet, very stylishly got up, about 5ft long by 2ft wide, with a door in front, and a hinged lid at the top. The inside has a very comfortably shaped couch made of hardwood laths, with spaces between so as to allow of the free circulation of the hot air; underneath the couch is a hot-air chamber.

When the bather has seated himself upon the couch he can then close the door and lower the lid, as shown in Fig. 2, which is shaped to fit the neck, and has also two circular apertures with sliding doors for regulating the heat, and also for passing the arms through, so as to read or smoke, etc., while enjoying the pleasures of the Turkish bath.

3 A very ingenious invention comes from Germany, which enables the user to rest as comfortably and safely as if lying on a bed, as it provides a rest for head, neck back, and elbow at the same time. The invention will be readily understood from our illustration, and it is claimed for it that the appliance is especially useful in the case of travelling for long distances by rail. It is also easily packed away in a small parcel, which can be carried in the pocket. It is claimed that by using the invention the traveller will hardly feel the shaking of the railway carriage while he can at any time by means of a single turn change his position as he likes by leaning to the right or left, or sitting straight, but in any case there is a firm support for his head.

4 A construction measuring 4ft by 3ft, supported by four legs 4ft in height, will give us the required space, and if made of steel quarter-inch tubing, will have all the strength needed. The rider sits in a seat like that of a bicycle, suspended by steel wires from the top frame, with which his shoulders are roughly about on a level.

The four horizontal propellers have their bearing on the vertical posts just below the upper frame, thus bringing the lifting power as far above the centre of gravity as possible. The vertically moving propeller revolves on a shaft behind the shoulders of the rider, midway between the side bars of the top frame.

5 Fixed under the window on the top floor, or on a lower floor if preferred, the apparatus is covered by a dressing table top which entirely hides it from view. It is thus always ready for use. On an alarm of fire the table top is removed and the apparatus thrown out of the window ready for action. That operation is exceedingly simple, and if done with alacrity takes about eight seconds. If using a large size apparatus two adults or three children can be lowered at one time.

Picture	Headline	Text
1		
2		
3		
4		
5		

Now answer these questions in your own words:

1 What design feature of the Turkish bath allows the bather to read a book?

2 How is the fire escape apparatus stored when not in use?

3 What means is used to raise the 'aerial machine'?

4 What is the German invention intended to prevent?

5 Why is it necessary to learn to balance when using the 'new method of locomotion'?

6 Why is it important to apply the brake on the front wheel before bringing the rear one forward?

▶Text 1 ·
Does technological progress work backwards?

Read the following text and see if you can sum up the writer's argument in one sentence.

The bath was invented before the bath plug. The bath plug could not have been invented before the bath, except as a small object with which to play ice hockey. The order in which inventions are made is very important, much more important than has ever been realised, because we tend automatically to think that later
5 inventions are better than earlier ones. A moment's thought will show this is not so. If, for example, a solution to today's urban traffic problems was proposed in the shape of a small man-powered two-wheeled vehicle which would make the motor car look like a cumbersome over-powered device, a space rocket trying to tackle suburban problems, we would greet it as a great technological break-
10 through. 'Bicycle makes car obsolete!' we would cry. Unfortunately, the bike came first, so we shall always unconsciously see it as a cruder version of the car.

Other things which may have been invented too early are the airship, the radio, the railway train, the piano-roll player and the cuff-link.

Consider also the zip. Zips represent a technological advance on buttons, being
15 faster and more complete. They are also more liable to come adrift, break, jam, malfunction, stick and catch. Buttons can only go wrong if the thread is faulty. Even then, buttons can be mended by the user. Zips rarely can.

from an article by Miles Kington in Vole

Now complete these statements by choosing the answer which you think fits best.

1 If the bicycle were to be invented now, the car would appear

    a unsuitable for its purpose.
    b in advance of its time.
    c unnecessarily expensive.
    d too fast for safety.

2 The airship and the radio are examples of things which

    a were not fully appreciated at the time of their invention.
    b are more suitable for use now than when they were invented.
    c have been neglected in favour of more recent inventions.
    d are less suited to their purpose than earlier inventions.

3 According to the writer, buttons are preferable to zips because they

    a are more convenient.
    b are more reliable.
    c cost less to replace.
    d are safer to use.

▶ Text 2 · Spanner in the robot's works

Read the following article about industrial robots and then decide *what aspect* of the subject is dealt with in each paragraph. For example, the first paragraph deals with the *origin* of the machines.

The contemporary industrial robot, in the eyes of politicians and others, may wear the halo of high technology, but it came into being to meet a rather mundane need. 5 In the booming labour market of the early 1960s it became increasingly difficult to find people willing to do boring, repetitive and unpleasant jobs. What was needed was not a machine which could master elabor- 10 ate human skills, but one which could provide the mindless manpower demanded by mass production.

What had to be learnt, and proved well within the robot's capacity, were se- 15 quences of precise movement of the arm and hand. Such sequences were relatively easily programmed into a computer memory, especially after the advent of the microprocessor freed robots from their 20 dependence on the giant mainframe computers of the 1960s. But however impressive, even uncanny, a robot may appear to the layman as it repeats a series of movements with flawless precision, it is 25 in fact operating blindly and by rote.

Repetitive manipulation is, of course, a skill common to many machines: what differentiates the robot is that it makes use of an articulated arm analogous to the 30 human limb and that it can be reprogrammed to perform a whole variety of tasks without the need to redesign or adjust its mechanical components. There are, however, a limited range of applications in 35 which a manipulator arm, operating blindly and without intelligence, is useful.

Whatever its task, a robot is dependent for its effectiveness upon a whole supporting cast of automated machines. Every- 40 thing must be presented to it in consistent positions and orientations; it can only operate in a world of guaranteed predictability. The need to provide an automated environment has so far restricted robot use

45 to large scale industry; businesses such as specialist machine shops, producing small batches of many different items, have little incentive to set up the paraphernalia of conveyors, jigs and electronic communica- 50 tion which a robot requires.

Those who leap to the conclusion that the provision of more and more robots is a guaranteed elixir of industrial health should also be aware that there is a sub- 55 stantial body of opinion which argues that, rather than being the universal worker of the future, the robot is no more than a stop-gap expedient forced upon us by the limitations of insufficient and inadequate 60 automation. Automation, the argument goes, achieves its really spectacular successes when it abandons the attempt to do things in ways based on human skills and finds solutions that are quite novel and 65 intrinsically mechanical. Replacing wire circuits, which are fiddly for human beings and virtually impossible for machines to assemble, with printed circuits which machines can manufacture with ease is an 70 obvious example. The need for robots arises, it is suggested, only because imperfect automation has left a number of gaps in the industrial scheme of things which require the particular skills of the human –

75 or robot – hand. But this is a temporary state of affairs which will be remedied when a new generation of automated equipment dispenses totally with anthropomorphic methods.

80 Against this view are those who argue that the robot has the potential to climb the ladder of skills and intelligence so rapidly that it will outpace any conceivable advances in automation. Moreover, it is 85 claimed, the arguments in favour of 'hard' automation ignore economic realities. Industry will not be able to afford the kind of investment that is required to install complex, special-purpose machines, with all 90 the attendant risks of premature obsolescence if products or methods suddenly change.

The robot offers a sensible half-way house; it provides an economic (and rela- 95 tively reliable) substitute for human labour while also having a degree of flexibility that is attractive. What has yet to be established is that robots have it in them to advance from the status of blind, preprogrammed 100 serfs to that of a skilled and adaptive labour force, capable of learning new tricks and acting on their own initiative without the need for human tutelage at every stage.

from an article by Piers Burnett in The Times

Look at paragraphs 1–4 and find words or phrases which mean the same as:

a was designed (1) ....
b ordinary (1) ....
c flourishing (1) ....
d arrival/appearance (2) ....
e mysterious (2) ....
f non-expert (noun) (2) ....
g faultless (2) ....
h from memory (2) ....
i connected by joints (3) ....
j similar (3) ....
k parts (3) ....
l quantities (4) ....
m encouragement (4) ....
n complicated arrangement (4) ....

Now complete these statements by choosing the answer which you think fits best.

1 This article makes it clear that, contrary to popular opinion, robots

  a were designed to replace human labour.
  b have been in use for many years.
  c have fairly limited skills.
  d cannot be classed as high technology.

2 After the 1960s, robots became more

  a convenient to use.
  b accurate in operation.
  c widely used.
  d consistently reliable.

3   Robots differ from other machines in that

   a they react like human beings.
   b they need little maintenance.
   c they have a limited number of applications.
   d they are easy to switch from task to task.

4   Robots are not suitable for use in specialist machine shops because they

   a involve a substantial investment in equipment.
   b are not designed to produce small items.
   c take up too much floor space.
   d take too long to install.

5   Those who doubt the robot's future see it as merely

   a a money-saving measure.
   b a short-term necessity.
   c an amusing curiosity.
   d a passing fashion.

6   Printed circuits are an example of a development which

   a will soon be replaced by more advanced processes.
   b is especially suited to robot production.
   c does not follow traditional production methods.
   d still has several areas for improvement.

7   Those who defend robots argue that

   a they will develop at the same rate as automation.
   b they will reduce the level of unemployment.
   c they are a more practical solution than automation.
   d they have more intelligence than we realise.

▶ Focus on writing 1

> Imagine that you are a social historian living 100 years from now. Write an article for a popular magazine describing what everyday life was like in the distant 1990s. (*About 350 words*)

Notes

1   The topic calls for an imaginative perspective on contemporary life. That perspective may come from a society which is technologically more sophisticated than ours or from one that is not.

2   Reference to features of your twenty-first century society (which of course your readers are more than familiar with) will help maintain the necessary perspective.

3   The viewpoint of the writer should be clear. Do you regard the lifestyle of the twentieth century citizen with amused scorn, with pity or with envy, for example? Do you see it as quaint, nostalgic, admirable, primitive or funny? You may well find that different aspects of life prompt different reactions, of course.

4   Consider the possible approaches. Specific illustrations often help to bring life to an account. 'A typical housewife' might be used as an example or perhaps better still, a particular housewife whose diary has been preserved. Documentary evidence would be normal in an article of this kind. What other types of documentary could there be and what light would it throw on our society?

5   Don't forget to use your introduction and conclusion to frame your account.

▶Text 3 · The price of progress

I was listening sleepily to that ingenious contraption, my digital clock radio, the other morning, when I half-heard one of those items that infects your day. It was about a new invention. A genius has decided that we wait too
5 long at supermarket check-outs, and so he has developed a considerate computer to let the brain take the strain. It all involves weighing, and tearing off special little tags from each item you buy, and feeding them into a machine and weighing again.
10 Now I can recall a time when there were a few long queues in supermarkets, because the companies ploughed their profits into employing *two* people at each check-out: one to ring up and the other to help you speedily pack. Remember? It was also when every garage
15 was staffed by friendly men who filled the car up, checked the oil and even did the tyres, before an infernal machine encased a solitary soul in glass by the till, reading off the digits and charging you accordingly. It meant jobs for them; and for you . . . *people* who had the
20 time to be jolly, grouchy, helpful or saucy.

Maybe you believe in that sort of progress. But I would like to smash the dreadful machines. I simply cannot understand why otherwise intelligent humans have gone computer-mad. It starts early: teachers despair of time-
25 telling when all the kids sport hideous digital watches that peep, play tunes, start and stop, even show firework displays, but instil no sense of the hands moving majestically round a clock face. No more 'Happy Families'; computer toys bark at them in Americanese
30 and cost a fortune in batteries. Instead of learning mental arithmetic they grow up thinking that calculators are their right.

As adults, they drivel on about Space Invaders, and learn a dead vocabulary that owes nothing to Shakespeare
35 or Milton. Boring, mindless, boring. As for thinking, our computers will do it for us.

Computers breed laziness and discontent. A couple came to my house and gazed in disbelief at the battered old Olympia on which I'm typing this. 'Gosh, we'd have
40 thought you would have a word processor by now.' I go to a library and see my beloved dusty manuscripts and old newspaper cuttings replaced by gleaming terminals, so you cannot actually handle the stuff. Then I hear from a friend that he is actually contemplating spending money
45 on a cosy 'home computer', so that all the little details of his life can be stored in its nasty cold brain. As for organising, our computers will do it for us.

All the science fiction fantasies of computers taking over the world, or being used to plot some devious
50 overthrow of government are not far from the truth I see all around me. Myths are rooted in a need to explain to ourselves the workings of the universe, and of human nature. That modern myth foretells the insidious corruption of man by his own dinky[1] little invention.
55 The computer generation (God help them) assumes that it is *better* to calculate, buy petrol, tell the time, work out your holiday plans, pay your bills, and even shop, with the aid of a computer. After all, our civilisation is founded, now, on the certainty that we can kill by remote
60 control, and a computer error could unleash Armageddon.[2] The age of the computer is the age of dehumanisation. Significantly in my old (c. 1969) Oxford dictionary the word does not exist except as a subheading – a *person* who computes or calculates. Now the person has gone.
65 As for feeling, our computers won't do that for us.

from an article by Bel Mooney in the Sunday Times

Notes [1]dinky = small and charming   [2]Armageddon = final battle marking the end of the world

1   Explain the phrase 'ingenious contraption' (line 1).
2   What does the writer mean by an item 'that infects your day' (line 3)?
3   How effective does the writer seem to think the new invention will be, and why?
4   What is wrong with the service which the writer receives at garages these days?
5   What does 'It' in line 18 refer to?
6   Explain in other words why teachers disapprove of digital watches.
7   What might 'Happy Families' have been?
8   Why does the writer think that the new vocabulary, learnt by adults, is 'dead'?
9   In what way do computers 'breed laziness and discontent'?
10 What are the 'gleaming terminals' at the library?
11 Explain 'to plot some devious overthrow of government' (lines 49–50).
12 Explain the phrase 'rooted in' (line 51).
13 What is 'that modern myth' (line 53)?
14 Why does the writer see the dictionary definition of a computer as significant?
15 Summarise in 50–100 words the writer's complaints about computers. (See STUDY BOX – Summary Writing on page 127.)

LANGUAGE CHECK

Dependent Prepositions 6: Preposition + Noun

Here is a list of 16 words or phrases, some of which have been used in texts in this unit. Write in the preposition which precedes them.

Check your answers with your teacher or in the dictionary so that you have an accurate reference list for the future.

.... the basis of/that	.... one's own
.... business	.... other words
.... chance	.... pressure
.... control of (2 possibilities)	.... possession
	.... present
.... all costs	.... purpose
.... debt	.... use (= being
.... fire	used)
.... the one hand	.... the whole

---

▶ Focus on grammar · Modal verbs 2

For general comments on modal verbs see *Focus on grammar Unit 4, pages 62 and 63*.

Ability   Look at these examples from Texts 1 and 2:

The bath plug *could not have been* invented before the bath.

it *can* only operate in a world of guaranteed predictability

Industry *will not be able* to afford ...

Can, could and *be able to* express mental or physical ability.

Present – *can* is more commonly used than *be able to*. The latter tends to suggest particular difficulty:

eg How many languages can you speak?

Are you able to concentrate on your work when the children are at home?

How often are you able to get home on leave?

Past   – in affirmative sentences, there is a distinction between the use of *could* and *was/were able to*.

Could is only used to express general ability:

> eg Whenever you passed their house you could hear them arguing!

> I could never find a taxi when I wanted one.

For specific instances of ability, *was/were able* is used:

> eg Were you able to find a taxi?
> (Note: *did you manage to* would also be possible.)

In negative sentences, *couldn't* can be used in both general and specific cases of ability. *Wasn't/weren't able to* is also possible and again, often suggests an element of difficulty.

PRESENT, PERFECT and FUTURE – since *can* has no infinitive, these tenses are formed with *be able to*.

COULD + PERFECT INFINITIVE

> eg I *could have been* famous once.

In this case, ability existed but wasn't realised. There may be a conditional element:

> eg I *could have been* famous, if only I'd been given a chance.

Remember also the possibility of a reproach with this form:
(*Focus on grammar Unit 4*)

> eg You *could have opened* the door! You saw that I had my hands full.

Obligation   Look at these examples from Text 2:

> What *had to* be learnt . . . were sequences of precise movements.

> Everything *must* be presented to it in consistent positions . . .

> Those who leap to the conclusion that . . . *should* also be aware . . .

1 MUST

a MUST VS. HAVE TO

Must expresses an 'internal' obligation, one which comes from the speaker.
Have to expresses an 'external' obligation, one which is more remote and impersonal.

Compare the following sentences:

> I must get to the bank today. (I'm short of money)

> I have to see the bank manager this afternoon. (He asked me to call in)

> You must pay your rent a week in advance. (Landlady speaking)

> You have to pay a deposit against breakages. (Accommodation agency explaining particular conditions)

b MUSTN'T VS. DON'T HAVE TO

Mustn't expresses negative obligation:

> eg You really mustn't talk to your father like that!

Don't have to expresses an absence of obligation (compare the use of *needn't* below):

> eg You don't have to have a comprehensive insurance policy for your car (by law) but it's a good idea.

c OTHER TENSES

In the *past*, obligation is expressed by *had to*. Absence of obligation is expressed by *didn't have to* or *didn't need to*. (See NEED on page 164.)

In the *future*, *must* can be used when the obligation already exists:

> eg I must do well in my exams next month.

Will have to is used when the obligation will only occur in the future (usually as a result of a condition):

> eg If I fail my driving test first time, I'll have to take it again.

163

2 NEED

NEED TO expresses a weaker obligation than *must* or *have to*.

It exists both as a modal auxiliary and as an ordinary verb but its use as a modal auxiliary is mainly limited to:

   a Questions in the present tense:

     eg Need you be quite so untidy?

   b Negative sentences in the present tense expressing lack of necessity:

     eg You needn't bother to go to the Post Office. I've got some stamps.

   c Needn't have done (see below).

DIDN'T NEED TO VS. NEEDN'T HAVE

There is a difference in meaning between these two forms. Compare the following sentences:

   a I *didn't need to* hurry because I was in plenty of time.

   b I *needn't have* hurried because the meeting started much later than scheduled.

In the first sentence, it wasn't necessary to hurry and the speaker *didn't* hurry.
In the second sentence, the speaker *did* hurry although he later discovered that it hadn't been necessary.

3 SHOULD/OUGHT TO

Should and *ought to* express obligation, duty or advice. Though they are very similar in meaning and can sometimes be interchangeable, *ought to* tends to carry more weight, suggesting moral obligation rather than mere advisability.

     eg You should always wear protective glasses when you use a sun-ray lamp.

     You really ought to apologise, you know. You were in the wrong.

As with other modal verbs, the past is formed with the perfect infinitive:

     eg I suppose I should have let you know I was coming.

     You oughtn't to have lost your temper like that. It was inexcusable.

Exercise Rewrite the following sentences by replacing the part in blue with the correct form of one of the modal or ordinary verbs in the sections on *Ability* and *Obligation* in this Unit. Make any other changes necessary.

   a I *was supposed to* finish the report by today but now they *will have no choice but to* wait for it.

   b Luckily enough, I *managed to* get hold of some tickets which had been returned to the box office.

   c *We weren't obliged to* wait a long time in the doctor's surgery. The receptionist told us to go straight in.

   d *It was in your power to* do a lot more to help people than you did.

   e *It's important for me* to come to a decision soon. Otherwise I might lose the chance.

   f I miss having a view. In my last house *it was possible to* see for miles on a clear day.

   g If you want to apply for a council improvement grant, *it is compulsory to* fill in Form RYC 44.

   h When *will it be possible for you to* deliver the new computer?

   i *It wasn't necessary to* buy all those provisions. We're only going for a weekend, not a month!

   j *It was thoughtless of you not to give* me a hand with the washing up. After all, it was your friends we had to dinner, not mine!

   k Is it really *necessary for you to* ask my advice about every little matter?

   l *Don't bother to* make out a receipt. I only throw them away.

   m Do you think *it would be advisable for me to* book a seat in advance?

   n Perhaps *it would have been wise to* think of the consequences before you told the boss to drop dead.

▶ Communication activity · The description game

Look at the following description:

> This object is shaped like a very thin cylinder. One end tapers to a sharp point and the other is blunt with an oval hole in it. It's made of metal.

What is it? What is it used for?

Now work with a partner to describe different objects in the same way.

Instructions:

One of you should look at List A on page 199 and the other at List B on page 200. Do not look at each other's lists!

The first student should describe an object from the list as accurately as possible, concentrating on the shape and the relation of one part to another. Do *not* give the size, unless asked, and do *not* say what the object is used for.

The second student should try to draw the object as it is described. You may ask questions to check that you have understood correctly but you must not ask what the object is or what it's for. You should then guess what the object is and, if you're correct, you must describe *clearly* how it's used.

Each correct first answer scores *2* points for the guesser and *1* point for the describer.

Take it in turns to describe and guess.

▶ Focus on listening 1

The world's most valuable mineral

1 Discuss the following questions with a partner. How many can you answer from your general knowledge?

a Why is sodium chloride known as 'common salt'?

b Why has salt been described as 'the world's most valuable mineral'?

c What is the percentage of common salt in sea water?

d How is salt used to prevent road accidents in certain conditions?

e Where is salt still used as a form of money?

f What are the two main forms in which salt is found?

g What are the two largest salt water lakes in the world?

h What is a 'saltern'?

i How is most of the world's salt obtained?

j Why is magnesium carbonate added to table salt?

2 Now listen to a short talk on salt and give the correct answers.

▶ Focus on register

Could this product kill millions?

ICI has announced the discovery of a new fire-fighting agent to add to their existing range. Known as WATER (Wonderful And Total Extinguishing Resource), it augments existing agents such as dry powder and BCF (bromine-chlorine-fluorine) which have been in use from time immemorial. It is particularly suitable for dealing with fires in buildings, timber yards and warehouses. Though required in large quantities, it is fairly cheap to produce and it is intended that quantities of about a million gallons should be stored in urban areas and near other installations of high risk ready for immediate use. BCF and dry powder are usually stored under pressure, but WATER will be stored in open ponds or reservoirs and conveyed to the scene of the fire by hoses and portable pumps.

ICI's new proposals are already encountering strong opposition from safety and environmental groups. Professor Connie Barrinner has pointed out that, if anyone immersed their head in a bucket of WATER, it would prove fatal in as little as three minutes. Each of ICI's proposed reservoirs will contain enough WATER to fill 500,000 two-gallon buckets. Each bucket-full could be used 100 times so there is enough WATER in one reservoir to kill the entire population of the UK. Risks of this size, said Professor Barrinner, should not be allowed, whatever the gain. What use was a fire-fighting agent that could kill men as well as fire?

A local authority spokesman said that he would strongly oppose planning permission for construction of a WATER reservoir in this area unless the most stringent precautions were followed. Open ponds were certainly not acceptable. What would prevent people falling in them? What would prevent the contents from leaking out? At the very least the WATER would need to be contained in a steel pressure vessel surrounded by a leak-proof concrete wall.

A spokesman from the fire brigades said he did not see the need for the new agent. Dry powder and BCF could cope with most fires. The new agent would bring with it risks, particularly to firemen, greater than any possible gain. Did we know what would happen to this new medium when it was exposed to intense heat? It had been reported that WATER was a constituent of beer. Did this mean that firemen would be intoxicated by the fumes?

The Friends of the World say that they had obtained a sample of WATER and found it caused clothes to shrink. If it did this to cotton, what would it do to men?

In the House of Commons yesterday, the Home Secretary was asked if he would prohibit the manufacture and storage of this lethal new material. The Home Secretary replied that, as it was clearly a major hazard, local authorities would have to take advice from the Health & Safety Executive before giving planning permission. A full investigation was needed and the Major Hazards Group would be asked to report.

from an article by Norman Mischler in the Sunday Times

1 This article is probably a light-hearted reaction to

a ICI's announcement of its new product developments.
b the introduction of new chemicals for fire-fighting.
c recent outcries against new industrial products.
d recent reports about a fire at a chemical plant.

2 The new product is intended to

a replace the existing range of agents.
b improve the agents presently in use.
c supplement the agents presently in use.
d be used when other agents are unavailable.

3 Professor Barrinner's argument illustrates how

a statistics are used to confuse people.
b pressure groups try to mislead people.
c academics often distort the facts.
d logic can be carried to absurdity.

4 The local authority spokesman called for

    a thorough investigations.
    b vigorous protest.
    c complex regulations.
    d strict safety measures.

5 The Home Secretary's response was to

    a express concern about the new product.
    b suspend production of the new product.
    c give the development his general approval.
    d deny the need for any action to be taken.

▶ Focus on writing 2

Write a balanced discussion on the following topic:

> 'Computers breed laziness and discontent' (Bel Mooney). How true
> is this of modern technological innovations in general?
> (*About 200 words*)

Notes

1 In what sense can computers be said to 'breed laziness and discontent'? Refer back to Text 3, if necessary, for ideas.

2 What is the counter argument? In what ways have computers improved the quality of our lives, for example? Could they be said to stimulate us rather than make us lazy, in some situations?

3 Can you draw any conclusions from your comments above? Is the use to which the computer is put significant, for example?

4 What other inventions can you think of which are in everyday use? Domestic gadgets and appliances like vacuum cleaners, for example.

5 What are the negative effects of these inventions on the user? Do their benefits compensate?

6 What overall conclusion can you draw in the light of the points that you have made?

STUDY BOX
Phrasal Verbs 6

Look at these examples from this unit:

1 *The computer generation assumes that it is better to . . .* **work out** *your holiday plans . . . with the aid of a computer.* (Text 3)
work out means 'plan or decide' here.

    NB **work out** can also mean:
    a 'calculate' eg *Have you* **worked out** *how much we owe?*
    b 'have a good result' eg *I hope things* **work out** *for you.*

2 *All the science fiction fantasies of computers* **taking over** *the world . . .* (Text 3)
take over means 'assume control over'.

3 *They also use bricks of salt as a single piece or* **broken up** *into smaller sections as a hard currency . . .* (Listening 1)
break up means 'to break into small pieces'.

NB **cut up, chop up, break up, divide up** and **split up** all have this meaning.

▶ Focus on listening 2 · The salterns of Brittany

You are now going to hear a talk about the salterns of Brittany. The talk is in two parts. Before each part, study the questions below so that you will be able to answer them as you listen.

Part 1   **1** The diagram below represents the layout of the saltern system. As you listen to the first part of the talk, write the letters A–G next to the appropriate label below the diagram.

        2 Complete the sentence which follows the diagram.

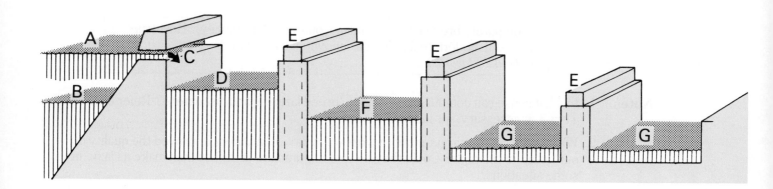

concentration beds	....	level of spring tide	....
lock	....	crystallisation bed	....
storage pond inlet	....	normal high tide	....
storage pond	....		

If the normal salt content of sea water is taken as approximately 3%, the salt content of the brine reaching the crystallisation beds is . . .

Part 2   While listening to the second part of the talk, write the numbers 1–6 by the steps in the production of salt below, to show the order in which they happen. Two of the steps below are not correct. *Cross these two steps out.*

.... cleaning and renovation of salterns

.... removal of water from tops of beds

.... piling of salt between beds

.... smoothing and beating of salt

.... preconcentration period

.... piling of salt on the edges of ponds

.... drainage of water through bottoms of beds

.... harvesting of salt

▶Vocabulary practice

Review   Choose the word or phrase that best completes each sentence.

1 It's only a small flat but it .... my needs perfectly.

   A settles   B meets   C supplies   D fills

2 After working for the Foreign Office, I must admit that ordinary clerical work seems rather ....

   A tasteless   B common   C stale   D mundane

3 My job is so enjoyable and generously paid that I have little .... to look for promotion elsewhere.

   A incitement   B influence   C incentive   D instigation

4 What on earth made you risk your life and .... by driving that fast?

   A limb   B liberty   C death   D health

5 You look so much like someone I knew years ago – it's quite ....

   A unlikely   B uncanny   C unspeakable   D unnatural

6 I think we can .... with the usual formalities since we all know each other already.

   A dispatch   B dispose   C discharge   D dispense

7 He works for a company which makes some of the electrical .... of Concorde.

   A constituents   B ingredients   C components   D elements

8 Tie that suitcase securely onto the roof if you don't want it to .... adrift half way down the motorway!

   A fall   B come   C fly   D get

9 If you wait a moment, there'll be another .... of loaves, fresh from the oven.

   A batch   B collection   C bunch   D bundle

10 Don't .... to any conclusions before you know the full facts.

   A rush   B dive   C leap   D fly

11 He's by no .... unintelligent. He's just lazy!

   A consideration   B way   C means   D degree

12 She's suffering from a .... of iron and needs to take a course of tablets.

   A defect   B deficit   C default   D deficiency

13 The .... of our business is done by mail order.

   A mass   B bulk   C range   D gross

14 Wheat and coffee, like copper and gold, are major trading ....

   A commodities   B articles   C materials   D stocks

15 Once the air warms up, the snow should start to ....

  A dissolve   B defrost   C liquefy   D thaw

16 I've been tracing my family history and I've discovered that one of my .... fought in the battle of Waterloo.

  A predecessors   B descendants   C ancestors   D forerunners

17 He made very little money in the early years as he chose to .... his profits back into the business.

  A plough   B sow   C plant   D dig

18 When he turned up in a .... new sports car, I thought he must have won the football pools!

  A glittering   B glowing   C shimmering   D gleaming

19 I carry all my important documents in a .... old briefcase so as not to attract thieves.

  A hammered   B battered   C trampled   D punched

20 My parents always tried to .... a sense of integrity into me.

  A instil   B infuse   C inlay   D inset

21 I sometimes despair .... ever seeing him again.

  A of   B about   C over   D at

22 She has asked me to .... her sincere thanks to you for what you have done.

  A report   B convey   C transfer   D confide

23 I've sent your brothers straight to bed and .... you, my lad, I'm stopping your pocket money for a month.

  A as far as   B for   C as for   D about

24 If he didn't receive royalties on that book he wrote to .... his tiny income, he simply wouldn't survive.

  A expand   B augment   C amplify   D contribute

25 The government has introduced .... new currency controls which will make it difficult to holiday abroad.

  A striking   B extreme   C strong   D stringent

Phrasal verbs: Match the following phrasal verbs with their meanings, then check your answers on page
SET   199.

1	set about	*a*	establish
2	set in	*b*	cause to explode
3	set off	*c*	intend
4	set off	*d*	start a journey
5	set off	*e*	attack/cause to attack
6	set out (*not* in the sense of 'to start a journey')	*f*	display
7	set out	*g*	begin to deal with
8	set to	*h*	start something happening
9	set up	*i*	start and seem likely to continue
10	set (up) on	*j*	begin a task with determination

Now choose the appropriate phrasal verbs to complete the following sentences:

1 It looks as if the rain has .... for the rest of the day.

2 If you could .... your specific proposals in a letter, we will give them our attention.

3 Don't you dare come near my house or I'll .... the dog .... you!

4 Could you give me some advice, please? I'd like to know how to .... claiming a tax allowance.

5 If we .... at dawn, we should reach the coast by midday.

6 The whole family .... energetically and by the end of the morning most of the weeds had been cleared from the garden.

7 It was just the funny way he spoke which .... me .... laughing. I couldn't help it.

8 The government has .... a scheme to help small businesses with advice.

9 Don't .... any fireworks too near to the house, will you?

10 He originally .... to beat the land speed record, but weather conditions were unfavourable.

The prefix 'out-'   The prefix 'out-' can be added to some verbs to give the idea of 'more than' or 'to a greater degree than'. An example occurs in Text 1:

> . . . the robot has the potential to climb the ladder of skills and intelligence so rapidly that it will *outpace* any conceivable advances in automation. (move at a more rapid pace)

Choose one of the verbs below to fit the sentences which follow:

do	manoeuvre	stay
class	number	weigh
live	shine	wit

1 Look, are you sure your parents won't mind me spending another day here? I don't want to out .... my welcome!

2 He foolishly hoped to out .... the police by changing his address every few weeks but they caught up with him in time.

3 I did my best in the pentathlon but, to be honest, I was hopelessly out ....

4 Your safety is a consideration which out .... all the others in my mind.

5 He was out .... in his attempts to gain control of the company by the other major shareholders.

6 One performance in the play out .... all the rest and I'd say the actress concerned had a promising future ahead of her.

7 Opponents of the motion out .... those in favour by 2 to 1 when the vote was taken.

8 She out .... her brothers and sisters by more than twenty years.

9 Seeing all the pound notes in the collection box, and not wanting to be out ...., he put in a cheque for £10.

▶Grammar practice

1 Fill in each of the numbered blanks in the passage with one suitable word.

We live surrounded by objects and systems that we .... (1) for granted, ... (2) which profoundly .... (3) the way we behave, think, work, play, and in general lead our .... (4). Look, for example, at the place in .... (5) you are reading this now, and see how much of .... (6) surrounds you is understandable, how much of it you could .... (7) build yourself or repair if it .... (8) cease to function. When we start the car or .... (9) the button in the elevator, or buy food in the supermarket, we .... (10) no thought to the complex devices or systems that .... (11) the car move, or the elevator rise, or the food appear on the shelves. .... (12) this century we have become increasingly .... (13) on the products of technology. They have already changed our lives: at the simplest .... (14), the availability of transport .... (15) made us physically less fit than our .... (16). Many people are alive only because they have been given immunity to .... (17) through drugs. The vast .... (18) of the world's population relies .... (19) the ability of technology to provide and transport food. We are .... (20) to feed or clothe or keep ourselves warm without technology.

from 'Connections' by James Burke

2 Fill each of the blanks below with a suitable word or phrase:

a You can borrow the car as .... it back by midnight.

b He accused me .... a liar.

c How could he .... my telephone number? It wasn't even in the directory.

d She offered me an aspirin but I told her I .... two already.

e They had three children, the eldest .... emigrated to Australia.

f I was exhausted after the flight and I really appreciated .... at the airport by my uncle.

g The house is beginning to look shabby. It's high time I .... painted.

h You look absolutely frozen. You .... ages for the bus.

i He asked me .... and I told him it was the 12th of September.

j It's no .... force the lid off. You'll only break the bottle.

UNIT 10 The consumer society

▶ Lead-in

Look at the following advertisements:

We replaced our gas back boiler with something far more sophisticated. A gas back boiler.

When the time comes to replace your old gas back boiler, other ideas may momentarily cross your mind.

You could, for instance, consider housing a new boiler in the kitchen. But the sheer cost and inconvenience involved in re-laying pipes and floorboards can make the whole experience anything but uplifting.

And even after the dust has finally settled, the reduced space in your kitchen may leave you hankering for the cosy arrangement you had before.

Far better then, to utilise your existing pipework and opt for a more sophisticated solution.

Take a look at the new Baxi Bermuda range, for example, and it becomes abundantly clear that the most stylish way to replace your gas back boiler is with one of ours.

There are nine superb Bermuda firefronts, ranging from the ultra modern to the unashamedly traditional.

Including four of the most realistic living flame effects you're ever likely to lay eyes on. Each one sitting in front of a boiler which powers all your household heating and hot water requirements in dependable Bermuda fashion.

And you can even change the look of your firefront at any time in the future. Bermuda Renewals allow you to update your existing Bermuda firefront, without having to replace the boiler.

BAXI BERMUDA
Nothing takes its place.

1 What image has the advertiser tried to create for his product by showing it in this setting?

2 List all the features which have been carefully designed to suggest that particular image.

3 What sort of people is the advertisement aimed at? What age and income group is it most likely to appeal to?

4 What other products can you think of which are advertised in a similar way?

On the left, Mrs Sinclair's old dishwasher.
On the right, Mrs Sinclair's new Servis dishwasher.

For nigh on 12 years, Mrs Sinclair's dishwasher had performed perfectly.

Without so much as a murmur it would stand, bent over the sink, washing everything spotlessly clean.

Then, one day, the inevitable happened. "This is insane" said the dishwasher. "Every day I wash up dozens of dishes. Not to mention knives and forks and pots and pans. In a year, it must run into thousands. Life's too short."

That, briefly, is why the Sinclairs decided to buy a dishwasher. Why they decided to buy a Servis dishwasher is another story altogether.

"It was the obvious choice really. My Servis washing machine these past ten years has been absolutely wonderful. Oh, there's been the odd thing now and again, but it's never really given any trouble.

However, quite apart from her faith in our products and our 700 strong team of after sales servicemen, Mrs Sinclair did find several other reasons for choosing a Servis dishwasher.

"It's big enough to take a whole day's washing up, so we usually only have to have it on in the evenings. And it takes all the pots and pans too. And you don't have to mess around rinsing things before you put them in or anything daft like that."

Finally, we asked Mr Sinclair if he didn't think it was a bit of a luxury owning a dishwasher.

"That's what everyone says" he replied. "But the way I look at it is this. No one thinks it's a luxury to have a washing machine. And you only use it once or twice a week.

A dishwasher you use every single day of your life."

Take a seat Mr Sinclair, you'll never have to wash up another dish again. Ever.

If it ever lets you down, we won't.
Servis

---

1 What are the visual differences between this advertisement and the previous one?

2 What is the main appeal of the picture and the caption together?

3 How would you describe the style of the 'copy' (text) and what has the writer done to make it both readable and persuasive?

4 What *facts* do we learn about the machine and what is merely suggested about it?

Work in pairs to answer the following questions:

1 Glamour and humour are two of the appeals which advertisements try to make for us. What other appeals do they make? Think of typical advertisements for:

   a washing powder   *c* cigarettes

   b toothpaste   *d* stereo hi-fi equipment

2 In what other ways, apart from advertising, are we persuaded to buy one product rather than another?

▶Text 1 · The development of advertising

During the early stages of the Industrial Revolution, advertising was a relatively straightforward means of announcement and communication and was used mainly to promote novelties and fringe products. But when factory production got into full swing and new products, eg processed foods, came onto the market, national advertising
5 campaigns and brand-naming of products became necessary. Before large-scale factory production, the typical manufacturing unit had been small and adaptable and the task of distributing and selling goods had largely been undertaken by wholesalers. The small non-specialised factory which did not rely on massive investment in machinery had been flexible enough to adapt its production according to changes in public demand.
10 But the economic depression which lasted from 1873 to 1894 marked a turning point between the old method of industrial organisation and distribution and the new. From the beginning of the nineteenth century until the 1870s, production had steadily expanded and there had been a corresponding growth in retail outlets. But the depression brought on a crisis of over-production and under-consumption – manufac-
15 tured goods piled up unsold and prices and profits fell. Towards the end of the century many of the small industrial firms realised that they would be in a better position to weather economic depressions and slumps if they combined with other small businesses and widened the range of goods they produced so that all their eggs were not in one basket. They also realised that they would have to take steps to ensure that once their
20 goods had been produced there was a market for them. This period ushered in the first phase of what economists now call 'monopoly capitalism', which, roughly speaking, refers to the control of the market by a small number of giant, conglomerate enterprises. Whereas previously competitive trading had been conducted by small rival firms, after the depression the larger manufacturing units and combines relied more and
25 more on mass advertising to promote their new range of products.

A good example of the changes that occurred in manufacture and distribution at the turn of the century can be found in the soap trade. From about the 1850s the market had been flooded with anonymous bars of soap, produced by hundreds of small manufacturers and distributed by wholesalers and door-to-door sellers. Competition grew
30 steadily throughout the latter half of the century and eventually the leading companies embarked on more aggressive selling methods in order to take custom away from their rivals. For instance, the future Lord Leverhulme decided to 'brand' his soap by selling it in distinctive packages in order to facilitate recognition and encourage customer loyalty.

Lord Leverhulme was one of the first industrialists to realise that advertisements
35 should contain 'logical and considered' arguments as well as eye-catching and witty slogans. Many advertisers followed his lead and started to include 'reason-why' copy in their ads. For example, one contemporary Pears soap ad went into great detail about how the product could enhance marital bliss by cutting down the time the wife had to spend with her arms in a bowl of frothy suds. And an ad for Cadbury's cocoa not only
40 proclaimed its purity but also detailed other benefits: 'for the infant it is a delight and a support; for the young girl, a source of healthy vigour; for the young miss in her teens a valuable aid to development...' and so on. As the writer E. S. Turner rightly points out, the advertising of this period had reached the 'stage of persuasion as distinct from proclamation or iteration'. Indeed advertise or bust seemed to be the rule of the day as
45 bigger and more expensive campaigns were mounted and smaller firms who did not, or could not, advertise, were squeezed or bought out by the larger companies.

from 'Advertising as communication' by Gillian Dyer

Now complete these statements by choosing the answer which you think fits best.

1 An example of a product which might well have been advertised during the early stages of the Industrial Revolution is

a a cooking utensil.
b a new child's toy.
c tinned fruit.
d household soap.

2 The small-scale manufacturers of this period did not need to advertise because

    a there was no competition between different firms.
    b customers bought goods directly from the factory.
    c the demand for most goods was fairly constant.
    d they were not committed to producing one type of product.

3 It is explained that during the depression small businesses combined in order to

    a spread their commercial risks.
    b gain control of the market.
    c increase their profits.
    d finance mass advertising.

4 The account of the soap trade in paragraph 3 illustrates how

    a products came to be distributed by travelling salesmen.
    b products came to be given separate identity.
    c leading manufacturers produced an excess of goods.
    d wholesalers drove their competitors out of business.

5 The Pears soap advertisement suggests that, compared with similar products, Pears soap

    a is more economical to use.
    b is more pleasant to use.
    c makes the task less difficult.
    d makes the task less lengthy.

6 Early twentieth century advertising differed from previous mass advertising in that it

    a contained more factual information.
    b included more pictorial detail.
    c relied more on appearing rational.
    d relied more on memorable phrases.

All these notices represent advertising 'gimmicks' – offers or incentives which catch your attention and encourage you to buy a product.

Would *you* be influenced by any of them? Why/Why not?

What other examples of gimmicks can you think of?

▶Text 2 · A marketing revolution

1 Read the following passage and answer the following questions:

a What does the new advertising campaign offer?
b What is new about the offer that it makes?
c How does the writer feel about the new development?

The first time it appeared it didn't seem possible: a poster promising new school equipment for those children who collected labels from the cans of a certain
5 brand of baked beans.

Since then a pox of advertising billboards has confirmed the gist of the softsell. It seems that things are now so bad in the aftermath of public sector spending
10 cuts that a multi-national company was inviting us to eat our way to our children's education facilities.

If the state no longer proposes to provide, perhaps God has disposed the com-
15 mercial hearts of giant business to find a way of doing so and making money at the same time; but oddly the implications of this recent advertising campaign have attracted no comment. Apathy, or indeed
20 gratitude makes it unremarkable that the breakdown of a social service has led private enterprise capitalists to mask the deficiencies of government-funded departments.

25 Yet this is a marketing revolution. Gimmicks and give-aways have gone before, but the moral overtones of selling on the basis of making penny-pinched mothers aware that the more beans they buy, the
30 better their children's school facilities will be, is something else again.

The baked beans company is not the only concern selling on the basis of helping family tight-spots in other ways. Take the
35 chocolate ad on television, offering vouchers for rail tickets or lawnmowers if the kids eat enough bars. But the baked beans company is different in that it is

actually plugging a hole in the state dam.
40 We are all used to supporting the lifeboats or guidedogs for the blind, but the need to help a full-blown department of a democratic state takes Robin Hood into the realms of Kafka.

45 Recently there has been a shift in attitudes – or at least emphasis – among the multi-nationals themselves. They have begun to admit, rather than hide, how powerful they are as a social force. The
50 trouble governments take just to have them build factories or set up shop in their countries demonstrates their political clout; now they are tending to set up departments within themselves, such as
55 the 'Division for International Social Action' at General Motors, or Shell's recently formed committee to take care of social responsibility for the company. Conscience is beginning to make commercial
60 sense.

The baked beans poster campaign, though, raises questions which could shift marketing out of psychology and into domination. It has changed the accepted
65 selling philosophy that you try to make people choose a particular brand or product by giving away a plastic submarine or a picture of a famous cricketer. This campaign – coming at a time when everyone is
70 pressed for money as unemployment rises and the value of earnings evaporates in inflation – adds the element of guilt. If you do not spend the money, your child may be deprived at school; if you buy another
75 brand of beans, which might be cheaper, will the school go without?

from an article by Jane McLoughlin in the Observer, London

2 When you have read the passage through once, look at it again and do this exercise:

Look at paragraphs 2–6 and find words or phrases in the passage which mean:

a widespread appearance (2)   ....
b general meaning (2)   ....
c advertiser's persuasive message (2)   ....
d period following (a bad event) (2)   ....
e business (5)   ....
f financial difficulties (5)   ....
g filling (5)   ....
h fully-developed (5)   ....
i influence (noun) (6)   ....

177

Now complete these statements by choosing the answer which you think fits best.

1 The writer was surprised when she saw the new poster because the offer it made was so

   a generous.

   b unusual.

   c amusing.

   d dishonest.

2 The circumstances which prompted the new advertisement were

   a a decline in the standards of teaching.

   b a reduction in the budget for education.

   c an increase in the numbers of unemployed.

   d an improvement in the rate of inflation.

3 The new advertisement differs from others in that its offer

   a is aimed at adults.

   b is not connected with the product.

   c concerns a worthwhile cause.

   d concerns public welfare.

4 The importance of the multi-national companies can be seen from the fact that governments

   a are keen to attract them to their countries.

   b are anxious to restrict their political influence.

   c co-operate with them in providing social services.

   d encourage them to take a responsible attitude.

5 What worries the writer about this new development in advertising is that it could

   a remove a responsibility from the government.

   b lead to a decline in educational facilities.

   c exert an unfair pressure on the consumer.

   d have a damaging effect on children's diet.

▶ Focus on writing 1 · Discussion

Write a balanced discussion on the following topic:

> What are the arguments for and against modern advertising methods? Are there any controls which you think should be imposed on advertisers? (*About 350 words*)

STUDY BOX
Actual vs Actually

1 *The baked beans company is* **actually** *plugging a hole in the state dam.* (Text 2)

actually is used here to indicate something which is surprising.

2 *People overestimate the frequency of the dramatic causes of death and underestimate the undramatic and unpublicised killers which* **actually** *take a greater toll of life.* (Unit 5, Text 1)

actually here means *really.* It stresses the *true* situation compared with what people wrongly imagine. (It does not mean *now* or *at present.*)

actual is used in the same way.

> eg *The police expected about 1,000 demonstrators but the* **actual** *number was much greater.*

3 **actual** is also used to refer to the most important part of what you are describing or discussing.

> eg *We should aim to arrive at 4.30 even though the* **actual** *check-in time isn't until 5 o'clock.*

4 **actually** is also often used in conversation to draw attention to what you are saying, or to introduce a new point.

> eg *I'm just in the middle of a meeting* **actually**. *Can I call you back?*
>
> **Actually**, *I've been meaning to ask you something . . .*

▶ Text 3 · The strange new taste of tomorrow

Have you ever eaten any of the following?

snails	jelly fish	hedgehog
frogs legs	haggis	camel
sea weed	raw fish	snake

1 If you *have,* what did they taste like? Would you eat them again?
2 If you *haven't,* which would you consider trying, and which not? Give your reasons.
3 What reasons are there for our prejudices about food?
4 Could these prejudices ever be harmful?

Read *Part 1* of the text to find out:

a Why did the Ministry begin looking for a new species of fish?
b Why was the new fish of interest to food producers?
c How commercially successful was it?
d Why?

Part 1

Food science, unfortunately, is not always dealing with what is acceptable to the public. The word 'new', such an exciting concept in other areas of advertising, causes only apprehension when applied to food. A new food? For science can open up a world of novel proteins, new methods of animal husbandry and feeding-stuffs, new crops and new meat and fish to eat. But the food trade can say no, and that is that. They know the extent to which the public attitude to food is guided by social and religious taboos, childhood conditioning, simple prejudice and preference.

We spend the best part of £40 million a year researching into farming and fishing and growing and the range of discoveries is extensive and fascinating. We grow apples like raspberries and harvest them with machines after two years: we are learning to trick cows into having twins and sheep into lambing twice a year by fiddling with their summertime. We're marvellously equipped to utilise everything from sea weeds to weed seeds.

The men at the Ministry of Agriculture Food and Fisheries have been alarmed by the overfishing of international waters – we can expect a 20% drop in catches soon. So they have been making sorties to discover possible new species of fish. With an eye on the unilateral fishing limit claims, they picked on the deep Atlantic shelf which hugs the West coast of Ireland, and they came up with a curious-looking deepwater fish, the grenadier.

What happened? The MAFF told Birds Eye and the big fishfinger producers that they had discovered a fish which lent itself to the same treatment as cod, which is the basis of fishfinger production. At this point, Graham Kemp, head of Birds Eye press, consumer and information services, started to sound out the Press, mentioning that Birds Eye was thinking of incorporating a new range of fish in fishfingers. Privately, he said: 'We'd put ground-up cod's head in our products if we thought the housewife would accept it.'

It was eventually John Waterman, long-serving Head of Information at Torry Research Station, Aberdeen, who announced the 'exciting' news at a Press-conference. Now, Waterman happens to be one of the world's most knowledgeable people on the subject of fish names, and he knew that the grenadier fish was best known as the rats-tail, John Waterman replied truthfully that it was, but they wished it to be known as the grenadier.

So he judiciously chose one of the fish's more pleasant names. Asked by the Press at the conference if the grenadier was not better known as the rats tail, John Waterman replied truthfully that it was, but they wished it to be known as the grenadier.

COULD YOU EAT RATS-TAIL? asked the headlines in the papers and TV. Big joke. But Waterman was not laughing because the thousands of pounds spent on the sea search was down the drain. Birds Eye, noting the public reaction, said it had no intention of using rats-tail in fishfingers. What a thought. And in a sudden panic it stopped labelling its fishfingers 'white fish' and put them out as pure 'cod'.

Read *Part 2* to find out:

a What seems to be the key to the success of new food products?
b How is this success achieved?
c What product is a good example of this process?

Part 2

At the Food Research Institute, Norwich, Liaison Officer, Arnold Tomalin says research can only go so far: it provides the information but we live in a society where it is left to the entrepreneur to decide whether or not to take it further.

Of course, Tomalin is right. When people vote with their pay packets in High Street shops every week they make peculiarly conservative choices.

There is no doubt that scientists can find new food alternatives, but who will find it worth their while to present them to a reluctant public?

Big Business – Unilever can do it, for one. Unilever's research covers everything from salmon fishing in Scottish lochs to putting Texturised Vegetable Protein in meat pies; from sucking the last scraps of flesh off a cod's backbone to turning the world's cheap oils into hydrogenated butter-gold. It cost Unilever £250,000 in gas chromatography and allied research to identify and synthesise the 22 separate unique flavour components to get the butter taste into their margarine.

It is obvious that a product like hydrogenated palm and coconut and herring oil could not have achieved world-wide acceptance without a boost from the persuaders and perhaps it is there that the whole key to food acceptance lies.

If it had not been for the last decade or so of brilliant advertising campaigning, how could margarine have climbed out of the hole it found itself in at the end of the war? If Unilever can get people to eat their marge surely there can be no limits to the possibilities of brilliant research allied to clever advertising.

Jeremy Bullmore, the creative director of Britain's largest advertising agents, has no illusions about what food acceptance is. 'We sell the myth about food rather than the reality'. So, the advertiser is concerned with generating this excitement in products. He has to confess you can't do this in food by proclaiming its novelty. But it's a challenge which will come.

'We're talking about foods that haven't evolved. They'll need to be marketed in shapes which are familiar. Like marge. They could have had a product which was clear, a kind of jelly, or a blue margarine, but it wouldn't have been acceptable. So they made it look like butter.

The truth is, says Bullmore, that times change, 'It's really a matter of what's acceptable and what's not. Who's right and who's wrong about snails and eels and so on. A friend of mine, a great ornithologist, bought a book in France and opened it at the Robin. It began: 'this charming little songster is best served . . .'

from an article by Michael Bateman in the Sunday Times

1 Explain 'apprehension' in line 5.
2 What does the research into farming and growing seem to have been aimed at, judging by the achievements mentioned (Para 2)?
3 What does the writer mean by 'we're . . . equipped to utilise everything from sea weeds to weed seeds.' (lines 26–28)?
4 Why did the MAFF choose the deep Atlantic shelf for its research?
5 Explain the phrase 'lent itself to' (line 44).
6 Explain the phrase 'sound out' (line 49).
7 What does Graham Kemp's private remark suggest about food producers' attitudes?
8 Why was John Waterman not amused by the Press reaction to the new fish?
9 Why did Birds Eye decide to change the label on its fishfingers?
10 Explain in other words 'they make peculiarly conservative choices' (lines 96–97).
11 Why is it unlikely that margarine would have achieved public acceptance without help?
12 What does 'there' (line 120) refer to?
13 What does 'it' in 'it's a challenge' (line 140) refer to?
14 What was the likely reaction of Bullmore's friend to the section on the Robin in the book, and why?
15 Summarise in 50–100 words what the passage tells us about public attitudes to food. (See STUDY BOX – Summary Writing on page 127.)

▶ Focus on grammar · Review of reported speech

1a When statements, questions, commands, requests and other utterances are *reported later*, with a *reporting verb in the past*, the original tenses move one step back in time. This basic rule can be summarised as follows:

present tense → past tense
present perfect tense → past perfect tense
past tense → past perfect tense
future tense → conditional
future perfect tense → conditional perfect

The past perfect tense cannot move back in time so stays the same. Conditionals and subjunctives also remain unchanged. See 3 on page 183.

Look at these examples from Text 3 and:

  a underline the verb forms which have been reported
  b say what the original words were (direct speech)

  1 The MAFF told Birds Eye . . . that they had discovered a fish which lent itself to the same treatment as cod . . .

  2 Graham Kemp started to sound out the Press, mentioning that Birds Eye was thinking of incorporating a new range of fish in fishfingers.

  3 Asked by the Press . . . if the grenadier was not better known as the rats-tail, John Waterman replied truthfully that it was, but they wished it to be known as the grenadier.

b *Expressions of time and place* may also change. Typical changes are as follows:

here → there   yesterday → the day before
now → then   last week → the previous week
this → that   next Sunday → the following Sunday
ago → before

Changes depend on the circumstances of the reporting, so common sense, rather than rigid rules, must apply.

c Sentences in reported speech are often longer than the original and may combine several elements using *link words* like *and*, *but*, *so*, *because* or participles like *adding that*, or *explaining that*

Exercise 1 Change the following sentences into reported speech. Use linking words where possible and use your discretion when deciding whether to change or omit the words in italics:

  a 'He went out at 10 o'clock *yesterday morning*,' she explained, 'and nobody's seen him since then.'

  b 'I just don't know what to do *now*,' she cried. '*This* news has come as a complete shock.'

  c 'There's nothing on at the cinema *at the moment* that I want to see. In fact, the last time I went to the cinema was two years *ago*,' she told me.

  d 'Phone me *next Sunday*. I hope to have more information by then,' he told me.

  e 'I'll stay *here* by the 'phone for the *next* ten minutes. They may call again,' she said.

2 When the reporting verb is in the present tense, the tenses *do not change*.

  eg 'I've got a job in London and I'm moving there next month.'

  (It's Helen on the 'phone and) she says she's got a job in London and she's moving there next month.

  Now report Helen's news, imagining that it's some weeks later.

3 Conditionals and subjunctives which do not relate to time *do not change*.

> eg 'If I had enough money I'd buy it.' – He said that if he *had* enough money, *he'd buy it*.
> 'I wish I could remember his name.' – She said she wished she *could remember* his name.
> 'I'd rather he were coming too.' – She said she'*d rather* he *were coming* too.

Try moving the verbs in blue one step back in time. What difference does it make to the meaning?

4 Orders and instructions change either to:

> *a* an infinitive construction introduced by 'told', 'ordered' etc.
> eg 'Sit down' – He told me to sit down.
> 'Don't say a word' – He told me not to say a word.

> or *b* a construction with was/were (not) to (see *Focus on grammar 2, Unit 8*).
> eg 'Wait in this room until you are called'.
> They said I was to wait in the room until I was called.

5 Auxiliary verbs

> *a* The following auxiliary verbs always change:
>
> *can/cannot – could/couldn't*
> *may   – might*
> *will/shall   – would/should*

> *b* The following auxiliary verbs *do not change* when they are used with the meanings given below.

might	He said he might come later
could/could not (to express possibility or impossibility)	She said the key could be lost.
should/ought to (to express advisability or expectation)	I told him he should be more careful.
must (to express a conclusion)	He said I must be joking.
must (not)/need not (to express obligation or lack of obligation)	She told me I needn't stay late.

> *c* *Did not need to* changes to *had not needed to* but *needn't have* doesn't change.

Exercise 2 Change the following sentences into reported speech. Use link words where possible.

a 'You might catch the 6 o'clock train, if you hurry.' (They told me . . .)

b 'I couldn't have a small dog as a pet. My flat's too small.' (I explained . . .)

c 'You must be exhausted! You haven't had a break all day.' (She exclaimed . . .)

d 'You ought to ask for a pay rise. You've brought the company a lot of business.' (He told me . . .)

e 'As I was only going for the day, I didn't need to pack a suitcase.' (She said . . .)

f 'You needn't have waited up for me. I'm quite capable of letting myself in.' (He told us . . .)

g 'I'd rather you didn't tell anyone what I've just told you.' (He said . . .)

h 'I may be able to give you a lift but I won't know until the morning.' (She explained . . .)

i 'I couldn't find my door key. That's why I broke a window.' (He told the policeman . . .)

j 'She should be delighted when she hears the news.' (They told us . . .)

k 'You must always ask for a receipt when you pay by cash.' (He told me . . .)

l 'If I could help you, I would. I'm not in a position to do so at the moment.' (He said . . .)

6 Requests and suggestions

a Reporting verbs like *ask*, *beg*, *warn* etc (see list below) take a *personal object+full infinitive*.

eg He | asked | us to wait for him.
      | begged |

b When *ask* is used to report a request for permission, it is followed by *if+subject+could/might*.

eg We asked if we could record the speech.

c *Suggest* takes either a *gerund* or a *that clause* (normally with *should*).

eg She suggested | organising a protest meeting.
      | that we should organise a protest meeting.

d *Recommended* may take a *possessive+gerund*:

eg He recommended our visiting the City Museum.

More usually, it takes either a *pronoun+full infinitive* or a *that clause*:

eg He recommended | us to visit the City Museum.
      | that we should visit the City Museum.

Exercise 3

ask	warn	suggest
beg	encourage	recommend
advise	forbid	
urge	invite	

Use one of the introductory verbs above to report each of the following sentences. Each of the verbs should be used only once. Use link words where appropriate.

a 'Please sit down and make yourself at home,' our hostess said.

b 'Don't touch the Record button', my friend said. 'You could erase the tape.'

c 'You really must take the matter up with your solicitor. It could be very serious,' my brother said.

d 'I should pay a visit to the Citizen's Advice Bureau. They'll be able to tell you what your rights are,' she said.

e 'If you're eating at Mario's, try the squid. It's delicious!' they told us.

f 'No one is to use a dictionary during the test,' the teacher said.

g 'Please don't forget to let me know when you've arrived safely,' my aunt said. 'I'll be worried to death unless you do.'

h 'May we come in?' said the two visitors.

i 'You could try the corner shop. They sometimes stay open late on Saturday,' the man said.

j 'Go on, enter for the exam,' he said. 'You've nothing to lose and it'll be good experience for you.'

7 Reported questions

a Questions with yes/no answers are reported with *if* or *whether*:

eg 'Will you be late home?' – She asked | if | I would be late home.
      | whether |

b Questions with question words (How, When, Who etc) are reported with the same question word:

eg How long are you staying? – They asked how long I was staying.

c The auxiliary *do* is not used in reported questions and *normal word order* is followed:

eg 'What does the word 'supersede' mean?' – I asked what the word 'supersede' meant
   'What is the time?'   – I asked what the time was

Exercise 4   Complete the customer's part in the following dialogue:

Shopkeeper: Good morning, Madam. Can I help you?

Customer: ....

Shopkeeper: I see. Well what exactly is the problem?

Customer: ....

Shopkeeper: And how long ago did you buy it?

Customer: ....

Shopkeeper: Could you let me see the receipt, please?

Customer: ....

Shopkeeper: Well I'm afraid you'll have to produce it. We can't make any exchanges without a receipt.

Customer: ....

Shopkeeper: OK. Well, if you could let me have the cheque number, I think I can authorise an exchange.

Customer: ....

Shopkeeper: Oh no. We never refund money, I'm afraid. The best I can do for you is to give you a credit slip.

Customer: ....

Shopkeeper: But you wouldn't have to use it to buy a similar article. You could buy anything in the shop you wanted. A computer game for the kids, for example.

Customer: ....

Shopkeeper: Don't try to tell me about your rights! I suppose you've been watching one of those consumer programmes on television! I'd advise you to take the credit slip before I change my mind and refuse to co-operate at all.

Customer: ....

Now write a letter to the consumer advice programme 'How Can We Help?' on your local television channel. Use reported speech to report the relevant parts of your conversation in the shop.

▶ Communication activity · Consumer law quiz

Broadly speaking the TRADE DESCRIPTIONS ACT makes it a criminal offence for a trader to give a false or misleading description of what he is selling. That sounds simple enough. But not all descriptions are covered by the Act. This quiz will give you an idea of the main things covered – and the main loopholes. When you have finished, turn to the key on page 199.

Work with a partner to discuss the following situations.

You buy a shirt labelled:

The shirt turns out to be a mixture of cotton and viscose. There has been a breach of the Trade Descriptions Act.

TRUE OR FALSE

This man asked for a suit that his wife would like – she thinks it's awful. The salesman has committed an offence.

TRUE OR FALSE

A trader gives a misleading description to goods he advertises in the *Sunday Verbiage* – which has a circulation of 2½ million. He has committed 2½ million offences.

TRUE OR FALSE

You see this description in an estate agent's advertisement.

The house turns out to look like this:

The Trade Descriptions Act has been breached.

TRUE OR FALSE

A watch is described as 'A Divers Watch'. It is not waterproof, but has been manufactured by 'Divers and Co'. An offence has been committed because the description 'A Divers Watch' implies the watch is waterproof.

TRUE OR FALSE

Garston Whinge, the writer and broadcaster, sells his bicycle to a bike shop – and describes it as 'only two years old, with low mileage'. He has had it for 10 years. Mr Whinge has committed an offence under the Act.

TRUE OR FALSE

The bike shop owner, knowing Garston Whinge to be an upstanding citizen, does not bother to check the description and repeats it when selling the bike. The shopkeeper has now committed an offence.

TRUE OR FALSE

You buy a cellophane-wrapped book with a picture of a pop-star on the front. When you get home, you find you've bought a Greek dictionary. The bookshop has committed an offence under the Trade Descriptions Act.

TRUE OR FALSE

The used car dealer has committed an offence.

TRUE OR FALSE

You go on holiday to a hotel which, in the brochure, looked like this. When you arrive you find the swimming-pool dry and filled with rubble. The tour operator has committed an offence under the Act.

TRUE OR FALSE

▶ Focus on listening

You are going to hear a short programme which deals with consumers' affairs. As you listen,

   a complete the table below which summarises the programme's contents. Put × where information is not available or not applicable. You may put more than one letter in a box. Use the key below.

   b answer the questions which follow.

1

ITEM	1	2	3
COMPLAINT FROM	Mrs Stewart	Mrs Bowen	Mr Walters
CONSUMER AREA[1]	MO		
GOODS CONCERNED	pushchairs etc	suit	stamps
PROBLEM[2]		g	
AMOUNT PAID			

Key

[1]Consumer area
Retail   – R
Mail Order – MO
Service   – S

[2]Problem

Retail and Mail Order
a goods not received
b goods not satisfactory
c goods damaged on delivery
d goods sent unsolicited
e other

Service
f goods lost
g goods damaged
h service unsatisfactory
i service overpriced
j other

2 Mrs Stewart wasn't satisfied with the pushchair when she received it because it

   a was more difficult to assemble than she'd expected.
   b wasn't as strongly built as she'd expected.
   c was cheaper than the one she'd ordered.
   d was smaller than the one she'd ordered.

3 Mrs Stewart ordered extra goods in order to

   a show them to potential customers.
   b open up a shop of her own.
   c obtain a special discount for bulk orders.
   d supply them to customers at a profit.

4 An investigation is now being made by

   a the newspaper where the advert appeared.
   b the Post Office.
   c the police.
   d the programme itself.

5 Mrs Bowen's complaint is that her son's suit

   a is now too tight for him.
   b is now too shabby to wear.
   c has been discoloured.
   d has been destroyed.

6 Jack, the programme's adviser, feels that responsibility lies with

 a the dry cleaners.
 b the manufacturers.
 c both the cleaners and manufacturers.
 d the consumer herself.

7 Mr Walters returned the package because

 a there had been such a delay in its delivery.
 b he didn't think the stamps were worth the money.
 c he didn't want to join a stamp club.
 d he knew he hadn't ordered it.

8 The letter he received threatened to

 a inform his employer's of his debt.
 b damage his credit-worthiness.
 c have him made bankrupt.
 d retrieve the money from him at home or at work.

LANGUAGE CHECK
Prefixes

A **prefix** is a letter or a group of letters which can be added at the beginning of a word to make a change in meaning.

1 Look at the following groups of words, and try to work out what the *general* meaning of the prefix in each case is. (The words in **bold** come from texts in this unit.)

a-	ab-	ad-	anti-	co-/com-/con-
apathy	abandon	**advertisement**	antibiotic	**component**
amoral	abdicate	**admit**	antisocial	**combine**
atheist	abnormal	advance	antipathy	**conglomerate**
				competitive

dis-	mis-/mal-	pro-	syn-/sym-	uni-
disappear	**misleading**	**promote**	**synthesise**	**unilateral**
disadvantage	misbehave	**proclaim**	sympathy	universal
disapprove	mischance	**propose**		unity
discredit	mishandle	**provide**		
	malformation			

2 Now match the following ten meanings to the prefixes above:

with/together; from/away from; bad/wrong; without; to/towards; supporting/in favour of; one/the same; opposed to/against; sharing (with)/together; negative/opposite.

3 Say what the words in *italics* in the following sentences mean:

a After twenty years the organization was *disbanded*.
b Before we all leave, let's *synchronize* our watches. It's now 10.04.
c The engineer says there's a *malfunction* in the generator.
d He drove round the ring road in an *anticlockwise* direction.
e Most people's faces are *asymetrical*.
f Even as a child he showed a natural *propensity* for crime.
g My arrival in Athens *coincided* with a public holiday.
h He *abstained* from eating for five days.
i People at *adjoining* tables looked at her in astonishment.
j "Who wants to go?" he asked the class. "We all do," they said in *unison*.

▶ Focus on register

Below is a consumer's guide to four typical pets:

Small dogs (110 in survey)

Price High – in survey typical range from £75 to £350 (mongrels cheaper).

Running costs Fairly high – cost of food averaged £6 a week, vet's fees £75 last year, licence and registration fees £8, basket or other equipment, etc £50, and boarding (if needed) around £7 per day.

Maintenance Quite a lot – average one hour a day.

Enjoyment time Long – average four hours a day.

Durability Good – average nine years. Maximum about 14.

Satisfaction High – more than 90 per cent very satisfied. The few who would not get another had various reasons – including the irreplaceability of the pet, the time needed to look after it and difficulties when going away.

Hamsters (42 in survey)

Price Cheap – about £5.

Running costs Very low – less than 35p a week for food. Few other expenses, but some members paid £18 or more for a cage etc.

Maintenance Very little – average eight minutes a day.

Enjoyment time Little – mostly about 10 minutes a day, but an hour or two for some members.

Durability Poor – usually less than two years. Maximum about four.

Satisfaction Average – most members would buy again, although some complained of lack of response.

Useful information Hamsters are nocturnal. They are solitary animals – two or more will fight, regardless of sex. Need exercise – either from exercise wheel in cage or by being let out (but note that they tend to hide, are accident-prone, and eat furnishings if given the chance). Can bite your finger if poked at them. If a hamster gets too hot or too cold it can *appear* to be dead. Keep cage clean and wash hands after handling: some hamsters have infections such as salmonella which can spread to humans.

Rabbits (70 in survey)

Price Fairly cheap – about £15.

Running costs Low – average £1.50 a week. Other expenses averaged about £10 a year.

Maintenance Moderate – average 20 minutes a day.

Enjoyment time Usually little – 20 minutes a day or less, but up to an hour for some members.

Durability Fair – average four years, but can live much longer. Maximum about 12.

Satisfaction Average – but about half would not get one again, mainly because children have outgrown them, but also because of work involved and other reasons such as destructiveness.

Useful information Metal or plastic hutches are best – wood gets smelly. They need exercise outside the hutch, and something to gnaw on, to prevent teeth from getting too long. Rabbits should be lifted by the scruff of the neck, not the ears, with the hind-quarters supported. They can bite and scratch.

Horses and ponies (23 in survey)

Price Very expensive – typical range £300 to £1,500.

Running costs Very high – food costs depend on grazing available. Our average £60 a week. In addition: vet's fees averaged £70 last year, insurance £100, registration etc £50, equipment and other expenses (including shoeing) £400 and, of course, stabling if you have not got space at home.

Maintenance A lot – average one hour 12 minutes a day, but a few spent three hours.

Enjoyment time Quite long – average 2¼ hours a day.

Durability Very good – average 15 years. Maximum about 25.

Satisfaction Very high – almost everyone was very satisfied, and three out of four would buy again.

Useful information Buying privately is safer than going to a horse sale unless you have professional help; don't buy without getting a vet's opinion. Some ponies can live out all year round – cheaper than stabling. A stable-kept horse needs exercising and grooming daily. For a young child get a well-schooled pony at least six years old, and be prepared to change to a larger mount in a few years.

1 Which pets would be the least trouble to look after?
   A Small dogs   B Hamsters   C Rabbits   D Horses and ponies

2 Which pets are likely to have the longest life-span?
   A Small dogs   B Hamsters   C Rabbits   D Horses and ponies

3 Which pets are likely to provide the least companionship?
   A Small dogs   B Hamsters   C Rabbits   D Horses and ponies

4 Which pets might the owners become particularly attached to?
   A Small dogs   B Hamsters   C Rabbits   D Horses and ponies

5 Which pets are likely to need most medical attention in a year?
   A Small dogs   B Hamsters   C Rabbits   D Horses and ponies

6 Which pets seem to be liked mostly by younger children?
   A Small dogs   B Hamsters   C Rabbits   D Horses and ponies

7 Which pets could constitute a health risk?
   A Small dogs   B Hamsters   C Rabbits   D Horses and ponies

8 Which pets need regular opportunity to bite steadily?
   A Small dogs   B Hamsters   C Rabbits   D Horses and ponies

▶ Focus on writing 2 · Report

Look at the extracts from the consumer's guide to pets.
a What is unusual about the sub-headings?
b What points are covered by the headings *Maintenance, Enjoyment time* and *Durability*?
c What questions do you think that pet owners were asked in order to provide information for each of the headings?

Using information from the extract below and from the first extract in *Focus on register*, together with your own ideas, write a report on:

> The relative suitability of dogs and caged birds as pets for elderly people, living alone. (*About 200 words*)

REMEMBER

Style – your report should be written in a neutral, expository style without the tongue-in-cheek humour of the consumer's guide.

Organisation – Decide on the main factors to be considered when choosing a pet for an elderly person. These will probably go beyond the points in the consumer's guide. Arrange your points in order of priority.

Budgerigars (and canaries)
(112 in survey)

Price Fairly cheap – usually £13 for budgerigars, canaries more.

Running costs Usually less than £2 a week for food. A cage is needed but other expenses are unlikely to be significant.

Maintenance Very little – average eight minutes a day.

Enjoyment time Rather little – less than 20 minutes a day for most people, but longer for some. Overall average was 1¼ hours.

Durability Fairly good – average 6½ years. Maximum about 14.

Satisfaction Average – assorted reasons given by those who would not get another.

Useful information Seed diet may need added vitamins, and some grit is needed to help digestion. Food should be continually available. The bigger the cage, the better. Avoid draughts, direct sunlight, fumes and too much temperature variations. Should not be handled too much. To teach a bird to talk, keep it separate from other birds, and give it lots of attention.

Make notes for each animal under the headings above.

Devise a suitable introduction and a conclusion which will summarise the main issues and make qualified recommendations.

▶Vocabulary practice

Review   Choose the word or phrase that best completes each sentence.

1 There has been a .... in the sales of new houses since mortgages became more difficult to obtain.

   A dive   B slump   C downfall   D crash

2 We can expect to treble our turnover once the January sales get into full ....

   A force   B flight   C speed   D swing

3 The government has spent £1 million on an advertising .... to encourage energy conservation.

   A campaign   B promotion   C operation   D enterprise

4 We managed to .... the last economic depression by cutting down our workforce.

   A weather   B surmount   C override   D float

5 I advise you to take .... to ensure that all your property is adequately covered by insurance.

   A means   B actions   C steps   D dealings

6 Let's hope that the new year will .... in a period of prosperity for everyone.

   A admit   B usher   C show   D introduce

7 It would cost an enormous sum to .... such a production in the theatre. Just think of the costumes and special effects involved!

   A raise   B release   C enact   D mount

8 She wants to make it clear that her course was in Fine Arts as .... from Graphic Art.

   A distinct   B separate   C different   D discrete

9 An advertising .... should be short, striking and easily remembered.

   A caption   B motto   C slogan   D epigram

10 We took the scenic route, a road which .... the coast for 50 miles.

   A surrounded   B adjoined   C bordered   D hugged

11 There is a .... of plant which is found only in this particular valley.

   A species   B specimen   C class   D breed

12 When the children .... their toys, I donated them to a charity.

   A outdated   B outgrew   C outlasted   D outwore

13 I'm rather .... for time at the moment. Couldn't we talk about it tomorrow?

   A stretched   B pinched   C pressed   D strained

14 The child has been .... of affection for so long that she hardly knows how to respond to love.

A withheld   B deprived   C denied   D excluded

15 I didn't know which .... of soap powder you used, so I just bought the supermarket's own.

A mark   B brand   C label   D make

16 There's been a .... in public opinion as far as the arming of the police is concerned.

A turn   B motion   C shift   D drift

17 At first I found it difficult to get used .... on the other side of the road.

A to drive   B to driving   C driving   D being driven

18 I tried to .... my disappointment at losing by cheering the winner loudly.

A mask   B hide   C shield   D veil

19 He joined a computer dating scheme but so far it hasn't .... a suitable partner.

A come by   B come across   C come up with   D come round to

20 I've tried .... with the knobs on the television but I can't get the picture back.

A juggling   B fiddling   C shuffling   D tampering

21 Have you thought what the .... might be if you didn't win your case in court?

A applications   B bearings   C implications   D connotations

22 I think I'll .... out my father and see if he would lend me his car for a few days.

A chance   B probe   C check   D sound

23 I thought I saw water in the distance but it must have been an optical ....

A error   B illusion   C delusion   D deception

24 This is a cut of meat which .... itself to long, slow cooking.

A lends   B suits   C adapts   D offers

25 What's that awful noise?   It's only the dog .... on a bone.

A nibbling   B teething   C gulping   D gnawing

Phrasal verbs:
COME

Match the following phrasal verbs with their meanings:

1	come about	*a*	find or meet by chance
2	come across	*b*	inherit
3	come across	*c*	begin to accept
4	come at	*d*	become ill from
5	come by	*e*	obtain
6	come down with	*f*	produce
7	come in for	*g*	make a particular impression
8	come into	*h*	receive/suffer
9	come out in	*i*	happen
10	come round	*j*	attack
11	come round to	*k*	show symptoms
12	come up with	*l*	regain consciousness

Check your answers on page 199.

Now choose the appropriate phrasal verb to complete the following sentences:

1 The play .... quite a lot of criticism when it first opened.

2 How exactly did you .... this painting? It's very like one that was reported stolen.

3 Give him time. He's sure to .... our way of thinking in the end.

4 I .... a small fortune when my uncle died but I managed to squander most of it, I'm ashamed to say.

5 As soon as I opened the garden gate, the dog .... us with teeth bared.

6 On the very first day of the holiday he .... in a rash.

7 In desperation we employed a private detective and he .... some quite valuable evidence.

8 She .... as rather nervous at the interview but I don't think we should count that against her.

9 How did it .... that you were travelling on that train to Istanbul?

10 When I .... after the accident, I couldn't remember what had happened.

11 Both the children .... measles at the beginning of the summer and we had to postpone our holiday.

12 We .... some marvellous deserted beaches on our touring holiday in south west Ireland.

▶Grammar practice

1 Fill each of the numbered blanks in the passage with one suitable word.

In its simplest sense the word 'advertising' means '.......................... (1) attention to something', or notifying or informing .... (2) of something. You can advertise by .... (3) of mouth, quite informally and locally and without incurring great .... (4). But if you want to inform a large .... (5) of people about something, you might need to advertise in the more .... (6) sense of the word, by .... (7) announcement. If you .... (8) a notice in a local newsagent's shop, design a poster or .... (9) some space in a local newspaper, you are likely to .... (10) the information you wish to communicate to the attention of more people than if you simply .... (11) the word around friends and neighbours. You could .... (12) further and distribute leaflets as well, get someone to .... (13) a placard around, even .... (14) on local radio and .... (15) a publicity stunt. However, you might not be .... (16) to simply convey certain facts and .... (17) it at that. You might wish to .... (18) a bit of emphasis or even to exaggerate the facts by .... (19) to people's emotions. And this is of course .... (20) all the controversy about advertising in its current form arises.

from 'Advertising as Communication' by Gillian Dyer

2 Finish each of the following sentences in such a way that it means exactly the same as the sentence printed before it.

EXAMPLE: 'Can you hear me?'
ANSWER: I asked *if he could hear me.*

a 'I'm sorry I didn't ring you to say I'd be late.'
He apologised . . .

b Although he was very tired, he agreed to play tennis.
Tired . . .

c I didn't realise how much he was influenced by his brother.
I didn't realise the extent . . .

d 'I never told anyone about your scheme,' he said.
He denied . . .

e It was wrong of you to scare your mother like that.
You oughtn't . . .

f He's likely to leave before the letter arrives.
By the time . . .

g The window cleaners haven't called for at least six months.
The last time . . .

h 'Where on earth have you been all this time?'
She demanded to know . . .

i The suitcase was extremely heavy but he managed to lift it easily.
Despite . . .

▶ Lead in and Communication Activities · Answers and Role B

| UNIT 1

**Communication
activity
Role B**

Business has not been too good lately and your boss has not been too complimentary about your salesmanship. There are two houses (marked *) that he would particularly like you to sell as they have been on the books for a long time. You know that some sellers will accept a lower price but your commission is based on the selling price so you are interested in persuading the buyer to pay as much as possible.

Look at the house descriptions below with your notes and then try to persuade your customer to buy one.

17 OXFORD AVENUE. £68,000 *throughout!*
A semi-detached house in a suburb 3 miles from the city centre but with good bus services. Has three bedrooms, lots of cupboard space, a small garden and a garage. Needs redecoration.

22 GREEN STREET £84,000 *(seller will take reasonable offer)*
A large detached house with four bedrooms in a quiet suburb 20 minutes walk from the city centre. Good condition throughout and central heating. Sizeable garden and double garage. *garden badly neglected*

1 CORONATION ROAD ✱ £64,000 *(price has already been reduced – get rid of this one)*
A terraced house in the city centre. Two bedrooms and one storeroom which could be converted into a third bedroom. The interior is in good condition but the roof is in need of repair. Large attic. Small courtyard to rear. *in a slum area*

ROSE COTTAGE ✱ £66,000
A picturesque country cottage, 8 miles from the centre of the city on a bus route. Huge garden and beautiful views. 1 double and 2 single bedrooms. Space to build a garage. Open fire for burning logs. *– but tiny!* *Only 2 buses a day*

FLAT 1, GEORGE HOUSE £74,000 *(No offers)*
Large basement flat in attractive building. Three bedrooms. Reasonable condition throughout although bathroom needs modernising. Central heating. Garage. Large garden to the rear and small courtyard to the front. 10 minutes walk from centre. *damp*

| UNIT 2

Lead-in answers

	%		%
The respect of colleagues	93	Being part of a team	69
Learning something new	92	Being praised by your superiors	68
Personal freedom	91	Being promoted	62
Challenge	89	Making money	62
Helping other people	88	Status in your organisation	58
Security	79	Exercising power	28
Working conditions	74	Social status	25
Meeting people through work	71		

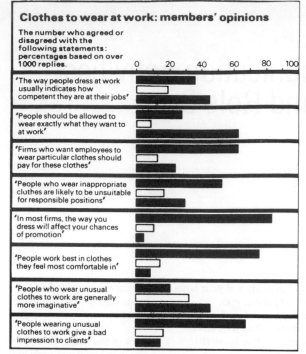

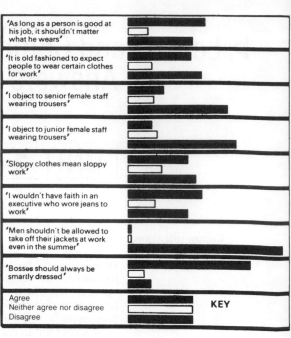

Clothes to wear at work: members' opinions

The number who agreed or disagreed with the following statements: percentages based on over 1000 replies.

'The way people dress at work usually indicates how competent they are at their jobs'

'People should be allowed to wear exactly what they want to at work'

'Firms who want employees to wear particular clothes should pay for these clothes'

'People who wear inappropriate clothes are likely to be unsuitable for responsible positions'

'In most firms, the way you dress will affect your chances of promotion'

'People work best in clothes they feel most comfortable in'

'People who wear unusual clothes to work are generally more imaginative'

'People wearing unusual clothes to work give a bad impression to clients'

'As long as a person is good at his job, it shouldn't matter what he wears'

'It is old fashioned to expect people to wear certain clothes for work'

'I object to senior female staff wearing trousers'

'I object to junior female staff wearing trousers'

'Sloppy clothes mean sloppy work'

'I wouldn't have faith in an executive who wore jeans to work'

'Men shouldn't be allowed to take off their jackets at work even in the summer'

'Bosses should always be smartly dressed'

KEY
Agree
Neither agree nor disagree
Disagree

The outfits *Which?* members judged most suitable for different jobs plus assorted comments from personnel officers in banks, advertising agencies etc.

1 most suitable for:
researcher, possibly clerk

'too casual': bank and building society

'quite acceptable': advertising agency

2 most suitable for:
clerk, doctor, insurance salesman

'quite acceptable': bank

'not smart enough for middle management but suitable for personnel manager': 29-year-old tool maker

3 most suitable for:
researcher or designer

'certainly not acceptable': bank

'only suitable for someone doing say night duty': building society

'OK for the machine and print room': media

4 most suitable for:
designer

'maybe OK for computer staff, they tend to get away with being more trendy': bank

'looks the creative type': ad agency

'you'd get complaints, because it's too sloppy': building society

5 most suitable for:
schoolteacher

'may just be acceptable for behind-the-scenes staff': bank

6 most suitable for:
clerk

'fine unless meeting public': building society

'quite OK': ad agency

7 most suitable for:
architect, schoolteacher

'certainly not turtle neck jumpers': bank

'quite OK': ad agency

8 most suitable for:
bank manager, but acceptable for all except designer

'very acceptable, how we expect our staff to look': bank

UNIT 3

Life or death in the Alps - suggested solution

1 Pack of flares – to signal your whereabouts to potential rescuers

2 Thermal ski gloves – to prevent frostbite, which could otherwise attack very quickly

3 Two litres of water per person – to prevent dehydration, a major cause of hypothermia. Eating snow would require too much energy to melt.

4 Chocolate – to maintain body temperature and energy levels in freezing conditions

5 Nylon rope – for use during difficult stages of the descent – likely to have several other uses

6 Magnetic compass – to prevent the group from going round in circles in low cloud or blizzard

7 First aid kit – the bandages in the kit can be used to wrap around the feet and hands for extra warmth

8 Goggles – to protect the eyes from the wind, and from the glare of the sun off the snow if the weather improves

9 **Swiss army knife** – likely to have a variety of uses

10 **Cigarette lighter** – could be used to start a fire if suitable combustible material is found; light to carry

11 **Five foam pads** – the best means of keeping warm at night will be to build a snowhole if no natural shelter is found – the pads can be used to insulate the shelter

12 **Plastic paddle** – to reduce the energy needed to dig a snowhole

13 **Life raft** – if inflated, it could be used for shelter, and to attract attention if the weather clears, but would need two people to carry it down the mountain, using up too much energy

14 **$800** – could be used to start a fire in emergency – will be needed on arrival back in civilisation!

15 **Map** – not much use – could be used to start a fire

UNIT 4

Lead-in answers

1C 25–29. Men are also most likely to marry in this age group.

2B 2 people. 1 person household: 27%; 2 person: 34%; 3 person: 16%; 4 person: 16%.

3D 80%. Less than 5% registered serious dissatisfaction.

4C more likely. Single men are four times more likely to be admitted to mental hospitals while single women are 2½ times as likely.

5C more likely. Both men and women are slightly more likely to die from heart attacks.

6 False.

7 True. More women than men emphasised confidentiality and trust; more men than women emphasised pleasure in a friend's company, going out with a friend and having a friend in one's home.

Communication activity answers

Situation 2

2a Assertive, because you accept and acknowledge the compliment.

2b Non-assertive, because you do not accept the compliment. You say it's nothing special although it's the first time you've worn it and you really do like it.

2c Non-assertive because you do not accept the compliment.

Situation 3

3a Assertive, because you tell the assistant exactly what you want. While acknowledging his/her point of view, you still want to return or exchange the item.

3b Aggressive, because you accuse the assistant of wasting your time.

3c Non-assertive, because you don't want this faulty merchandise.

Situation 4

4a Non-assertive, because you don't tell your colleague you're tired of doing his/her work. You agree to help even though you don't want to.

4b Aggressive, because you make accusations.

4c Assertive, because you express how you feel and what you plan to do.

Situation 5

5a Assertive/Non-assertive. This response gets two ratings because the non-verbal behaviour is assertive. You smile to show your interest, but your verbal behaviour is non-assertive; you don't say anything.

5b Assertive, because you go and introduce yourself.

5c Non-assertive, because you won't meet your neighbour by just watching.

Communication activity Role B

1 A friend of yours keeps borrowing small sums of money and never pays you back. He/she now owes you several pounds and you don't want to lend him/her any more until you have been paid back. You have plenty of money, including small change, so don't make excuses! Your partner speaks first. (**A**)

2 You have invited an old friend to dinner and taken quite a lot of trouble over the cooking. You've even baked your own bread! There are several things he/she hasn't tried yet and unless he/she has a second helping of the casserole, there will be a lot left over. You speak first.

3 Your doctor has just given you a prescription. You want to know what the prescription is for and what the potential side-effects might be. Your doctor is generally quite vague on these issues. You speak first. (**A**)

4 You borrowed a friend's car to collect a package from the post office and promised to return it by 5.30 pm. You did some shopping as well which has made you a bit late but you put some petrol in to make amends. You speak first.

5 You lent a friend a record recently. You didn't mind because you know he/she's very careful and would really appreciate the recording which is a historic one and no longer obtainable in the shops. Your partner speaks first. (**A**)

197

UNIT 5

Lead-in answers

Voluntary risks
1 smoking
2 motor cycling
3 car racing
4 car driving
5 rock climbing
6 drinking

Involuntary risks
1 influenza
2 leukemia
3 being run over
4 lightning
5 atomic power
6 falling aircraft

UNIT 6

Lead-in answers

1b 10 years old. (The age of criminal responsibility is 8 in Scotland and 10 in Northern Ireland.)

2b Theft and handling stolen goods. The proportions are given in the diagram below.

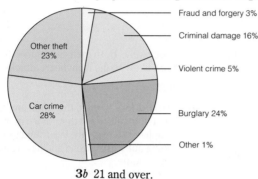

Fraud and forgery 3%
Criminal damage 16%
Violent crime 5%
Other theft 23%
Car crime 28%
Burglary 24%
Other 1%

3b 21 and over.

4d Theft of motor vehicles. (Figures in millions: burglary, £601; theft from another person, £6; theft by an employee, £613; vehicle thefts, £1,772; shop-lifting, £20.)

5d Other family member. (Murderers: friend/ acquaintance, 28.5%; spouse/lover, 26.5%; other family member, 16%; stranger, 20%.)

6c Sharp instrument. (Shooting, 8%; hitting/ kicking, 22%; sharp instrument, 35%; strangulation, 15%; other, 8%.)

7b 60.

8c Fine. (Probation, 19.5%; prison, 12%; fine, 32%.)

9c More than four times as likely.

10 False.

Communication activity Role B

Suspects

One of you has been contacted by the police about the break-in because you used to work part-time at the camera shop until recently. You left after a row with your boss about your wages.

You had nothing to do with the break-in of course, but the problem is you can't tell the police where you *really* were that evening without getting someone else into trouble. In fact, you and your friend spent the evening playing the guitar and singing at a local pub until midnight. You know and like the landlord of the pub and you know he could lose his licence if the police discovered he had kept his pub open after the legal licensing hours (closing time is 11.00 pm in your town). You are determined not to mention the pub in case enquiries there cause problems for the landlord.

You and your friend went swimming at the local sports club until about 7.45 pm and from there you went on to the pub. You both live in the same house and you got back at about 12.30 am. You think a neighbour probably heard you arrive because the alsatian on the ground floor started barking when it heard you.

Together, you must work out a convincing alibi for the time between 7.45 pm and 12.30 am. The most important thing is that your two stories correspond in every detail. Any discrepancy would cause suspicion.

Vocabulary practice answers

Phrasal verbs: **1** – *c*; **2** – *h*; **3** – *j*; **4** – *g*; **5** – *i*; **6** – *b*; **7** – *a*; **8** – *f*; **9** – *d*; **10** – *e*.

UNIT 7

Communication activity Role B

You are in charge of Adult Education at a technical college. You like to have as large a number of evening classes running as possible and also to have some more unusual classes each year rather than just the ever-popular French Conversation and Local History.

On page 200 is a list of the courses which you are planning to run this year with brief descriptions and details of class times, course length and fees.

On the right side are your notes on how many enrolments there have been so far. (There is a *maximum* of 20 and a *minimum* of 12 in each class.)

Some classes are already full or nearly full; some are so popular that you know there will be no difficulty in filling them. You want to try and dissuade people from joining these as far as possible.

Other classes (marked *) have had very few enrolments and will have to be cancelled unless you can encourage a few more people to join them.

Study the list and make any extra notes you want to; then be ready to deal with your first enquirer.

UNIT 8

Vocabulary practice answers *Phrasal verbs:* **1** – *h*; **2** – *g*; **3** – *j*; **4** – *f*; **5/6** – *a/c*;
7 – *e*; **8** – *i*; **9** – *b*; **10** – *d*.

UNIT 9

Communication activity List A

1 a toothbrush	**6** a tripod
2 a telescope	**7** a garden fork
3 a pipe (for smokers)	**8** an axe
4 a frying pan	**9** a drum
5 a saw	**10** a grandfather clock

Vocabulary practice answers *Phrasal verbs:* **1** – *g*; **2** – *i*; **3/4/5** – *b/d/h*;
6/7 – *c/f*; **8** – *j*; **9** – *a*; **10** – *e*.

UNIT 10

Communication activity answers

1 Answer: TRUE   Most factual descriptions of goods and services are covered by the Trade Descriptions Act – such things as materials, ingredients, dimensions, strength, claims about who uses the product (eg 'Royalty') and claims about the history of the product (eg 'one previous owner').

2 Answer: FALSE   Most descriptions of fact are covered by the Act, but expressions of subjective opinion aren't.

3 Answer: TRUE   Each copy of the newspaper counts as one offence – though, in practice, multiple prosecutions don't normally take place.

4 Answer: FALSE   Descriptions of houses are not covered by the Act.

5 Answer: TRUE   A description has only to be misleading, not necessarily false, for an offence to be committed. The trader doesn't have to have any intention of being misleading.

6 Answer: FALSE   Descriptions made by private individuals not in the course of business are not covered by the Act.

7 Answer: TRUE   The description is inaccurate. And it is up to those making descriptions to check that they are not false or misleading. Relying on the good name of Mr Whinge is not enough.

8 Answer: FALSE   Misleading descriptions of the character or content of books, films, magazines and records, unless actually false, are not usually covered by the Act.

9 Answer: TRUE   A trader can commit an offence if he makes a false or misleading statement – even if he is buying rather than selling.

10 Answer: FALSE   provided there was a reasonable chance, at the time the tour operator drew up his brochure, that the swimming-pool would be in use on the date of your holiday.

With goods, a trader may be convicted if he makes a misleading statement – even if he sincerely believes it to be true. It's up to him to check the statement before making it. But with services (such as a holiday) a trader who makes a false or misleading statement commits no offence so long as he has reason to believe that his statement is true.

Vocabulary practice answers *Phrasal verbs:* **1** – *i*; **2/3** – *a/g*; **4** – *j*; **5** – *e*; **6** – *d*; **7** – *h*;
8 – *b*; **9** – *k*; **10** – *l*; **11** – *c*; **12** – *f*.

PAYMENT OF FEES BY INSTALMENTS
Where a course lasts more than 11 weeks, half the fee can be paid at the beginning of the first term, and half at the beginning of the second.

POTTERY
2 classes: Complete beginners only.   Mon. 16/20
Mon 5.45 - 7.45   Develop your own ideas or follow a theme each week.   Tues. 19/20
Tues 7.30 - 9.30   Small charge for materials, <u>payable in advance</u>.
24 meetings
fee: £26.90

LANDSCAPE PAINTING
Mon 6.30 - 8.30   For beginners and experienced painters.   6/20   *
20 meetings   Study the composition of trees, figures, animals as well as water, sky.
fee: £25.60   It is hoped that part of the course will be held outside.

ANTIQUES APPRECIATION
Mon 7.45 - 9.15   Covers styles from Greek to Art Deco.
10 meetings   Includes furniture, clocks, glass, pottery, silverware and books.
fee: £9.60   Tells you how to start a collection.   9/20 *

BASIC COMPUTING
Tues 7.00 - 9.00   Introduces complete beginners to simple programming and considers
10 meetings   possible applications.   16/20 Plenty of interest
fee: £25.00   in this class.

BEGINNERS' RUSSIAN
Tues 6.00 - 7.30   Course has an emphasis on listening and speaking.
20 meetings   Teaches you how to use everyday Russian in practical situations.
fee: £25.00   Students will need to buy the coursebook.   4/20   *

PERSONALITY DEVELOPMENT
Wed 7.30 - 9.00   A review of Freudian and post-Freudian theories of personality
11 meetings   development within the family context from childhood to adolescence.
fee: £24.00   2/20 Looks in real danger.

SHORTHAND
Wed 7.00 - 9.00   An opportunity to learn the Pitman system from the start or to
20 meetings   improve your existing speeds.   13/20
fee: £24.00

CHESS FOR BEGINNERS
Fri 6.00 - 7.30   Course covers the history, development and basic theory of chess.
10 meetings   The accent is on practice and play.
fee: £9.60   Students will be expected to provide their own chess sets.
                                      10/20   *

SOFT FURNISHING
Thurs 7.00 - 9.00   How to make attractive chair and sofa covers, cushions, curtains,
11 meetings   lampshades and similar items.
fee: £13.20   Students will be expected to provide their own materials.   15/20

CAR CARE
Fri 7.00 - 9.00   Understand the basic workings of your car.   20/20 Put any
11 meetings   Simple maintenance and get-you-home techniques. more enquirers
fee: £13.20   on waiting list.

UNIT 9

▶ **Communication**
   activity
   List B

1 a ladder
2 a tennis racquet
3 a pencil
4 a comb
5 a garden spade

6 a guitar
7 a paintbrush
8 a thermometer
9 a spanner
10 a wheelbarrow

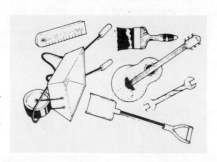

Exam Practice · Listening

▶ Home improvements

You are going to hear a radio interview with George Neal, an estate agent, who is talking about home improvements. It is in three parts.

Part one   Which of the following items in a house would be considered fashionable, according to George Neal? Tick (✓) the appropriate boxes.

plastic kitchen chairs	☐	beige bath, sink, WC	☐
an antique pine kitchen table	☐	floral wallpaper	
an old-fashioned cooker	☐	plain pale blue tiles	☐
a traditional bath	☐		

Part two   Complete the following table to show what effect (if any) different home improvements can have, according to George Neal, when it comes to selling your house. Put a tick (✓) in the correct column in each case.

Inside	Adds Value	No Effect	Easier to Sell	Harder to Sell
gold taps				
loft conversion				
downstairs WC				
kitchen/dining room				
fitted cupboards				
carpets + curtains				

Outside	Adds Value	No Effect	Easier to Sell	Harder to Sell
swimming pool				
conservatory				
climbing plants				
fountains				
fast-growing trees				

Part three   In this final part, say whether the following statements are **true (T)** or **false (F)**:

If you own a cottage which you want to sell in the future, George Neal's advice is to

	T	F
a make sure it's structurally sound		
b concentrate on the first impression the cottage will make		
c install hand-carved kitchen units		
d remove any inappropriate modern features		
e build on an extension for an extra bedroom		
f spend up to 50% of the price of the cottage on renovation		

201

▶ Time is money

You are going to hear an interview with Adrian Burchall, a *horologist*, or clockmaker. As you listen, answer the following questions:

1 Which of the following does Adrian specialise in repairing? Tick (√) the correct boxes.

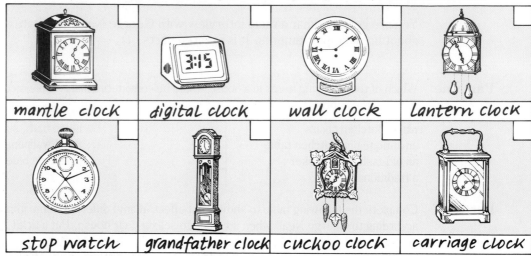

mantle clock	digital clock	wall clock	lantern clock
stop watch	grandfather clock	cuckoo clock	carriage clock

2 The part of a clock which tends to suffer worst from bad storage is
   a the face
   b the mechanical parts
   c the outer case
   d the hands

3 The chief cause of damage to clocks in storage is
   a careless handling
   b dirty conditions
   c wood eating insects
   d wet conditions

4 In Adrian's story, the new verger* went to the church the first time in order to
   a see if the clock was working
   b collect some important equipment
   c learn how to carry out his job
   d find out how his predecessor was feeling

5 The clock stopped because the old verger
   a wasn't able to wind it
   b forgot to wind it
   c didn't know how to wind it
   d didn't know he had to wind it

6 Adrian told the story to illustrate how some people
   a fail to look after their clocks properly
   b imagine their clocks have human characteristics
   c waste his time with trivial problems
   d damage their clocks through ignorance

7 The police will look at a grandfather clock in a house that's been burgled because the thieves may have
   a left evidence inside
   b caused it to stop
   c damaged the case
   d stolen the pendulum

8 Adrian suggests that the work of a clockmaker is not very
   a demanding
   b satisfying
   c useful
   d profitable

*A *verger* is a person whose job is to look after the building and contents of a church.

▶ Himalayan kingdoms

You are going to hear a conversation between Steve Berry, who runs a new company which specialises in arranging treks in the Himlayas, and a customer. It is in three parts.

**Part one
Basic
Information**

Answer the following questions:

1 What is the preferred age range of the company's customers? From .... to ....

2 At what age is a medical certificate required? ....

3 The treks are graded according to difficulty. Complete this list of the three main factors:

    a _The number of hours per day_   **b** ....   **c** _The number of high passes_

4 At what height do the majority of people feel the effects of altitude? .... feet.

5 What is the main effect of altitude that people experience? ....

**Part two
The Route**

As you listen, you must:

1 show where the following places can be found, by marking the symbols below in the correct place on the map.

King's Palace Ⓟ Airport (2) ✗ Hotel Ⱨ Monastery Ⓜ

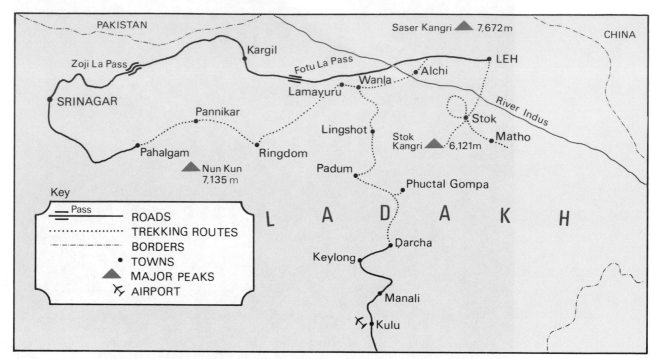

2 give the altitudes of the following:

Zoji La Pass   13,500 feet
Fotu La Pass   .... feet
Stok Kangri Base Camp   .... feet

3 give the time it takes to do the following:

climb Stok Kangri   ....
descend Stok Kangri   ....

**Part three
Costs and
Booking**

Answer the following questions.

1 Which of the following does Steve say is *not* included in the price? Tick the correct box(es) (✓)

local transport	☐	international flights	☐
climbing equipment	☐	meals during the trek	☐
hotel accommodation in Delhi	☐	camping equipment	☐
accommodation during the trek	☐	dinners in Delhi	☐

2 Complete this table showing the various extra costs:

	£5.00
INSURANCE	
	£20.00
SPENDING MONEY	

3 The dates of the next *Himalayan Summit tour* are from .... to ....

4 Booking must be made ....

▶ A many-sided therapy

You are going to hear a radio interview with Martin Matthews, who works in the healing profession. It is in two parts.

Part one Before you listen:
a look at the drawings below and make sure you know the names of the various parts shown.
b read through the questions below. The first two are based on the interview as a whole.

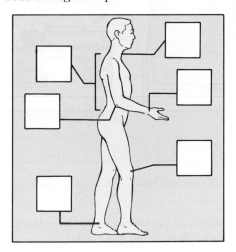
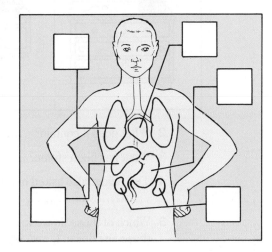

1 Show which parts of the body Martin mentions during the interview by ticking (√) the boxes.

2 Martin Matthews is   *a* a physiotherapist   *b* a doctor   *c* an osteopath   *d* a psychologist

3 He believes that
  a the liver is the cause of most illnesses   *c* pain-killing drugs are the key to treatment
  b the body is capable of curing itself   *d* most illnesses are psychological

4 He may need to advise his patients on   *a* exercise   *b* drinking habits   *c* hygiene   *d* diet

5 People often come to see him
  a because their doctor sends them   *c* after trying other forms of treatment
  b because they are in great pain   *d* in order to have X-rays taken

6 Martin explains that when he sees new patients, he first talks to them to
  a make sure they aren't seriously ill   *c* find out if their illness is imaginary
  b make them feel relaxed and at ease   *d* explain how his treatment works

Part two Say whether the following statements are **true** (**T**) or **false** (**F**):

T   F

1 Mark's back is actually hurting now.

2 His back first hurt when he was a small child.

3 He can't suggest a reason for the problem.

4 The pain he has now lasts longer than the pain he had when he was younger.

5 He used to exercise to get rid of the pain.

6 His back usually hurts most in the evening.

7 Certain sitting positions can make the problem worse.

8 He only feels the pain in one particular place.

9 He's also been having problems with stiff legs.

10 Martin asks Mark to undress.

▶ Another crime statistic

You are going to hear a conversation between a householder, Anna Clark, and a police officer. It is in three parts.

Part one 1 Where was the box that Anna thinks the thieves touched?

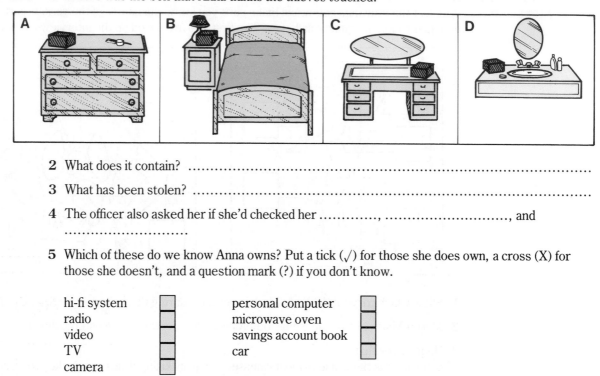

2 What does it contain? ....

3 What has been stolen? ....

4 The officer also asked her if she'd checked her ...., ..., and
....

5 Which of these do we know Anna owns? Put a tick (√) for those she does own, a cross (X) for those she doesn't, and a question mark (?) if you don't know.

hi-fi system ☐   personal computer ☐
radio ☐   microwave oven ☐
video ☐   savings account book ☐
TV ☐   car ☐
camera ☐

Part two 1 Complete the crime report form below.

WESSEX CONSTABULARY

CRIME REPORT / REGISTER

1. Offence ...... Domestic Burglary ......

2. To whom reported ...Redfield Police Station...

3. Time reported .... Date reported ....

4. Name of aggrieved person ....

    Date of birth ....

5. Address ....

    Telephone number ....

6. Time of offence ....

    Place of offence ...at above address...............

7. Type of premises ....

8. Means of entry to premises ....

9. Property stolen .... Value ....

    Description of property stolen ....

10. Officer attending scene .... number ....

206

2 Now, from the information you have heard, say which of these plans represents Anna's flat.

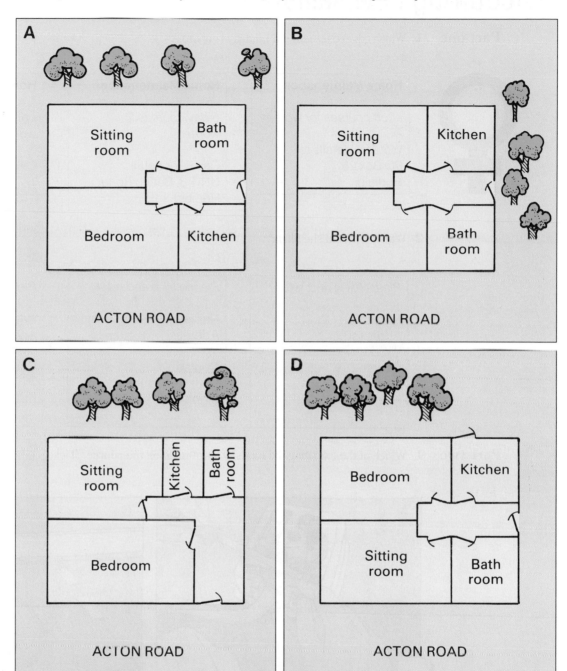

Part three **1** Say whether the following statements are **true (T)** or **false (F)**:

T F

a The lock on the front door was a strong one.

b Anna's flat had been broken into before.

c The door handle has also been damaged.

d She's planning to stay the night with a friend because she feels nervous.

e The officer doesn't think there are any useful clues to be found at the house.

f The officer thinks the break-in must have been carefully planned.

g The officer thinks the break-in may have been a joke played by a friend of hers.

▶ Acquiring new skills

Part one   **1** Which advertisement did Lindsay reply to?

A

> **Home Maintenance**
>
> *short courses for women*
>
> Write for details to:
> PO Box 25,
> Horfield.

B

> **Home Maintenance**
>
> *6 day courses for women*
>
> Call in for details:
> UNIT 3, Beech Road,
> Horfield.

C

> **Home Maintenance**
>
> *part time courses for women*
>
> Call 567123 for details.

2 Which form did she fill in?

A

> *Please fill in and return*
>
> Name.............................
> Address.........................
>
> Course..........................
>
> Fee enclosed:
>
> ....

B

> *Please fill in and return*
>
> Name.............................
> Address.........................
> ....
>
> Course..........................
>
> Signature:
>
> ....

C

> *Please fill in and return*
>
> Name.............................
> Address.........................
> ....
>
> Course..........................
>
> Exams passed:
>
> ....

Part two   **1** Which of the following did Lindsay learn to do on the course? Tick (√) the correct boxes.

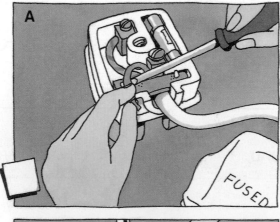

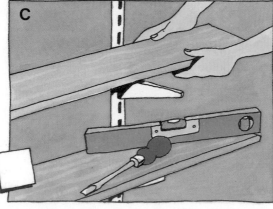

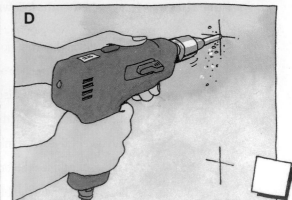

2 Write the correct letters.

    a Which 2 skills did Lindsay find most frightening at first? ………….

    b Which skill did she think would be particularly difficult before she tried it? ………….

    c Which skill does she think might save her a lot of money? ………….

Part three   Complete this table to show the other courses available.

	Course	**Additional Information**
1		
2		runs at a different centre
3		—

▶ Your friendly local radio station

You are going to hear some extracts from breakfast programmes broadcast by GWR, a local radio station in the West of England. You will also hear the programmes' presenters talking about their work. As you listen, answer the following questions:

1 Here is a list of items that might be heard on breakfast programmes. As you listen to the recording as a whole, tick those which you hear or you hear someone mention.

Which did you hear?		Which did you hear someone mention?	
time check		weather reports	
daily recipe		record requests	
competition		public transport information	
health advice		local news	
gardening advice		world news	
birthday greetings		crime report	
sports information		traffic information	

2 Merging two local radio companies has resulted in
  a the need for more administration
  b the need for more expensive technical equipment
  c programmes which are more geared to local needs
  d programmes which are more professional

3 The time is .... when we hear about Swindon Town's hopes in the FA Cup replay match.

4 The Wiltshire programme is different because it has more .... than the other two programmes.

5 It also has .... presenters involved, unlike the other programmes.

6 One speaker explained that two areas had to be treated quite separately even though they were ....

7 The breakfast programme is designed to have sections of no more than .... minutes.

8 One speaker explains that he is only able to be so alert early in the morning because he
  a stands on his head
  b goes for a run
  c gets up very early
  d goes to bed early

9 Another speaker says that he's not very cheerful in the morning with
  a his colleagues
  b his family
  c the listeners
  d his friends

10 Another speaker explains that he needs to be an egotist because
  a he gets up so early in the morning
  b he has to tell a lot of jokes
  c he gets no audience response
  d he has so many admirers

▶ Something to complain about

You are going to hear a conversation between two friends, Lindsay and Jenny. As you listen, answer the following questions:

1 Which of the following did Lindsay buy?   **2** Where did the equipment leak from?

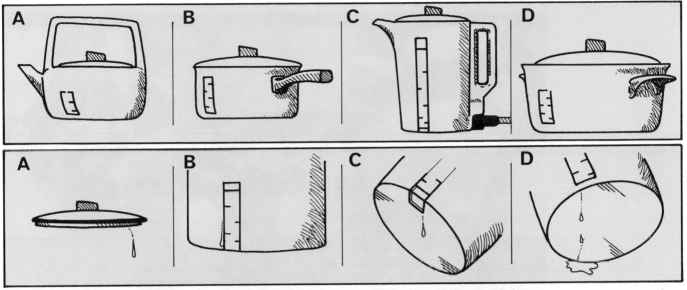

3 When she took the equipment back to the shop, she had owned it for
a a few weeks   *c* a year
b about six months   *d* more than a year

4 The shop wouldn't repair the equipment because
a she hadn't got a receipt   *c* the guarantee was out of date
b they said it was a design fault   *d* they said she had damaged it

5 Look at the 12 statements below. As you listen, you must:
a decide which *nine* are correct, and tick them.
b number them in the order in which they happened 1–9.

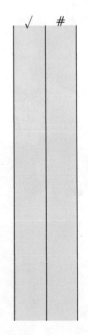

She wrote to the manufacturers

She spoke to the manager in the shop

The manufacturers sent her a form to fill in

She contacted the shop's head office

She spoke to an assistant in the shop

She telephoned the manufacturers

She went to the shop where she had bought the equipment

The local agents replaced the equipment

She sent the manufacturers' letter back to them

The manufacturers sent her letter back to her

The equipment was repaired free of charge

She spoke to the manager on the telephone

6 The unhelpful attitude of the people she dealt with made her feel
a helpless   *c* miserable
b more determined   *d* less optimistic

Exam Practice · Interview

▶ Interview Practice 1

Photographs   Look at the photographs below.

a Describe and compare   – the people and settings.

b Talk about   – how you think the people are feeling.
– what is involved in achieving success in a chosen sport.

c Discuss   – the responsibilities top sporting figures might have towards their sport and their fans.
– whether it's possible to take sport too seriously.
– whether sport brings nations together or keeps them apart.

Passages What do you think the following passages refer to and where might they have been taken from?

What do they illustrate about different approaches and attitudes to sporting activity?

1 *The great fallacy is that the game is first and last about winning. It's nothing of the kind. The game is about glory. It's about doing things in style, with a flourish, about going out and beating the other lot, not waiting for them to die of boredom.*

2 A less likely candidate for Self-Contained Underwater Breathing Apparatus than this happy paddler would be hard to find. I'm a swimmer of stamina but no power or style. I have the athletic prowess of a land-locked duck, and I never take more exercise than is required for survival in London. All this I explained to George Hurley, my Bajan Dive Master.

3 First you must keep a daily log. Without a training and racing diary, you cannot see your pattern, and so cannot see clearly the reasons for success or failure. The log should record the total distance run, the distance and time, if known, of the fast stretches, the weather conditions and, in particular, your reaction to the day's training. It is said that the Eskimos have 40 different words for snow because snow plays such a vital role in their daily lives. In the same way, there is an almost infinite range of ways of describing a run.

Communicative Activities

1 Discussion

Read the letter opposite which appeared in a newspaper as part of a public debate about the role of sport in the school curriculum in Britain.

What other reasons can you suggest for including team games, and sport generally, in the school curriculum? Are there any arguments *against* having team games in the curriculum?

Which games/sports do you feel are most appropriate for school children to take part in, and why?

Did you take part in any games/sports while you were at school? What were your feelings about the experience? Has the experience had any effects on your later life?

From Mr John James
Sir, The minister for sport and plenty of others need to be reminded that team games in schools grew out of an exercise in simple economics: they were (and still are) a device to occupy the largest number of pupils with the minimum of supervision for the longest period of time.
Yours faithfully,
JOHN JAMES,
Oak Cottage, Westonbirt, Tetbury, Gloucestershire.
April 9.

2 Expressing Opinions

Which of the following sporting activities do you consider to be:

– the most/least exciting to watch?
– the most/least fun to take part in?
– the most/least physically demanding?

- athletics
- baseball
- boxing
- cricket
- fencing
- football
- golf
- ice hockey
- ice skating
- tennis
- table tennis
- swimming
- surfing
- judo

213

▶ Interview Practice 2

Photographs   Look at the photographs below.

a Describe and compare — the people, the animals and the settings.

b Talk about
- how the photographs make you feel.
- the kinds of relationship between people and animals which are shown in the pictures.

c Discuss
- whether people should have to pass a test before they can own an animal?
- whether animals should have rights, as people do? If so, what are these?
- when the relationship between people and animals works best?

Passages What do you think the following passages refer to and where might they have been taken from?

How do they relate to the general theme of Man's Relationship with Animals?

1 Candie and Sweetie wear collars encrusted with semi-precious stones. They are bathed twice weekly and are brought in for me to see at the slightest sign of any irregularity of habits. They have been indulged all their life and have never been taught the basics of responsible behaviour. They are hopelessly dependent on their leader, Mrs Parsons, and they show it. When they are brought in to see me they play 'If you leave me I'll scream' because they are helpless without their boss dog, who happens to be a person.

2 The agent of the rhino's destruction is man. Yet the rhino is not being killed for its meat, nor is it succumbing to a change in its habitat. The rhino is being killed for its horn. The rhino's glory – the knob of modified hair and skin at the end of its nose – is the cause of its decline. For the rhino's horn is prized around the world because of mystical properties attributed to it by many cultures.

3 *Dogs aren't the only species with the power to soothe. Aaron Katcher, from the University of Pennsylvania, is investigating the effects of introducing an aquarium to a dental school. Measuring the heart rates of people who watched fish before their operation showed that they were significantly more relaxed than the control group who didn't.*

Communicative Activities

1 **Discussion**

> ***The only way*** we can bring about any healthy and relaxed meeting between people and captive animals is to scrap the whole concept of the zoo and start again. Start with the animals, not the people. Start by asking what justification there is for ever keeping animals in cages.

What are the arguments against zoos?

What are the arguments for them?

What alternatives to the conventional zoo can you suggest?

What are the other ways in which people can learn about animals?

2 **Rank Ordering**

You work as a part-time reporter for a students' magazine and your editor has asked you to write one or more articles which would be of interest to animal lovers. Interviews with any of the following people can be arranged. Put them in order according to how interesting you think their stories might be. Give reasons for your decisions.

- farmer
- pet shop owner
- dog breeder
- lion trainer from a visiting circus
- champion jockey
- elephant keeper from the local zoo
- beekeeper
- angling enthusiast
- wildlife film maker
- vet
- bird-watcher
- university zoologist

If you were asked to contrast two animal specialists in the same article, which two would you choose?

If you were asked to add some personal experiences of your own, what would you write about?

▶ Interview Practice 3

Photographs   Look at the photographs below.

a Describe and compare — the people and settings.

b Talk about — whether all the works qualify as 'art'.
— the different approaches to art they represent.

c Discuss — how an artist like Van Gogh, who had difficulty in making ends meet when he was alive, would feel about the enormous sums his paintings command today?
— the fact that very valuable works of art are often bought as investments by corporations rather than by galleries or individuals.
— whether the state should provide financial support for young artists.

Passages What do you think the following passages refer to and where might they have been taken from?

What different interests in art do they illustrate?

1 There really is no such thing as Art. There are only artists. Once there were men who took coloured earth and roughed out the forms of a bison on the wall of a cave; today some buy their paints, and design posters for the hoardings; they did and do many other things.

2 *I don't think I've ever walked out on a portrait, but I always have a clause that either of us can opt out if we don't get on. You can paint a very successful portrait of someone you dislike: but if it's to be bland, middle-of-the-road nothing, then I'd rather not do it. I flatly refuse to paint young children; their faces aren't interesting enough. Not enough has happened to them.*

3 SOMETIMES the culprits bite off more than they can chew. Thieves who made off with old master paintings worth £7 million from the dealers Colnaghi in New York were specialists in opportunist break-ins through skylights, and were horrified to discover the value of their haul when they read the newspapers the next day. These paintings have been recovered.

Communicative Activities

1 Expressing Opinions

What I dream of is an art of balance, purity and serenity, devoid of troubling or depressing subject matter, an art which might be for every mental worker, be he businessman or writer, like an appeasing influence, like a mental soother, something like a good armchair in which to rest from mental fatigue. (Henri Matisse, 1908).

Do you agree that art should be like 'a good armchair' or do you think it should challenge the viewer?

Can you think of any great works of art which are 'troubling or depressing'? Do you think it's possible for a work of art to depict ugly or even revolting subject matter?

How would you choose a picture for your own home? To match the colour scheme? To remind you of someone/something? To impress your guests? What other criteria would you use?

2 Discussion

Look at the cartoon below, which was published in a German magazine in 1898.

More Severe Punishments.
Prosecution: *'I submit that the criminal, in order to make his punishment more severe, should have modern pictures hung in his cell.'*

What does it illustrate about public reaction to unfamiliar approaches to art?

Have attitudes changed since this cartoon was published?

What aspects of modern art might make it difficult to appreciate?

Do you think people should be 'educated' to appreciate modern art? How could this be done?

▶ Interview Practice 4

Photographs   Look at the photographs below.

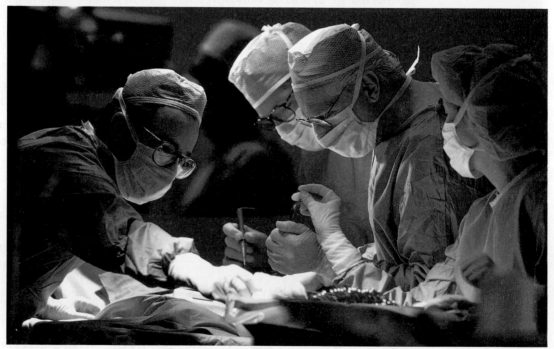

a   Describe and compare –   the people and settings.

b   Talk about   –   similarities and differences between the two groups and the
way they operate.
                           –   how the members might feel about each other.

c   Discuss   –   the different kind of groups which exist within society.
                           –   the importance of the sense of 'belonging' which
membership of a group can bring.
                           –   the harmful effects of some groups.

Passages What do you think the following passages refer to and where might they have been taken from?

What do they illustrate about different group relationships?

1 After England's defeat in the rugby world championship final, Dorrington hired a personal trainer and began working out three times a day to achieve the levels of fitness that spurred on the rest to follow suit. 'I think women as a group are better team members than men,' she said. 'We communicate better and are more compatible. We're also more perfectionist and take instruction better; so many men are real know-alls.'

2 At the centre of the estate is the most bitterly disputed area known as the War Zone, where buildings controlled by different gangs overlook each other like redoubts, separated by a bleak piece of tarmac dotted with children's swings and slides, known as the blacktop. This is the Cabrini-Green killing field, the scene of random shootings and pitched battles.

3 Of course, my mother will never have to struggle to survive on a pension. The joint family will provide for her; everyone's resources are pooled and shared, everyone is taken care of. When I see young people living in bed-sitting rooms, obviously unhappy and desperate to communicate with anyone, I'm glad I had my family to go home to in my single days. There was always someone in the house with time to listen, to sympathise or to laugh with me – to help me see things clearly.

Communicative Activities

1 Discussion

Read the poem opposite:

What is the poem about?

What are the essential qualities of leadership in your view?

Can leadership skills be taught?

Can you think of any leaders you have known or read about who embody/embodied these qualities?

> I wanna be the leader
> I wanna be the leader
> Can I be the leader?
> Can I? I can?
> Promise? Promise?
> Yippee, I'm the leader
> I'm the leader
>
> OK what shall we do?
>
> ROGER MCGOUGH

2 Decision Making

Imagine you have decided to start an English Club in your neighbourhood for people who want to get together socially and also practise their English. The following suggestions have been made for attractions the Club could offer:

- English language newspapers and magazines
- Screenings of English language films
- Talks by local experts and visiting speakers
- Library of English books and videos

How appealing do you think these ideas would be, and how practical are they in terms of cost and organisation?

What kinds of books and films would be most suitable? What topics for talks might be of interest to members?

What other ideas for facilities or activities could you suggest?

▶ Interview Practice 5

Photographs   Look at the advertisements below.

<table>
<tr><td>a</td><td>Describe and compare</td><td>– the two advertisements.</td></tr>
<tr><td>b</td><td>Talk about</td><td>– the contrasting styles and messages.
– how effective they are.</td></tr>
<tr><td>c</td><td>Discuss</td><td>– why people should be encouraged to use public transport.
– how they can be encouraged to use public transport rather than private cars.
– whether there are any other ways of getting about. How practical are they?</td></tr>
</table>

Passages What do you think the following passages refer to and where might they have been taken from?

What aspects of modern transport do they illustrate?

1 MOTORWAY MADNESS is reaching new levels of intensity. In America, frustrated drivers have taken to shooting each other. And last week in Britain a driver told how he was ambushed in his BMW while travelling in the outside lane of the M4. He was beaten up by the other motorists who wanted to overtake.

3 Every London driver now spends 111 hours a year sitting in stationary or slow-moving traffic. The total cost, in wasted time and fuel, is a staggering £1.4 billion – annual bill of £500 per vehicle. The capital's roads have become so clogged that in the heart of the city vehicles move at just 8 miles per hour – as slowly as horse and carts did 100 years ago.

2 The alarm system can be triggered by the doors, bonnet and boot, and incorporates an electronic sensor to detect movement inside the car. A continuity strip fitted on one side triggers the alarm if a window is broken. When the alarm is activated the ignition is immobilised. On the other side, laminated glass is fitted. Wheel-rotation sensors are fitted to detect movement if an attempt is made to tow the vehicle away, and another sensor detects any attempt to jack up the car to remove the wheels.

Communicative Activities

1 Discussion

Look at the cartoon below.

Discuss the point the cartoonist is making.

What makes people so attached to their cars?

How do car manufacturers encourage people to become so obsessed with cars?

What are the negative effects for drivers and for society?

2 Decision Making

You have agreed to help organise a project for children. The aim is to make them more aware of the adverse effects of road traffic on the quality of life in the community.

Think of practical activities the children could undertake to gather information about two of the following topics:

- why and how people move around in the local area
- noise pollution
- dangers for children playing in the street
- reduced social contact

▶ Interview Practice 6

Photographs   Look at the photographs below.

a Describe and compare – the people and settings.

b Talk about
- how you think the children are feeling.
- the differences in their lives and opportunities.

c Discuss
- the effects of poverty on childrens' lives.
- whether today's children get enough physical activity.
- the dangers of growing up too quickly.

Passages What do you think the following passages refer to and where might they have been taken from?

What do they illustrate about different parents' attitudes to their children?

1 But the crux of the matter is the attitude of coaches and parents to the sporting child. Too often children are treated simply as pocket adults. They are not. As Craig Sharp explains, 'They are *so* different, it is almost as if they were a third sex.' Children can become the vehicle of their parents' or coach's ambitions. The psychological pressures build up and by the time they are 16 half their life has been centred on a single goal.

2 What annoys me most about parents is their inability to say 'No'. Few take the time to explain to their children why certain behaviour is wrong, and as a result children are allowed to decide for themselves what they want to do and when to do it. They are allowed to stay up too late, watch unsuitable TV and have too many new toys. They don't need goods and goodies, they need their parents' time, which seems to be in increasingly short supply.

3

> ## COVENT GARDEN
> Like most parents, you probably want to be a train driver when you grow up. So we suggest you shunt down to the London Transport Museum in the Piazza. You can work the controls of a 1938 Tube train and operate points and signals. Come to think of it, why not take your children along too? They can join you in the cab and inspect the historic buses, locomotives and rolling stock.

Communicative Activities

1 Expressing Opinions

> *Children have more need of models than of critics.*
> Joseph Joubert

How do you interpret this remark? Do you agree with it? Why/Why not?

How would this principle work in practice?

How are children best disciplined when they are naughty?

How were you disciplined when you were a child? What effect did this treatment have on you?

2 Rank Ordering

You have been asked to look after two of your friend's children, a boy aged 7 and a girl aged 8, for a few hours. Look at the possible activities listed below.

Can you suggest any additional activities?

Put the activities in order of suitability, in your opinion. Give reasons for your choices.

- going for a walk
- going to the zoo
- buying them toys
- letting them watch a cartoon video
- telling them stories
- playing ball games in the garden
- letting them watch television
- giving them a cookery lesson
- giving them a jigsaw puzzle
- letting them draw and/or paint

Index

Key: *FG* – Focus on Grammar; *SB* – Study Box; *VP* – Vocabulary practice; *FW* – Focus on Writing; *LC* – Language Check.

▶ **A**
able to 162*FG*
expressing ABILITY 162*FG*
actual/actually 179*SB*
animal names as verbs 131*VP*
as if/as though 80*FG*
'-ate' suffix 72*VP*
avoid vs prevent 50*SB*

▶ **B**
had better 102*FG*

▶ **C**
can (ability) 162*FG*
   (permission) 62*FG*
clauses of time 124*FG*; reason 124*FG*
expressing COMPLAINTS 9*FW*
expressing CONCESSION 78*SB*
on condition (that) 44*FG*
CONDITIONAL 144*FG*
CONDITIONAL 244*FG*
CONDITIONAL 376*FG*
could (ability) 162*FG*; (in conditionals)
      76*FG*; (permission) 62*FG*;
      (possibility) 62*FG*

▶ **D**
dare + infinitive 102*FG*
DEFINING RELATIVE CLAUSES 117*FG*
describing a house 6*FW*
DIRECTED WRITING 46*FW*
DISCUSSION essay 64*FW*
do vs make 31*LC*
dread + gerund/infinitive 109*FG*

▶ **E**
or else (conditional link) 44*FG*

▶ **F**
facial expression (verbs describing) 53*VP*
few (with inversion) 41*FG*
for 25*FG*
forget + gerund/infinitive 109*FG*
FUTURE 139*FG*
FUTURE CONTINUOUS 139*FG*
FUTURE PERFECT 140*FG*
FUTURE SIMPLE 139*FG*
   (probability) 62*FG*

▶ **G**
GERUND 97*FG*
GERUND vs INFINITIVE 109*FG*
given (conditional link) 44*FG*
'going to' future 139*FG*

▶ **H**
hardly . . . when (with inversion) 40*FG*
have to vs must 163*FG*

▶ **I**
if – see conditionals
if only 79*FG*
imperative (in conditionals) 44*FG*; (in
         instructions) 87*FW*; 126*FW*

in case (conditional link) 44*FG*
INFINITIVE 102*FG*
-ing – see gerund
'ing' forms (participles) 124*FG*
describing injuries 93*VP*
writing INSTRUCTIONS 87*FW*; 126*FW*
inversion of subject and verb 40*FG*

▶ **J**
just 145*LC*

▶ **L**
let + infinitive 102*FG*
LETTERS: Do's and Don'ts 10*SB*
LETTER of complaint 9*FW*
little (with inversion) 40*FG*
look forward to + gerund 98*FG*

▶ **M**
make + infinitive 102*FG*
make vs do 31*LC*
may (permission) 62*FG*; (probability) 62*FG*
mean + gerund/infinitive 109*FG*
might (in conditionals) 76*FG*; (permission)
      62*FG*; (probability) 62*FG*
MODAL VERBS
   Ability 162*FG*; Obligation 163*FG*;
   Permission 62*FG*; Probability 62*FG*
must (certainty) 62*FG*
must vs have to 163*FG*

▶ **N**
NARRATIVE/descriptive 68*FW*; 103*FW*
need + gerund 97*FG*
      + gerund/infinitive 109*FG*
      + infinitive 102*FG*
      (as a modal verb) 164*FG*
didn't need to vs needn't have 164*FG*
no sooner . . . than (with inversion) 40*FG*
NON-DEFINING RELATIVE CLAUSES
   117*FG*
not only . . . but (with inversion) 40*FG*

▶ **O**
expressing OBLIGATION 163*FG*
only + adverbs of time (with inversion)
   40*FG*
ought to 164*FG*
'out-' prefix 171*VP*

▶ **P**
PARTICIPLES – see 'ing' forms
PASSIVE VOICE 13*FG*
PERFECT GERUND 97*FG*
expressing PERMISSION 62*FG*
PHRASAL VERBS
   (form and meaning) 30*FG*
   allow 51*SB*; break 101*SB*, 167*SB*; carry
   85*SB*; come 138*VP*, 193*VP*; cut 51*SB*,
   101*SB*; get 112*VP*, 151*SB*; give 51*SB*,
   85*SB*; go 129*SB*, 138*SB*; join 101*SB*;
   put 129*SB*, 152*VP*; send 129*SB*; set
   85*SB*, 170*VP*, 101*SB*, 129*SB*;

take 36*VP*, 129*SB*, 167*SB*; turn 128*SB*;
   work 167*SB*
prefer + gerund/infinitive 109*FG*
PREFIXES 188*LC*
dependent PREPOSITIONS
   verb + preposition 12*LC*; 104*LC*
   preposition + noun 41*LC*; 162*LC*
   adjective + preposition 69*LC*; 123*LC*
PRESENT CONTINUOUS (future) 144*FG*
PRESENT PARTICIPLE 97*FG*
PRESENT PERFECT 25*FG*
   (after time links) 144*FG*
PRESENT SIMPLE (conditional) 44*FG*;
            (future) 144*FG*;
            (after time links);
            144*PG*
prevent vs avoid 50*SB*
expressing PROBABILITY 62*FG*
description of a PROCESS 14*FW*
prosecute vs sue 61*SB*
provided that (conditional link) 44*FG*

▶ **R**
would rather + past 80*FG*; + infinitive
         102*FG*
recommend (in reported speech) 184*FG*
regret + gerund/infinitive 109*FG*
expressing REGRETS 79*FG*
RELATIVE CLAUSES 117*FG*
RELATIVE PRONOUNS 117*FG*
remember + gerund/infinitive 109*FG*
REPORT based on statistics 120*FW*
REPORTED SPEECH 182*FG*

▶ **S**
should (in conditionals) 44*FG*; (obligation)
         163*FG*; (in reported speech) 183*FG*
so/as long as (conditional link) 44*FG*
'-some' suffix 71*VP*
STATIVE VERBS 26*SB*
stop + gerund/infinitive 109*FG*
sue (vs prosecute) 61*SB*
SUFFIXES: 72*VP*; 71*VP*
suggest + gerund/'that' clause 184*FG*
SUMMARY WRITING 127*SB*
suppose/supposing (conditional link) 44*FG*
   + past 80*FG*
describing symptoms 93*VP*

▶ **T**
it's (about/high) time + past 80*FG*
try + gerund/infinitive 109*FG*

▶ **U**
unless (conditional link) 44*FG*

▶ **W**
want + gerund/infinitive 109*FG*
were to + infinitive (in conditionals) 44*FG*
expressing WISHES and REGRETS 79*FG*
I wish + past 79*FG*; wish + would 80*FG*
without (conditional link) 44*FG*
worth + gerund 98*FG*